To
John E. Fobes
and
John W. Holmes
doers, mentors, friends

Multilateralism in Multinational Perspective

Viewpoints from Different Languages and Literatures

Edited by

James P. Sewell
Professor Emeritus of Politics
Brock University, Ontario

United Nations
University Press

First published in Great Britain 2000 by
MACMILLAN PRESS LTD
Houndmills, Basingstoke, Hampshire RG21 6XS and London
Companies and representatives throughout the world

A catalogue record for this book is available from the British Library.

ISBN 0–333–71728–7 hardcover
ISBN 0–333–69814–2 paperback

First published in the United States of America 2000 by
ST. MARTIN'S PRESS, INC.,
Scholarly and Reference Division,
175 Fifth Avenue, New York, N.Y. 10010

ISBN 0–312–22915–1

Library of Congress Cataloging-in-Publication Data
Multilateralism in multinational perspective : viewpoints from
different languages and literatures / edited by James P. Sewell.
    p.   cm. — (International political economy series)
Includes bibliographical references and index.
ISBN 0–312–22915–1
1. International economic relations—Study and teaching.
2. International relations—Study and teaching.   I. Sewell, James
Patrick.   II. Series.
HF1411.M84   1999
337—dc21   99–38754
                                            CIP

This book is printed on paper suitable for recycling and made from fully managed and sustained
forest sources.

10   9   8   7   6   5   4   3   2   1
09   08   07   06   05   04   03   02   01   00

Printed and bound in Great Britain by
Antony Rowe Ltd, Chippenham, Wiltshire

Contents

Acknowledgements

This book began as a project of the United Nations University's programme on Multilateralism and the United Nations System. Project participants gratefully recognize UNU support and in particular the leadership of Robert W. Cox. We appreciate the unending encouragement of Tim Shaw. Gunnar R. Sewell deserves special thanks for his translations of two chapters. Robert W. Cox, Keith Povey, Tim Shaw, Craig Worden and an anonymous reader for UNU Press made valuable suggestions. Judith R. Sewell played a vital role throughout every phase of the project. Along with the contributors, they deserve credit for any of the book's merits. Only the editor deserves blame for its faults.

J. P. S.

List of Abbreviations

ACUNS	Academic Council on the UN System
CMEA	Council for Mutual Economic Assistance (COMECON)
ECA	(UN) Economic Commission for Africa
ECE	(UN) Economic Commission for Europe
ECOSOC	(UN) Economic and Social Council
ECOWAS	Economic Community of West African States
EU	European Union
FAO	(UN) Food and Agriculture Organization
GATT	General Agreement on Tariffs and Trade
G-7	Group of Seven (industrial democracies)
ICJ	International Court of Justice
IDA	International Development Association
IFC	International Finance Corporation
IFIs	International financial institutions
IMF	International Monetary Fund
MAI	Multilateral Agreement on Investment
MUNS	Multilateralism and the UN System
NAFTA	North American Free Trade Agreement
NATO	North Atlantic Treaty Organization
NGOs	non-governmental organizations
NIEO	New International Economic Order
NWI(C)O	New World Information (and Communication) Order
OAS	Organization of American States
OAU	Organization of African Unity
ODA	official development assistance
OSCE	Organization for Security and Cooperation in Europe
UN	United Nations
UNCED	UN Conference on Environment and Development
UNCLOS	UN Conference on the Law of the Sea
UNESCO	UN Educational, Scientific and Cultural Organization
UNEP	UN Environmental Programme
UNU	UN University
US(A)	United States (of America)
USSR	Union of Soviet Socialist Republics
WEU	Western European Union
WHO	(UN) World Health Organization
WTO	World Trade Organization

Notes on the Contributors

M. C. Castermans-Holleman is Senior Researcher associated with the School of Human Rights Research, Utrecht. Her team includes Professor dr. P.R. Baehr, Director, School of Human Rights Research and Professor of Human Rights, Utrecht University; Dr. D.A. Leurdijk, Research Fellow, Netherlands Institute of International Relations 'Clingendael', The Hague; and Professor dr. N.J. Schrijver, Professor of International Law, Free University, Amsterdam.

Alberto Cisneros-Lavaller was born in Argentina and completed his MA at the University of La Plata. His PhD was earned in Political Science/International Relations at the University of North Carolina (Chapel Hill). Dr. Cisneros-Lavaller has served as advisor on international petroleum strategies to Maraven SA (1989–1992) and as advisor to the President of Venezuela (1989–1992). He has taught at Catholic University (Caracas) and at the University of Illinois (Urbana). Among other publications, he has written *America Latina: Conflicto O Cooperacion*, 1987.

Yevgenia Issraelyan is Senior Researcher at the Canadian Department in the Institute of the USA and Canada in Moscow. Her PhD in History was earned at the Moscow State University. Research interests of Dr. Issraelyan are Canadian studies and gender studies. She serves as Chief Editor of the Russian Association for Canadian Studies Newsletter and as member of the Board of this association. Among her recent publications are *Canada and G-7*, 1997; *Canada and the United Nations*, 1995; and *Russian and Canadian Women: Challenge of the Modern World*, 1994, with Tatiana Zabelina.

Djamchid Momtaz is Professor of International Law at Tehran University and Legal Adviser to the Iranian Ministry of Foreign Affairs. He graduated from Paris University with a Doctorat d'Etat in Public Law and has served as visiting Professor in Paris, Grenoble and Geneva. He has represented Iran at many UN General Assembly sessions and specialized conferences, including UNCLOS III. His publications include numerous articles on the law of the sea, the law of armed conflicts, international waterways, and international environmental law.

Hassan Nafaa completed undergraduate studies in his native Egypt and three advanced degrees in Paris. Dr. Nafaa now serves as Professor in the Department of Political Science at Cairo University. He has also taught and held posts as visiting professor at a number of other universities. His publications span three languages, Arabic, French and English. Among these are books in Arabic which translate as *The UN: 50 Years After*, Kuwait, 1995 and *The Reform of the UN*, Cairo, 1995.

Károly Nyíri, now in Emeritus status, has served as Deputy General Director of the Institute for World Economics, the Hungarian Academy of Sciences, Budapest.

Ahmed I. Samatar is the James Wallace Professor and Dean of International Studies and Programming at Macalester College, St. Paul, Minnesota. Dr. Samatar has also lectured at a number of other institutions of higher learning, including the University of Amsterdam, Cornell, Harvard, Iowa, London School of Economics and Political Science, Somali National University, Toronto, Wellesley College, and York. He has written and or edited four books, notably *Somalia: State Collapse, Multilateral Intervention, and Strategies for Political Reconstruction*, 1995, and published over twenty articles. He edits *Macalester International*, a journal of undergraduate education and internationalism. Currently he heads a research project entitled 'Rethinking the State in Africa: African Perspectives'.

James P. Sewell is Professor Emeritus of Politics, Brock University, Ontario, and External Associate, Centre for International and Security Studies, York University, Ontario. He has authored *Functionalism and World Politics*, *UNESCO and World Politics*, chapter contributions to other volumes, and numerous articles.

Jean-Philippe Thérien is Associate Professor in the Department of Political Science, Université de Montréal. His research interests include international organizations, foreign aid, and international cooperation processes. He has published articles in several journals, including *International Organization*, *Global Governance*, *International Social Science Journal*, *International Journal*, and *Canadian Journal of Political Science*. He is the author of *Une voix pour le Sud: Le discours de la CNUCED*, Paris, 1990.

Zhang Xinhua is Professor, Director of the Centre for Policy and Strategic Studies (which he founded), and Director of the Department of Information Science, Shanghai Academy of Social Sciences.

Simultaneously he serves as Secretary-General, Shanghai Society for International Strategic Studies and as General Manager of Shanghai Vision Consultants, a private consulting firm that he formed. As a member he participates in the Chinese Political Consultative Conference and in the Chinese Society for Russian and Eastern European Studies. He has written several books and over 100 academic papers.

Introduction

This volume examines how multilateralism has been investigated within cultures and states in different parts of the world. Contributors divine the concerns that far-flung practitioners and scholars have found important, elucidating how these concerns evolve in shifting circumstances. We inquire into the sources, approaches and methods used by various analysts to investigate multilateralism, a term referring to many-sided institutional and organizing international relations. The lines of scholarship that converge in the study of multilateralism have for many years featured published work from the United States, just as the topics and terms of global discourse have reflected the strong influence of media based there. Our book strives to extend common awareness to other studies constituting the body of world literature on multilateralism.

To examine multilateralism invites preliminary reflection upon two matters. Consider first which fundamental units actually underpin the discrete studies assessed by contributors. On what level of analysis do surveyed writings basically proceed?

Today's Internet world political economy displays unmistakable many-sidedness.[1] States in their multiform relations cannot adequately convey this system. 'People in remote corners of the world who don't even know the names of their own capital cities know the name Coca-Cola', claimed this company's head of marketing in 1986. Globalization means vastly expanding markets, around-the-clock markets that highlight corporate entities in competition, alliance and consolidation. The electronically-networked modular assembly and delivery of products identifies but one emergent form of corporate relations. Daily interbank currency movements approximate $1.5 trillion.

Other kinds of international non-governmental organizations (NGOs) – voluntary associations of individuals defining themselves organizationally in order to act beyond state boundaries[2] – similarly proliferate and extend their circles of adherents and operations while weaving a capacious societal fabric. Individuals affiliated with NGOs contribute significantly to the literature on multilateralism. Besides acting as components of the globalizing economy and civil society, NGOs articulate interests within multilateral political arenas. Inside walled institutions they leaven multi-state policymaking with recommendations and perspectives unlikely to originate with governments – though governmental participants may come armed with suggestions already adopted from NGOs at home. In political arenas the intersocietal mingles with the intergovernmental upon more than one level, reminding the observer that in its intricacy and fecundity, our world infinitely surpasses a system analytically reduced to states.

Feminist literature in particular insists that we look well beneath the state and acknowledge the significance of everyday lives lived by transnationalized individuals, not least women the world over.[3] Interstate institutions that sanction inquiries into the most egregious or accessible domestic troubles nowadays expose malefactors and victims long screened from others' sensibilities. No longer can a head of state feel immune from indictment for war crimes and crimes against humanity. Media and the information revolution contribute formidably to the discounting of boundaries along with the multilateralizing of societies and the raising to prominence of individuals, including dissidents, deemed newsworthy. (Of course, such forces may prompt some to react by affirming what they proclaim as their singular identity.)

Notwithstanding its parochial origins, the Internet has come to epitomize multilateralism more than do markets, to the extent these remain distinct: beyond the threshold to admission, many participate, and no body dominates, let alone wields a unit veto in cyberspace. During what might be called today's dot-suffix era of communicating, 'domain' shows its adaptation to highly ambiguous territoriality. Already the Internet has facilitated activity by unofficial groups bringing political change on several continents. It has also linked the efforts of individuals in many lands – 'hordes of vigilantes', as Noam Chomsky admiringly dubs them – who oppose the Multilateral Agreement on Investment (MAI), or at least oppose what they regard as a stealthy approach to MAI by governments. In short, a multilateralizing world increasingly empowers and reveals all sorts of nonstate global actors.

The terms of reference for this present study encouraged investigation of significant multilateral forces through whatever forms or entities they operate. Authors were explicitly invited to understand multilateralism as embracing the intersocietal along with the intergovernmental. Specific references, for instance to Marxism and to functionalism, cued contributors to recognize studies of multilateralism that display class and other nonstate units of analysis such as transstate movements.

Yet clearly states matter,[4] as do the governments in whose names they act. Our contributors' investigations of existing work establish that most studies canvassed found states and governments to constitute, or at least to reflect most adequately, the firmament of (if not the key limitation upon[5]) multilateralism. Often herein, though by no means invariably, authors witness these governments enacting the dynamics of multilateralism within and around walled institutions. Whether as a baseline from which in future to reckon the state's further retreat, or as references by which in future to document its obdurate survival, the present study bequeaths points of departure that invite revisitation. Meanwhile, multilateralism, deployed as a concept open both to interstate and to intersocietal phenomena, has proved serviceable for our purposes.[6]

Note secondly that authors surveyed within chapter accounts do not invariably regard multilateralism as a *desirable* development. One might suppose that the term's '–ism' implies a commendatory endorsement. By no means, however, do literary selections uniformly bear out such a supposition. Indeed, some writings intimate that multilateralism names a perverse trend to be resisted.

More frequently, studies reviewed neither praise nor condemn multilateralism. They simply accept as given cross-borders institutions and other palpable multilateral formations, describing and sometimes analyzing, explaining and predicting further manifestations and their consequences. Similarly, many practically-oriented writings merely treat multilateralism as an established fact for policymakers. These selections evince neither extravagant satisfaction nor dissatisfaction with a multilateralizing system. Instead, policy advisories take for granted widespread awareness of a prevailing pattern of multilateral cohabitation. Tacit understandings inform this multilateral cohabitation: what goes around comes around, for instance; players must go along in order to get along. Perhaps writings in this vein can be called studies in *multilateralship*. Pragmatism stands out as their chief characteristic. In the concluding chapter I reflect upon this pragmatic quality characterizing much of the literature on multilateralism.

Earlier in the present decade, James A. Caporaso asked why the concept of multilateralism has not played a more prominent part in theorizing about international relations.[7] Our response differs from Caporaso's answer to his question and from implicit answers by other contributors to the volume in which it appears. Even though the United States has engaged extensively in organized international efforts forming multilateral structures, American policymakers have more commonly acted on the world unilaterally. American academics adapted to this 'real'-world circumstance. And since most published postwar theorizing about international relations heretofore originated in the United States, 'multilateralism' has had to wait its turn in the scholarly succession of concepts until evolving domestic conditions seemed auspicious – quite possibly only momentarily auspicious.[8]

Despite multilateralism's belated conceptual christening, its phenomena have not lacked theorizing and research. In the past scholars called these matters 'international organization' as a process and 'international organizations' as products of the process,[9] products that some observers saw impacting or feeding back to processes producing other kinds of products and by-products.[10] Moreover, international organization studies have often encompassed nonstate actors and social forces whose patterned configurations might be described as institutions without walls.[11] Caporaso's question merits our salute, yet we have not let it induce us to act on a belief that multilateralism began to be studied only after it came to be named. This book's authors could not accept such terminological over-determination, if only because we would then find ourselves bereft of materials pertinent to a scholarly work bearing our volume's title.

The United Nations University (UNU) project culminating in the present work has been dedicated to critical exposition of work on multilateralism that would encompass many points of origin while embracing languages and literatures well beyond North America. A reflective scholar or practitioner anywhere will have imagined that other observers, accustomed to their own respective polities' distinct experiences with multi-participant processes, command perspectives differing from his or her own. Herein the reader will find substance for such surmises. This book introduces writings that might otherwise remain little known beyond their original readership. Its commentaries provide an opportunity for the reader to view from divergent vantage points the multilateralizing world that we share; the varied ways that peoples seek to abide, sustain or reshape this world as they apprehend it; and the alternative means for making sense of their efforts.

No assertion of congruity attends our combined effort. Common questions were posed and tendered for authors' consideration:[12] What is the balance of interest in scholarly endeavors between emphasis on the UN system and on other forms of multilateralism? What is the balance among different disciplines? Do different groups of scholars deal with different functional scopes of multilateralism? What are the principal theoretical mindsets or -isms; are any of these in growing favour? Do scholars consider the future of multilateralism in terms of 'reform'[13] or do they offer a more radical critique? Augmented versions of these questions I address in the concluding chapter while reflecting upon informative convergences and divergences. But as will be evident well before the concluding chapter, authors' decisions on form and substance have enjoyed substantial latitude.

This freedom we sanctioned with the expectation that some measure of scholarly independence would evoke new or under-appreciated ways to comprehend multilateralism. A project that accounts for how observers variously see and act upon multilateralism must today explore phenomena that in their nature comprise many viewpoints. Wisdom counselled that individual inquiries into the study of multilateralism not be cramped by insistence upon particular angles, specific foci or identical procedures. We wished to avoid putting theoretical straitjackets upon contributors of different political and cultural backgrounds. Often they in turn have provided subtle critiques of our categorizations' fit by favouring alternative constructs. That which observers deem important to do and significant to study differs tellingly in divergent circumstances. What each omits may speak cogently, too. Thus the manifestation of differences was welcomed for the lessons this scholarly pluralism would extend, lessons that will most often proclaim themselves directly to the reader during the course of chapters to follow. In this respect we have honoured diversity more than conformity.

Put somewhat differently, we preferred to sacrifice a degree of coherence across the inner chapters in order to maximize the possibility of contributors' fresh insights and minimize the risk of editorial contamination. The framework of common questions has proved vital and productive, as we later conclude. Yet divergence from this elective framework also illuminates where authors are 'coming from', thereby enlightening us as to how perception and conception vary with the geopolitical or social or personal terrain on which the observer stands. Regard three examples. The Dutch chapter suggests implicitly how consensus on multilateralism as requisite to action for the Netherlands apparently devalues combative theorizing, leaves commentators indifferent to ideology, and prompts instead an overwhelming flow of instrumentalist writings on multilateral opportunities and how to play them. Venezuelan Alberto Cisneros-Lavaller apparently regards the remarkable nineteenth century legal and organizational origins of multilateralism in Latin America as a worthier claimant of scarce allocated chapter space than the much more recent *dependencia* literature. And the polemical case study by Djamchid Momtaz impresses one with its preponderant theme of injustice to Iran meted out by the UN Security Council and with its greater similarity to a *plaidoirie* than to academic pleadings ordinarily produced elsewhere. Despite its liabilities, the modest methodology of offering standard questions and interpreting unanticipated responses along with the reactions to assigned queries offers some compensation. We hope that our collective study prompts others' ventures into heterodoxy.[14]

Although we reached as far as possible, we cannot claim comprehensiveness. Literature stemming from research in state and cultural realms unrepresented here of course awaits inquirers beyond our domain of inquiry. Friends of this project as well as the editor long sought yet ultimately failed to elicit contributions examining literature from francophone Africa, Germany and other German-speaking areas, India and the Indian subcontinent, Japan, Mexico, and Scandinavia.[15] Many other bodies of literature on multilateralism also deserve treatment.

Aside from unanswered set questions and unaddressed domains of literature, significant expressions of multilateralism continue beyond the scope of contributions. For instance, thematic global conferences remain mostly unexamined, perhaps because of a dearth of major analytical works specifically on these conferences that could have spurred contributors' mental ruminations. Again, inclusive multilateral arrangements predominate over exclusive minilateral ones. Multilateralism and the United Nations System, the overarching UNU programme of which this volume is an outcome, by its title helps account for greater emphasis herein on works addressing universal-membership organizations than on works addressing limited-membership structures and groups. From some state vantage points, this emphasis may also reflect the actual relative importance of participation in larger and in smaller intergovernmental institutions. In any event, on the whole the essays evince more attention to United Nations units than to 'regional' and other particular-member institutions or to patterns of nonstate convergence, even though the project's terms of reference invite inclusion of all forms of multilateralism.[16] Finally, the burgeoning critical feminist and postmodernist literature surely must bear upon multilateralism in ways beyond those touched on here. In short, plenty of matter invites investigation by others.

Yet matter aplenty lies ahead. By this series of appraisals we honour Alexis de Tocqueville's admonition that without comparisons to make, the mind knows not how to proceed. Our examination of multilateralism begins with an interpretation of studies in the United States by James P. Sewell. Yevgenia Issraelyan then appraises writings in the Soviet Union and Russia. Inquiries in China are assessed by Zhang Xinhua. Jean-Philippe Thérien explicates French-language literature, more specifically that of France, Belgium, francophone Canada and francophone Switzerland, while drawing trenchant contrasts with English-language literature. Research in Egypt and elsewhere in the Arab world is scrutinized by Hassan Nafaa. Findings in the Netherlands are inventoried by Monique Castermans-Holleman, with contributions by Peter R. Baehr, Dick A. Leurdijk and Nico J. Schrijver. The literature of Hungary is assayed by Károly Nyíri. Alberto Cisneros-Lavaller peruses selected works in Latin America. A major matter of intense Iranian concern focuses the essay of Djamchid Momtaz, and A.I. Samatar dissects both soothing and blistering scholarly efforts of Africa. The conclusion draws inferences from the findings and silences of intervening chapters.

Notes

1 See for instance an early volume in the Multilateralism and the United Nations System (MUNS) series, Yoshikazu Sakamoto, ed., *Global Transformation: Challenges to the State System*, Tokyo: United Nations University Press, 1994.

2 'NGO' carries a broad connotation here. Caritas, the Human Rights Watch family, the International Council of Women, the International Union for Conservation of Nature and Natural Resources, and the World Confederation of Labour qualify as NGOs. So too do Bertelsmann, Cable News Network (CNN), DaimlerChrysler, General Electric, HSBC, Long-Term Capital, Microsoft, Mitsui and Unilever, as well as the Cali, Juarez and Tijuana cartels, and Hell's Angels. George Soros epitomizes non-governmentalism. Central bankers distance themselves from governments; see Steven Solomon, *The Confidence Game: How Unelected Central Bankers Are Governing the Changed Global Economy*, New York: Simon & Schuster, 1995.

   To categorize organizations as *non-governmental* does not necessarily mean that they form themselves unnurtured by the culture of a motherland, develop unimprinted and unfettered by the state, function uninfluenced by the government or governments of the day. Nor of course does the appellation 'non-governmental' mean that they refrain from striving to influence governments even while seeking to minimize governmental control. Their relative degree of multi*nationalism*, as suggested by the domains of their members, offers a different dimension pertinent when analyzing NGOs. Yet another variable germane to the dynamics of specific transnational associations shares a central concern underlying our study: How truly *multi*lateral are the decisionmaking processes of particular NGOs? How multilateral are the decisionmaking processes scrutinized in world literature on multilateralism? Thus NGOs of varied kinds constitute an integral part of global multilateralism, contributing to the many-sidedness of multilateral phenomena. At the same time, individual NGOs pose a comparative research agenda item sharing a key concern with the present work.

3 See for instance Cynthia Enloe, *Bananas, Bases, and Beaches: Making Feminist Sense of International Politics*, Berkeley: University of California Press, 1990. As Enloe suggests, to do this may very well transform our perception of what 'international politics' is.

4 Two contributing essayists refer to their home states not as 'it' but as 'she'.

5 Compare Amrita Basu, 'Introduction', in Basu, ed., *The Challenge of Local Feminisms: Women's Movements in Global Perspective*, Boulder: Westview, 1995.

6 For a sustained examination of societal multilateralism, see another volume in the MUNS series, Keith Krause and W. Andy Knight, eds., *State, Society, and the UN System: Changing Perspectives on Multilateralism*, Tokyo: United Nations University Press, 1995.

7 'International Relations Theory and Multilateralism: The Search for Foundations', *International Organization*, 46, Summer 1992, p. 599; also in John Gerard Ruggie, ed., *Multilateralism Matters: The Theory and Praxis of an Institutional Form*, New York: Columbia University Press, 1993.

8 Within the context of domestic political conditions, exigencies of the academic workplace affect the succession as well as the nature of concepts, notably in the US. Academia rewards conceptual origination, referred to grandiloquently as 'conceptualization'. Documented origination assures footnote credits throughout the life cycle of a concept, contributing directly to a scholar's 'seminal' (citation-spawning) potency and consequent professional renown. The scholar coins or rediscovers a term, then presents it as what Imre Lakatos calls a 'progressive problemshift' – optimistically distinguished from Lakatos's 'degenerating problemshift'. (The latter Lakatos deems 'unscientific' since a degenerating problemshift 'only offers a content-decreasing (linguistic) *reinterpretation*' by which a 'contradiction is resolved in a merely semantical, unscientific way'.) Lakatos, *The Methodology of Scientific Research Programmes: Philosophical Papers*, Vol. I, John Worrall and Gregory Currie, eds., Cambridge: Cambridge University Press, 1978, pp. 33–4. Once publication confirms private ownership of the concept, the author seeks further to promote and distribute it. Publication gatekeepers will already have eliminated ideas that are commonplace or extreme. Wide acceptance of the concept occurs if it meets the predilections of an establishment or network. When in the early 1970s the US government offered financial support for the study of 'interdependence', for instance, American scholars obliged with alacrity. Establishment benefaction assures that others will draw affirmative inferences and apply, exemplify or at least refer to the concept, rendering acclaim to the benefactor and citation tribute to scholars back along the distribution process. Academics and publishing houses find that prolonging while internationalizing the production run enhances their returns. Meanwhile, unbeknown to academics in the periphery who continue to teach the idea and illustrate it in their writings, quite possibly a replacement model has already entered the academic marketplace. Curiously, academic exigency puts a premium on 'new' concepts supplanting obsolescing ones even as domestic political exigency acts as a damper on fundamentally revised ways of seeing and explaining. Thus concepts tend to exhibit a pattern of marginal differentiation from predecessor concepts while following a tempo of expedited supersession. Conceptual volatility obscures an underlying steadiness of orientation.

9 Inis L. Claude, Jr., *Swords Into Plowshares: The Problems and Progress of International Organization*, 4th ed., New York: Random House, 1971, p. 4.

10 The literature descending from the seminal formulations of David Mitrany, notably his *A Working Peace System: An Argument for the Functional Development of International Organization*, London: Royal Institute of International

Affairs, 1943 and Chicago: Quadrangle Books, 1966, explores functional applications and side-effects. See, for instance, Richard Peck, 'Socialization of Permanent Representatives in the United Nations: Some Evidence', *International Organization*, 33, Summer 1979, pp. 365–90; Martha Finnemore, 'International Organizations as Teachers of Norms: The United Nations Educational, Scientific, and Cultural Organization', *International Organization*, 47, Autumn 1993, pp. 565–97; Lucian M. Ashworth and David Long, eds., *New Perspectives on International Functionalism*, London: Macmillan, 1998.

11 Compare Robert W. Cox and Harold K. Jacobson, *et al.*, *The Anatomy of Influence: Decision Making in International Organization*, New Haven: Yale University Press, 1973.

12 These questions stem from Robert W. Cox, Programme Co-ordinator, Multilateralism and the United Nations System, under the aegis of the United Nations University.

13 Varieties of 'reform' receive attention in Chapter 1 and Chapter 11, the widespread phenomenon of *displacement* associated with 'reform' in Chapter 11.

14 Perhaps future collaborators can programme a follow-up phase during which contributors justify their departure from the proposed conceptual framework, thereby providing readers with concrete and authoritative explanations instead of having them rely solely on the dubious conjectures of a fallible editor.

15 Chapter 4 by Jean-Philippe Thérien and Chapter 10 by A.I. Samatar go some distance to close the gap on francophone Africa. Though directed to questions rather different than those posed for the present study, two other volumes offer source citations useful in accessing world literature on multilateralism. *State, Society and the UN System* contains essays on Germany, India, Sweden, Romania, Chile, Jamaica and Sierra Leone. For notes to references on India, for instance, see Hari Mohan Mathur, 'India in the United Nations and the United Nations in India', pp. 93–7. See also Chadwick F. Alger, Gene M. Lyons, and John E. Trent, eds., *The United Nations System: The Policies of Member States*, Tokyo: United Nations University Press, 1995, which combines chapters on Algeria, Canada, France, Japan, the Netherlands, Nigeria, the UK and the US.

16 By their examples contributing authors show that they understand multilateralism to comprise all parts of the United Nations system as well as multilateral relations beyond it. Along with more commonly recognized units, the UN system includes the most independent-minded of specialized agencies 'brought into relationship with the United Nations' (UN Charter Article 57); the UN regional commissions; and UN field operations. Authors also touch on organizations with particular sets of participants (among these, various 'regional' organizations), whatever their purpose or purposes, and transstate private associations, including NGOs and cross-national movements.

Maple Stand and Owlshire   JAMES P. SEWELL

1
Congenital Unilateralism in a Multilateralizing World: American Scholarship on International Organization

James P. Sewell

American scholarship on international organization may be illuminated by tracing how the United States has adapted to a changing world. This initial chapter examines selected American writings on 'multilateralism'[1] chiefly in light of the abiding US practice of unilateralism. It contends that conceptual tailoring has sometimes enshrouded basic structural truths while gilding official rationales.[2] The chapter proceeds on these premises: politics matters; international organization forms an important part of multilateralism; and the proper study of international organization includes international organizations. My argument advances contentiously in keeping with the traditional American faith that assertiveness offers the surest path to provocation and thence to better explanation.

Limitations of space force limitations of scope. Many scholarly books cannot be cited, let alone criticized. Brevity obliges explanation to justify hard choices. Works cited here fit the argument advanced. The argument holds that theory follows practice, much as practice had followed exigency. Thus among the ration of references certain selections depict practice and others connote exigency. Writings on international political economy illuminate the chance and choice borne by exigency. Superior studies show profoundly how economic factors function and evolve, thereby cunningly expanding the range of material forces affecting governance and authentic political choice.[3] But economic factors as ordinarily construed do not present the only exigencies of political acts.[4] Cultural inheritance too shapes the desiderata or unrecognized wellsprings of action. Nor does politics concede all its autonomy to exogenous forces or reduce itself to the status of dependent variable. In turn, politics produces its own exigencies. Exigency, then, assumes various forms. In any event, here we aim to move beyond exigency, not to rest the case with exigency. Thus practice along with its rationale may come into focus.

A frequent premise of studies in political economy from across the political spectrum deems international institutions to serve as adjuncts of hegemony.[5] Multinational organizations thus supposedly constitute realms unsupportive if not barren of effectual many-sidedness. By such lights multilateral manifestations become epiphenomena that misdirect the observer toward false conclusions: more meets the eye than is really there.[6]

This chapter maintains that political factors bear important consequences for multilateralism and for any changes in the fashion by which observers perceive and act upon it. To follow politics, in any event, yields illumination of the American experience, notably American scholarship on international organization. No doubt differing accounts of American writings on multilateralism will offer alternative findings. Consider this chapter an invitation to correct misapprehensions no less than one to close gaps.

The design for our collective work envisages benefits from comparisons across a broadly-based ensemble of critical surveys. So too might a contribution on the literature from one particular country or culture yield benefits from comparisons drawn closer at hand with scholarship from kindred countries or cultures – as exemplified, for instance, in Chapter 4 on francophone studies by Jean-Philippe Thérien. Yet only passing contrasts with studies from elsewhere within the anglophone world can be ventured here.

The following paragraphs introduce two constants, the American vision of greatness as world leader and the US style of unilateralism. American scholarship on international organization is examined over time as the two constants persist while worldly variables change. In conclusion, summary contentions more general in nature are ventured.

Constants

The United States came later than some states to the experience of international organization. During and after the Second World War, however, US policymakers organized internationally with considerable dedication. To shrewd observers abroad it may have seemed that the manner of founding the United Nations, as successor to a League of Nations lacking US membership, was orchestrated in a manner to assure that the US would engage fully in the new post-cataclysm generation of multilateral institutions. The US did project a mighty presence at the creation, hosting formative meetings and shaping structures born of diplomatic conferences abroad,[7] but Americans hardly played the role of reluctant partners. Instead they saw the resurrected principal organs now headquartered mainly in New York, and the newest agencies allocated within North America and Europe, as manifestations of the *global leadership* that they were destined and implicitly mandated to provide. At last an historic vision of national greatness[8] could come actively to fruition on a grand stage. The United Nations system, along with organized 'regional' arrangements embracing particular sets of governments in the Americas, Europe and elsewhere, initially promised to serve as uncomplicated extensions of US foreign policy.

Their global leadership would affix Americans' attention over the years. Containment of the adversary within a bipolar system sanctified this preoccupation with leadership while the US domain remained truncated as the 'Free World'. The passing of the cold war opened fresh frontiers but also posed new challenges of meaning and motivation for Americans. Notwithstanding the loss of a single opponent to contain,[9] however, the fascination with leadership continues among attentive publics. Interested US citizens hardly cease to ponder the problems and opportunities, the general beneficence and particular burdens, the inevitability and yet the problematic future of their country's leadership.[10]

Today many voices question the wisdom of hands-on leadership. Some urge instead an isolationist version of 'city-on-the-hill' inspiration: America would set an example, beaconing forth this example to others, but its modelling would occur only from a position safely above the huddled masses below. Others stress the domestic and foreign costs of an indiscriminating fixation on global leadership, counselling highly selective commitments abroad rather than promiscuous attachment to sundry causes.

Issues about the wise domain of US preponderance continue to arouse debate.[11] For instance, Irving Kristol acknowledges several threatening problems to be dealt with by American overlordship, if not by direct action, but pronounces 'the European phase' of world history over and NATO 'an organization without a mission'. To reinvent this structure of commitment, says Kristol, would constitute 'a vast irrelevance. Let it slide into obsolescence.'[12] Jack F. Matlock Jr. warns the US against a 'mindless expansion of NATO' while continuing 'without strategic design' to 'inject itself into one crisis after another, treating much of the world as its protectorate'.[13] Ronald Steel calls for acceptance of 'the reality of the long-standing tradition of spheres of influence' – the US with its estates in the Americas, others with theirs elsewhere.[14] Many now counsel an adjusted realm for American leadership, but few in high places exempt leadership's exercise altogether. Retired Air Force Lt. Gen. Thomas Kelly, voice of the Pentagon during Desert Shield and Desert Storm, says with respect to a possible return engagement 'You don't have a right to do *nothing*.'[15]

At least one adviser, Richard Haass, would have US leadership serially regulate a geopolitically deregulated post-cold war world. Re-regulation would proceed through the timely marshalling of successive contact groups producing evanescent alliances, each tailor-made to thwart a looming threat to US interests. Prior instances include the Gulf War posse; the Somalia humanitarian force during its original, pre-mission-creep, Bush-administration phase, and presumably a foreshadowed US instigation of military retaliation if Serbian force were used against Albanian Kosovars, a warning issued to Yugoslav leader Slobodan Milosevic during the final month of the Bush presidency.[16] But NATO came to play a more durable role than that of contact group in regulating Serbia. The quest for a new purpose to ease NATO's identity crisis coincided with the reprehensible Serbian acts in Kosovo. Debate in the US addressed the uncertain quality of US alliance direction. In short, many variants illustrate a consuming concern: the possession of planetary leadership haunts the American political mind.[17]

Academics reflect the absorption with leadership, objectifying America's role as that of the hegemon ostensibly required to assure that the global system functions in an orderly manner. The prerogative of leadership as unilateral choice thus becomes verbally buttressed as the systemic imperative of hegemony. Leadership so conceived induces a supposition that the rules of the system exist mainly in order to constrain others. The systemic imperative of one's leadership also tempts an illusion of hegemonic immortality. Nobody disagrees that great powers have declined after having risen in the past, although some apparently see in US hegemony an end of history. American exceptionalism permits extraordinary understandings.

Intergovernmental organizations initially offered a means to exert leadership and later implied one means to fulfill what had been construed as the system's requirement for hierarchy. The US served as patron of multilateral organizations, a role perhaps justified to some by the faith that America offers the world a conscience and produces leaders capable of universal understanding. Hence their country's superintendence bestowed upon the world a marriage of power with morality and discernment. Any doubts about omniscience were lessened by the confidence that America and its allies enjoyed an essential like-mindedness. Kindred intent by the multitudes would obviate oppressiveness of hegemony by the one.

Never were organized multilateral contraptions the principal means to American ends. But at least, early on, they were regarded as useful vehicles. After all, these organizations had been designed for dispatch or parking at the will of the United States, even if Americans most often contrived that others would assume the driver's seat.[18]

In the beginning, the tractability of multilateral organizations to American guidance prompted little doubt on the part of the guides. The United Nations served Americans as an alter ego. Oral references to the UN frequently slipped out as 'the US'. Of course sceptical assessments of the UN's effectiveness soon grew more prominent, later to be overshadowed by disparaging remarks or worse on the value of the largest multilateral institutions.

Even when deemed benign, these multilateral institutions were seen by Americans to exist largely for the benefit of others. Organized internationalism initially appeared to reproduce such American traditions as voluntarism and charitable giving, albeit with bureaucracies interposed that threatened to absorb an overly large proportion of donations or even to subvert the realization of altruistic intentions. Still, Americans thought their remote control adequate to regulate help for foreign beneficiaries. The trick consisted in conceiving then launching a new system, bequeathing its operationalization to others. Prudent US origination would minimize the need for constant US involvement. To solve global problems once and for all by designing and setting up the appropriate mechanism appealed far more as a task than coping with obdurate difficulties by persevering management of joint effort.

Perceived distance between donor and recipients invited a stance and terminology of alienation. In due course the UN was reduced to 'it' and even to 'them'. This distancing would for instance in March 1998 lend partisan domestic plausibility to the charge by Senate majority leader Trent Lott that the Clinton administration had contracted out US foreign policy by authorizing United Nations Secretary-General Kofi Annan to carry a UN Security Council mandate to Baghdad. Even when held in highest esteem, the United Nations remained a congregation of needy supplicants for America to lead from afar, at least until 'they' would no longer be led.

The proclivity toward individualized action stands as a second American attribute significant for multilateral practice and theorizing. This pattern of international behaviour can fittingly if indelicately be called *congenital unilateralism.*[19] Unilateralism means the wont to act apart from others along with the justification for doing so. Superman needs no helpmate for his performances of justice; the Lone Ranger brooks only a Tonto walk-on as he rights wrongs along the frontier.

Observe that unilateralism embraces forcible and non-forcible conduct alike. Peacemaking no less than warmaking lends itself to solitary application by Americans. Indeed, warmaking increasingly invites at least virtual collaboration: basing and overflight permission; verbal licensing or its representation as multilateral legitimation; subsidies, including financial offsets for US defaults of UN dues. Peacemaking can still start with a single intermediary, and extraordinarily dedicated Americans such as Bill Richardson, Richard Holbrooke[20] and George Mitchell answer this calling. Yet especially when national stakeholder-ship grows to overshadow that of individual negotiator, the peace-maker's commitment may intensify to a self-assured sense of indispensability. To identify with the role of broker for peace evidently tempts growth of one's conviction that no other actor or institution could succeed.

Similar processes led to the buildup of US passion as designated sanctioner. Sanctions' pinpricks tweak foes and friends who stray 'off the reservation' or fail to follow the US 'road map'. Despite occasional throwbacks to earlier patterns, economic acts of displeasure have largely replaced gunboat diplomacy's cruder coercion. Collateral damage recognized to blindside both innocent peoples and unmobilized US interests renders unilateral sanctions' effectiveness increasingly problematic. Notwithstanding the important exception of Anglo-American leadership spurring NATO's concerted action against Serbia, however, the unilateral essence of US sanctions remains. Indeed, Americans may draw from the Balkans project that began in 1999 the lesson that multilateralism, even NATO multilateralism, should be avoided.

The spirit of crusade wielding a 'terrible swift sword' to compel peace typifies unilateralism. But by no means does global policeman stand as the only part whose possession generates a sense of ownership. Enfranchised broker, upholder of free trade, and protector of human rights suggest other roles that to Americans imply singular action. Literally or figuratively, the phrase 'calling the shots' encompasses these varied modes of unilateralism.

The unilateral way did not begin with Senator Jesse Helms or with President Ronald Reagan. From its formative years, the United States brought forward this habit and the quiet celebration of it, thereby discounting the support extended by European allies in facilitating the birth of the republic. George Washington, Thomas Jefferson and other early leaders[21] admonished Americans not to entangle themselves with foreigners.

When the oceans were broad, unilateralism worked. Early successes discouraged consideration of alternatives. Unilateralism proceeded from conduct unquestioning of the prototype and exhortations of founding fathers to the fixity of axiomatic principle. It acquired the profound power of cultural givenness manifested as embodied ideology.

This proudly self-reliant nation, suspicious of governance upon any level beyond the local community, lives largely oblivious to the extent its affairs intertwine with those of others. Unilateralism exacts and sustains an operating premise that US action will not precipitate others' reaction. Experience to the contrary has not shaken this working assumption.

In their drive to fast-forward the bounty of progress, Americans also disregard the grip of the past upon routines of the present. So deep-seated has the unilateral impulse become that Americans scarcely even ponder their penchant for solo performance. Questions about leadership stir debate on might, right, ambit; unilateralism happens. The conditioning of a unilateral reflex long antedated American engrossment with world leadership, though unilateralism and leadership, paradoxically, eventually became mutually supportive.

Unilateralism exemplifies the independence of a people whom Lincoln saw as 'conceived in liberty'.[22] It marks both the periods of relative stability and the recurrent episodes of constitutional paroxysm that afflict the American political system. Unilateralism translates equally as free rein in world affairs[23] and as freedom to remain aloof from world affairs. Thus unilateral behaviour characterizes both the interventionist and isolationist swings in US foreign policy. Over their history, Americans have gone it alone at home far more than they have gone it alone abroad.[24]

Republicans and Democrats alike show their proneness to operate unilaterally. At the outskirts of the broad American political centre, reactionaries and radicals mostly show the same inclination. Militias advocate isolationist unilateralism with a vengeance.[25]

With exceedingly rare exceptions, Congress applies[26] and the media insist upon this international stance. In turn their steadfast postures suggest that American publics generally share a bent to follow unilateral ways. Unilateralism's staying power implies that agents of acculturation socialize immigrants and perpetuate this leaning through oncoming generations.[27] The impact occurs immediately as well as indefinitely.

Congress and the media function as gyroscopes of unilateralism, instantly enforcing the propensity to act in exquisite isolation upon any public figure who might otherwise be tempted to deviate from the norm.[28] Yet this they can do only because the propensity prevails among their respective constituents. To operate in concert, let alone to enmesh one's country in sustained multilateral schemes, goes against the grain for those outside the Washington beltway as well as those inside it. For the people no less than their governments, to act alone comes virtually as second nature. In brief, the unilateral cast of mind functions as an integral part of the American political psyche.

One searches with scant comparative return for any other national actor whose character approaches the tenacity of unilateralism displayed by the US. Perhaps Israel offers the closest approximation, at least in terms of attitudes and an operational code that stresses self-reliance in foreign affairs. Americans themselves complain about the waywardness of France, Russia, Japan and occasionally India when these are seen to defect from 'the international community' in pursuit of selfish interests. Still, no major state has so persistently stood apart as the US, conducted extensive foreign affairs with indifference to others' scruples, and slighted their cooperation as principals.[29]

This quintessential American trait of unilateralism has deeply influenced scholarship on multilateralism. The relationship between practice and theorizing we examine within a context of changing global circumstances. Four periods I shall term **lordly unilateralism** (1941 to the late 1960s or early 1970s); **damage-control unilateralism** (the late 1960s or early 1970s to 1981); **aggressive unilateralism** (1981 to about 1989); and **floundering unilateralism/muddling multilateralism** (1989 to the moving present). Each period yields examples of how academic response meets 'real'-world challenge.

Applications

Lordly unilateralism names the US approach to multilateral organizations from wartime planning for the peace until the early 1970s. Lordliness means nobility, including guileless nobility. The term can also connote pride to the point of hubris in the form of arrogance and overbearingness. Some of each describe positions taken by those who acted in the name of the United States.

The US emerged very strong relative to others following the war.[30] Triumphal Americans sought to plan, construct and lead an order that would maintain the peace *and* sustain US pre-eminence.[31] Scholars played a part.

The newest generation of international organizations headquartered in New York and abroad received a tacit American prescription that might be summed up as good law, good government, and good administration. Uptown from the UN's New York headquarters, at Columbia University, Leland M. Goodrich emphasized good law and good government. Goodrich had completed graduate studies on government at Harvard and he recalled, years after retiring, that the founding of the United Nations reminded him of the founding of the American federal republic. An early book co-written by Goodrich provides a constitutional history of the UN Charter reminiscent of studies that do much the same for the US Constitution.[32]

Besides publishing many studies, Goodrich mentored a series of proteges, by no means Americans only, who themselves have made significant contributions as scholars, teachers and institution builders. At Yale, meanwhile, Walter R. Sharp published works on the proper administration of intergovernmental organizations.[33] Chadwick F. Alger subsequently prepared a report offering unpretentious and attainable recommendations as to how the United States might better meet the challenges of participating in the United Nations.[34]

These and other scholars set themselves the task of educating their students and the attentive public about the units comprising the emergent order of organized internationalism. That their studies *described* the new firmament more than analyzing or explaining it served the task they had set and also accomplished a necessary step toward deeper understanding.[35] Perhaps description seemed sufficient to them. In any event, abstraction through the use of acronyms for organizational names seemingly marked the extent of their theorizing about the practice of multilateralism.

The legal formalism of many early studies should not surprise the thoughtful onlooker. At the outset scholarship had little more to rely on than the record of multilateral diplomacy cast as conventional law as palpable evidence of what had been decided, by whom, how, and why. Moreover, walled institutions on several levels of action figured more within the academic balance of American political science during the 1940s and 1950s than after this discipline underwent its behavioural revolution.[36]

The judgments implied within early studies offer clues to scholars' minds at work. American pioneers in studying international organization carried implicit models of how things should be. These models embedded tacit norms for assessing the United Nations. British scholars traced and carried forward the failed experience of the League of Nations as a backdrop to their investigations of the postwar successor organizations, bespeaking a preference for history as the master means of assessment.[37] But Americans tended to rely implicitly on the mental image of their own federal republic as a basis for judging.[38]

Beyond the description of intergovernmental organizations, scholars often tendered their diagnoses and prescriptions through the evaluation of *problems*. These problems evidently arose from desires to grapple with the 'real' world as they perceived it more than from any urge to fabricate conceptual puzzles, let alone to conceptualize about conceptualizing.[39] To early scholars no doubt such problems seemed sufficiently relevant and challenging on their face to merit attention. Their defining of problems about international organization evoked readily recognizable entities and ailments. Among the problems addressed were the Soviet veto in the UN Security Council and the suspected national disloyalty of Americans within the UN secretariat. The American classic *Swords Into Plowshares* deals at length with six problems, and the enduring appeal of Inis Claude's book testifies to the timeless quality of its substance as well as the trenchancy of its realistic analysis.[40] *International Organization*, a quarterly journal, offered a forum in which scholars (mostly Americans) could inform interested parties about international organizations as such, their problems, and also their accomplishments and prospects. In addition this journal summarized activities of intergovernmental organizations and offered readers bibliographical leads to primary and secondary sources in order to facilitate better understanding.

Setting a pattern that would persist, studies during this period often treated *politics* as deleterious to the rightful functioning of intergovernmental organizations and as extraneous to the scope of scholarly investigation.[41] The American science of politics, at least as applied to intergovernmental organizations, left curiously little room for politics as explanation. Even with respect to the UN General Assembly, where political forces lurk tantalizingly near the surface, analyses sometimes implied less curiosity about politics than attention to other objectives within academia's world of its own.[42]

Some levels of politics American writers make explicit. Politics beneath the nation-state has always attracted scholars. How the United States government reaches decisions pertinent for international organizations forms a generic question that has often stimulated American studies.[43] Still, the American account of how the UN came to be implies cosmic determinations at the creation, when the firmament was wrought, followed by autonomous institutional perpetuation, like some self-winding mechanism powered from the energy by-products of minor administrative exertion.

It was thought that American founders made the most fundamental of decisions at the outset and enshrined these within the UN Charter. Bureaucratic caretaking was thereafter to have supplanted politics. Politics beyond the time of the UN's founding, particularly politics beyond the United States, would offend American sensibilities. These mental constraints on politics meshed with Americans' expectations about their leadership and with the visceral US resort to unilateralism. Stand-alone US guidance would eliminate the need for politics. Perhaps, too, an origin myth featuring the end of politics helped to sustain Americans' trust that after the creation they could revert to what President Warren Harding had, following the previous war, read as 'normalcy'. Americans yearn to establish once-and-for-all solutions to foreign-inspired problems so they can go freely about their lives, liberties and the pursuit of happiness as each may perceive it. Initially the new organization seemed to offer this possibility and thereby permit a return to business as usual.[44]

The cold war stirred practice and then theorizing. American studies followed the Truman administration's Marshall Plan and the organizing of collective self-defence alliances that embraced various parts of the world.[45] Those European-created institutions of the 1950s that would become today's European Union attracted contemporary scholarly attention, notably by Europeans who had resettled in the United States.[46] For a time others investigated integration,[47] especially European integration, though America-based studies became remarkably scarce as the uniting of Europe manifestly proceeded.[48]

David Mitrany's wartime *A Working Peace System*, which outlines and argues for the functional development of international organization, stands as one of multilateralism's seminal contributions of this waning century.[49] Mitrany did not shy from prescribing for the ailing system that he diagnosed. The Mitranian argument for discrete non-political multilateral units suited both the American disposition and the intergovernmental political requisites for accommodating pre-positioned, long-established agencies (UPU, ITU and ILO) within the nascent UN system. Mitrany's plea for separate functional agencies justified on apolitically acceptable grounds the politically necessary geographic distribution of freshly-created headquarters sites for new UN specialized agencies.

Mitrany's assessment began with the world as practitioners saw it, a world of states driven by power politics. His project purported to show

how, through material efforts rather than visionary planning, gentle and gradual progressive activities might transform the existing system. To some extent functionalism befuddled distinctions between realism and idealism. Hans J. Morgenthau endorsed it. William T.R. Fox commended its study. Claude's *Swords Into Plowshares* mounted a formidable attack on the functional approach, then showed consonance with functionalist thinking in its final chapter. Ernst B. Haas followed his pioneering work on European integration with an extravagant exploration of functionalism that sandwiched a discriminating inquiry into the International Labour Organization.[50] A contemporary study reached critical conclusions about functionalist expectations based on an investigation of the World Bank Group and the UN Development Programme.[51] Acknowledged or unacknowledged, Mitrany's notions would similarly influence innumerable investigations over the years.[52]

Elsewhere, the functional approach lent itself to claims on behalf of effective multilateral participation by the less powerful. Canadian practitioners made of it a 'functional principle'. This principle comprised two propositions: 'first, that the Great Powers are entitled to take the lead in international affairs but not to dominate them; and, secondly, control should be shared with such other powers as are able and willing to make a definite contribution to the particular object in view'.[53] The second proposition also subtly sanctioned Canadian disengagement when circumstances suggested this. Almost reflexively, however, Canadian leaders sought assured stations within the inner circles of multilateral institutions. The 'lapidary' approach of functional construction often lauded by practitioner-scholar John W. Holmes implied a strong distaste for blueprinted designs by the most powerful that could exclude the likes of Canada from any significant role. Canadians' emphasis on functional collaboration for building peace carried even to insistence on 'Canadian article' 2 in the NATO Charter by which members pledged their economic cooperation.[54] In Canada, too, scholarship follows practice, but Canadians practice multilateralism.[55] Former UN ambassador Stephen Lewis calls this multilateralism 'endemic to the Canadian character'.[56]

Damage-control unilateralism characterizes the period from the late 1960s or early 1970s until 1981.[57] No specific event marks the advent of this defensive phase of unilateralism, though growing friction between the US President and the UN Secretary-General over the war in Vietnam, along with the loss of some US capacity to muster General Assembly majorities, serve as convenient references.

What happened on these public fronts? In brief, Secretary-General U Thant lent credence to domestic charges that the administration of President Lyndon Johnson was misleading the American public about the possibility of a negotiated settlement in Vietnam.[58] Also, the General Assembly's decision in October 1971 to seat the mainland Chinese delegation presented a spectacular moment hinting at diminished ability by the United States to forestall whatever it did not want to emerge from this plenary organ.[59] Partly because of such tele-visible General Assembly dramas, sometimes spiced by a US spokesman harbouring domestic political ambitions while castigating the foreign wrongdoers, for many Americans the Assembly epitomized the entire United Nations constellation. This perception exaggerated the weakening of US influence and thereby added political inducement to official damage-limitation stances. President Richard Nixon's man John A. Scali resurrected the phrase 'tyranny of the majority' the better to impugn voting in the UN General Assembly.[60] Momentum built during the Nixon administration for the US to exit from membership in the International Labour Organization.[61] Administrations and congresses of both political parties during this period contributed to the batten-the-hatches effect.

The tendency to disengage by closing down connections with parts of the United Nations could come because Americans recognized that they controlled alternative channels for international action. At this time, neither multilateral legitimation nor the material collaboration of other UN members seemed necessary to pursue US aims. President Jimmy Carter, for example, saw himself as eminently successful, as did most Americans, in his solitary act of conciliating the political leaders of Israel and Egypt at Camp David.[62] On another front, Carter sought to advance human rights, 'the soul of our foreign policy', essentially through unilateral means – US foreign aid and trade concessions for human rights compliance, US retorsion (notably cessation of aid and trade concessions) for non-compliance.[63] A series of presidents waged the cold war in surer fashion outside a troubling UN than encumbered within its confines.

The United Nations now afforded little comfort to attentive US publics. For influential Americans the UN had become a hostile arena, 'a dangerous place', 'a place where lies are told'.[64] Better a do-nothing United Nations than one that meddled and infringed, the shunning of the UN seemed to imply. The Carnegie Endowment for International Peace in New York had for many years sustained a series of monographs bearing the generic title *International Conciliation* and during the 1950s facilitated a series of national studies examining UN participation by about twenty states.[65] It ceased support for the investigation of multi-lateralism, closed its Geneva and New York offices, and concentrated on Washington. Academics took actions appropriate to the times and their worldly circumstances. Politics had erupted where no politics had been recognized before; studies were commissioned and completed on the 'politicization' of intergovernmental organizations.[66] The United Nations no longer worked like it had before; studies on 'reform' proliferated.[67] In truth, politics obtains under all conditions, while 'politicization' appears during periods of perceived decline in control by established leadership. Similarly, the appeal of 'reform' tends to grow when an institution's changing ways serve the would-be reformer's interests less than before.[68]

A multinational scholarly collaboration examined the sources and manifestations of power with respect to intergovernmental organizations.[69] *The Anatomy of Influence* addressed ITU, ILO, UNESCO, WHO, IMF, GATT and UNCTAD. While not the first (and certainly not the last) inquiry to do so, this study took explicit and extensive account of non-state forces, especially economic forces. It encompassed private association actors (including NGOs, the media and experts), enfolding these with governments and international civil servants in comprising what the study's principal authors termed the 'subsystems' of international organization. Thus the work's examination of decisionmaking encompassed extra-governmental factors without effacing intergovernmental organizations or dissolving them into networks of networks.

As enmity between segments of the United States and parts of the United Nations developed, the professional cost of studying inter-governmental organizations grew. To write on US foreign policy, a subject of self-evident significance, tends to inoculate the American writer against charges of unscientific procedures. The universalism of American foreign affairs somehow qualifies as the universalism requisite for science, albeit a ptolemaic or otherwise flawed science from critical perspectives.[70] What passed as scientific standards apparently shifted for investigations of international organization that were undertaken as multilateral processes became increasingly (though still only marginally) resistant to American foreign policy. The number of published submissions on international organizations and especially on the United Nations declined in *International Organization*.[71] Low scientific yield in terms of 'systematic and testable theory' and 'cumulative' results[72] provided cover to retreat, regroup, reorient, and advance on a more promising front. In 1979 *International Organization* formalized a decade-long revision of the journal's 'thematic orientation and content', as its editor reported: 'We have completed a transition from a journal devoted to the study of international organizations, particularly the United Nations, to an international journal of "political and economic affairs".'[73]

Aggressive unilateralism denominates the period beginning with the Reagan administration in 1981 and continuing into the first part of the Bush administration, roughly until the end of the cold war. In-your-face posturing and hardball tactics characterized these times. Reaganites practiced unilateralism without tears and without apologies. UN ambassador Jeane Kirkpatrick personified Ronald Reagan's promises to stand tall while seated commandingly in the saddle.[74] The Reagan administration invaded Grenada, shelled Lebanon, bombed Libya, and sought by mining Nicaraguan harbours (thereafter ignoring the World Court), as well as by engineering a guerrilla movement, to overthrow the Sandinista government – unilateral acts that violated the UN Charter as well as other norms.[75] Reagan representatives took unyielding positions at and beyond the UN Conference on the Law of the Sea.[76] Having been encouraged to withhold funds as a means of controlling undesired UN outcomes, Congress would remain unabashedly niggardly and the US bill would mount in arrears well beyond the Reagan years.[77] The Reagan administration took the US out of UNESCO membership.[78] Kirkpatrick colleague Ambassador Charles Lichenstein, for once prompting doubt about his administration's sense of direction, invited any discontented UN members to 'consider removing themselves and their organization from the United States. We will . . . be at dockside bidding you a fond farewell as you set off into the sunset.'[79]

Academics had largely abandoned the field of international organization to non-academic educators. Without much critical challenge, the Heritage Foundation sponsored a series of publications besieging the United Nations system.[80] Reagan administration practitioners, some from the Heritage Foundation pool, likewise published contemporaneously or later to inform the public's understanding.[81] Others added their harsh judgments.[82]

Some careful scholarly books germane to international organization did appear and reappear during this period; of them, an illustrative few bear noting. A work by Richard B. Bilder offered a number of 'risk-management techniques' and counselled on protecting one's state against changes in the value of an agreement as well as 'against non-performance or inadequate performance' by others.[83] Harold K. Jacobson's *Networks of Interdependence* ended its second edition with this cautious conclusion: 'The most important issue . . . is not building up the authority of a universal membership, general purpose organization, but rather insuring that there are open and ample communications links among the major groups of states today'.[84] At the hands of M.J. Peterson the UN General Assembly received comprehensive, illuminating treatment.[85] Journalist Linda M. Fasulo and Johnson administration UN ambassador Seymour Maxwell Finger presented cameos of US representatives at the United Nations.[86] Lawrence S. Finkelstein edited a volume whose title promised at long last a sustained study of politics in intergovernmental organizations.[87] Richard L. Jackson, a practitioner, produced a detailed and richly nuanced study entitled *The Non-Aligned, the UN and the Superpowers* while the cold war still lent meaning to non-alignment and to superpowers heading two blocs.[88] Inis Claude's *States and the Global System* emerged shortly before the world underwent momentous change.[89]

Meanwhile, the quarterly journal previously relied upon by scholars in the field received a further cosmetic uplift. In 1983 its editorial board 'gave the new subtitle "Journal of Political and Economic Affairs" what amounted to top billing by reducing the title *International Organization* to *IO*'.[90] Friedrich Kratochwil and John Gerard Ruggie sought to explain why the field of international organization had, as they saw it, declined into 'irrelevance if not obscurity'. Kratochwil and Ruggie maintained that 'the fate of theory and the fate of practice were never all that closely linked after World War II'. They contended that the international organizational 'patient is moribund' and stated that 'the leading doctors' in the field 'have become biochemists and have stopped treating and in most cases even seeing' international organizations as 'patients'. The doctors' switch to biochemistry in their professional identification nonetheless offered payoffs for the present and significant promise for a more distant future: 'new discoveries have been made, new diagnostic techniques have been developed, and our understanding has deepened, raising the possibility of more effective treatment in the long run'.[91] Academics had left a dying cause in favour of more rewarding endeavours.

For many American academics, 'regime' became the charmed concept in their newest quest for deepened understanding immediately, effective (if problematic) treatment eventually, and scholarly recognition in any event. The term had referred to international arrangements during the era of last century's public international unions and beyond.[92] More recently it enjoyed usage with respect to US foreign policy, mostly in substantive sectors or issue-areas the functioning of which receive fewer headlines than do issues of war and peace. Of course regime also has a history of application within states, where it connotes a system of government or rule. And to *regiment* means to organize, order, discipline or otherwise subject to control.

Regime differs from *regimen*, though the two share some meaning. Both entail rules. The rules of a regimen, usually deduced previously by others and undertaken voluntarily, imply improvement in the well-being of the subject and thus in the subject's capacity to take advantage of life's chances through rigorous, self-disciplined adherence to these rules.[93] Regimen thus demands behavioural change yielding benefit to one's body – or body politic. Regime rules demand less dedicated compliance, at least for the regime leader.

The notion of regime heartened explorers of international 'principles, norms, rules, and decision-making procedures'.[94] To theorize about international regimes protected academics from professional stigmata while researchers approached what might otherwise be seen as international law. Likewise, to invoke the language of regime warded off criticism while academics followed, comfortably beyond institutional walls, matters that had previously been associated with the study of international organization. Regime, in short, facilitated reinvention befitting altered exigency.

The notion of international regimes also permitted discreet revisitation of older puzzles. Does the functioning of transstate efforts toward mitigating common problems that manifest low controversiality engender patterns of cooperation enabling more demanding regimes? Do regime participants learn or rehabituate so as to transcend steeper challenges? A security regime might seem impossible, though by small steps in raising confidence it could prove achievable. If so, in what time frame and with respect to what sequence of predecessor regimes might security be realized?

Regime as idea rationalizes regime as practice. The term forms a staple in the vocabulary of American foreign policy; its summoning enables scholars to identify with power. Without fundamentally altering unilateral ways, the US accommodated rhetorically to the growing need to bring others along. Thus for instance a regime was instituted to contain the threat of nuclear weapons. Regime thinking appeals to the American preference for laying down the law while finessing the burden of abiding laws laid down with others. From a position of leadership, Americans regard rulings more favourably than rules. A regime suits American liking because the hegemon largely establishes precepts by its actions and their justification by verbal embellishment, whatever may have been the 'procedures' prescribed for or ascribed to this regime.[95] Unlike formal general sets of regulations, then, they reflect a comfort level for the US that provides little cause to flout norms. Regimes, however, do tend to create obligations for others even though these do not necessarily bind or even pertain to the United States. They certainly do not fence in the US, and little empirical evidence demonstrates that they lessen an American sense of impunity. In sum, regimes broadly construed institutionalize privileges for their alpha even while they impose more demanding expectations upon followers.[96] Power enlists legal finery within regimes yet more effectively than without them.[97]

These features of regime met the designs of American academics. They dressed up unilateralism in sophisticated conceptual attire. From other vantage points, theorizing about regimes looked like the ideologizing of US foreign policy on behalf of the status quo.[98]

Floundering unilateralism/muddling multilateralism tenders a working title for the period from the cold war's end into the moving present. Developments in the world at large presented opportunities to change US practice. Initiatives by the Gorbachev government had in 1987 sent a clear message that the USSR wished to accommodate new realities within a United Nations context. The two superpowers cooperated in ending the Iran–Iraq war, meanwhile establishing (along with China, France and the United Kingdom, the three other permanent members of the Security Council) certain institutional conditions for a UN concert of great powers.[99] The collapse of the Soviet Union lowered the political cost at home for US presidents prepared to modify tried and true ways in order to meet unaccustomed circumstances. Increasingly after the cold war many Americans cared little about happenings abroad. Sporadically they found disturbing the phenomena serialized on their television screens, but for the most part the foreign paths taken by their political leaders, whether through or around the UN, mattered less than concerns about domestic needs and the accumulated effects of their neglect during the protracted global struggle. This period has witnessed some halting steps in adapting multilaterally to emerging situations. In particular, the convening of contact groups suggests official American hopes that just-in-time coalitions may share or assume responsibilities for coping with incontestably appalling events.

To some politically-active Americans, post-cold war actions by the Bush administration and especially by the Clinton administration seemed increasingly disoriented or confused. Neither administration undertook a publicized shift from unilateralism, though elements of multilateralism appeared fitfully in the piecemeal, stopgap adjustments of both presidencies to fresh challenges. President George Bush had invaded Panama without asking anyone's permission, but before displacing Iraqi forces from Kuwait he sought legitimation by the UN Security Council. Bush also practiced hat-in-hand diplomacy at many points outside the United Nations, reviving a multilateral makeshift pioneered less overtly by Reagan administrators in financing the Contra insurgency against the government of Nicaragua.[100]

President Bill Clinton's operatives scrambled by all possible means, including inaction under multilateral cover, to cope with or avoid inherited problems in more than one part of former Yugoslavia, with worsening situations in Somalia and Haiti, and with the graphic horrors of Rwanda. US Presidents since the Monroe Doctrine of 1823 had seen fit to act unilaterally and without prior notification throughout the hemisphere of the Americas. Clinton arranged authorization by the UN Security Council before animating replacement of the de facto government of Haiti. When in early 1998 domestic pressures mounted to launch a titanic assault against Saddam Hussein, an increasingly familiar pattern emerged. Seriatim bilaterals with consultative partners were presented as agreements by US spokespersons through announcements amplified by American media. This cumulative form of multilateralism US interpreters spun in order to contrive permission for making war.[101]

Notwithstanding multilateral gestures, the underlying unilateral disposition remained. For instance, the early reassurance Clinton extended to the advocacy group Americans for the Universality of UNESCO presaged no serious effort to rejoin the specialized agency. Other revealing vacillations followed. Clinton had announced a new policy of 'assertive multilateralism' in 1992 while calling for a rapid deployment force that could respond quickly to troubles the world over. Then-UN ambassador Madeleine Albright sought for a time to sell assertive multilateralism until, finding little domestic acceptance of the phrase, she repaired to 'burden sharing' as vindication.[102] Increasingly robust military action in Somalia took its toll on practice and principle alike. American servicemen died, and the pictorial indignities to their remains led Clinton to issue a prohibitive list of conditions for future US participation in UN military operations.[103] Clinton's list bespoke a new US retreat from multilateralism and as well seemed meant to curb peacekeeping-related UN operations commanded and staffed by non-American personnel. The effort succeeded tragically by fostering what appeared in retrospect like 'New York' indifference to the impending slaughter in Rwanda.[104] Assertive multilateralism as policy or slogan died a quiet death.

The US approach to hemispheric freer trade offers an example of ambiguous unilateralism or multilateralism by default. Clinton sought to add incrementally to the North American Free Trade Agreement (NAFTA) by negotiating one by one with the governments of individual state candidates. The process of expansion slated next to embrace Chile would have continued serially thereafter with other selected parties. But Congress denied fast-track authority to the Clinton administration – but one emblem of a weakened, diminished presidency – and the progression toward hemispheric freer trade took on a modestly multilateral character with a leisurely timetable pending renewed congressional permission for presidential trade initiatives.

One keen and well-connected observer sensed within the Clinton administration 'a certain exuberance' when the opportunity arose to 'do the unilateral'. It was said that these chances were eagerly seized upon, for instance by threatening trade sanctions as well as undertaking subsequent measures against Japan and by mounting missile attacks on Iraq. They provided relief from the limitations inherent in such ordeals as North Korean wrangles and Bosnian frustrations that appeared to be required yet exacerbated by multilateralism.[105] As the quadrennial US political cycle approached its 1996 presidential election phase, congressional measures to extend extraterritorial sanctions to those abroad who benefit from economic relations with Cuba, Iran or Libya – an extension of unilateralism by other means – received Clinton's endorsement. Yet Clinton aides seemed defensive when charged with what one called 'all this whining' about abandoning multilateral approaches. 'It's simply an unfair complaint,' said then-deputy national security adviser Samuel R. Berger. 'This is a Government...whose instinct has always been to do...things in a collegial way. To extrapolate from a few instances that the US is going unilateral is a bit ridiculous.'[106] Clearly deed and word presented a mixed picture.

Defensiveness about unilateralism perhaps showed itself because of the increasing outspokenness by allies opposing the extraterritorial measures. For example, such measures Canadian Minister of Foreign Affairs and International Trade Lloyd Axworthy termed 'bullying'. Thus potential domestic political gains from piling on more sanctions against Castro's Cuba and other renegade states[107] were offset somewhat by the events they set in motion that invited criticism of Clinton's world leadership.

A shortfall of Clinton leadership did serve as one charge by his main 1996 presidential opponent.[108] But the attack on Clinton's multilateral dalliance loomed larger. In announcing his own candidacy for President,

Robert Dole sounded a theme that would recur, with variations, through-out the long campaign: 'We must stop placing the agenda of the United Nations before the interests of the United States. And when we take our revolution to the White House...we will vow that American foreign policies will be determined by *us*, not by the United Nations.' Although the 1996 presidential election did not hinge on issues of foreign policy, both candidates' postures reconfirmed accustomed patterns: the world leadership obsession and the unilateral compulsion.

Contradictions have grown between evolving exigency and historic US practice. 'The spread of our companies to every corner of the world...will push us to take the multilateral route', said Dean Jeffrey Garten of the Yale School of Management, a sometime international negotiator for and official in the Clinton administration. 'We would like to do what we did in the cold war, to go to our allies and decree an outcome. You can't do it any more. Now there is always a huge amount of arm-twisting and tradeoffs.'[109] Multilateral means would facilitate the necessary bargaining to reach effective agreements, yet old tendencies persisted.

Media images accentuated a dilemma. As throngs of refugees fled hunger, disease, torture and execution, Americans pondered whether to deploy in harm's way their own young men and women in uniform so as to lead the new humanitarian-stabilization missions, or whether instead to stand aside and let others lead these multinational forces. Behind-the-screens prevention of UN efforts offered no allure as a third option; television would still show inhuman horrors and history would uncover the connivance permitting their perpetuation. Thus while lea-dership held its liabilities, so did either the foregoing of leadership or its subversion if undertaken by others.

NATO had seemingly presented a promising alternative to the UN for meeting selected challenges. The organization afforded a unified com-mand structure to sanction active US leadership. Its cold war cohesive-ness had impressed observers and its record of preventing aggression within the NATO domain was frequently extolled with undeniable supporting evidence. Yet the American disinclination toward multila-teralism, along with the genuine risk in Bosnia and elsewhere to Amer-ican military personnel and to American political support, made commitment even to NATO operations – especially ground operations – a matter of equivocation.[110]

New tasks for NATO promised no deliverance for Americans. The misfired US effort in Somalia long made alliance directors hesitate to arrest prominent war criminals throughout former Yugoslavia.

Moreover, NATO lacked experience and a clear constitutional mandate to ease complicated troubles within states, especially states beyond the Treaty's writ. NATO seemed to hold a reservoir of contingency plans containing more scenarios for war than scenarios for peace. An unpromising orientation to communal problems requiring third-party conciliation was suggested by the longstanding failure to resolve conflicts on Cyprus and elsewhere between NATO members Greece and Turkey. And the curtailed multilateralism of NATO, a multilateralism made more pointedly exclusive by the line drawn beyond newly-anointed eastern European members, gave non-member Russia little reason to support NATO military operations in Serbia by affirmation within the United Nations. In brief, the NATO alternative offered no remedy to relieve the sharpening quandaries of leadership.

During the Law of the Sea saga, Leigh S. Ratiner warned that if American 'leadership is abdicated and the world finds that it can proceed without us, it will not be easy for the United States to reclaim its influence'.[111] Multilateral processes led by NGOs and other governments to ban landmines and limit practices injurious to the biosphere presented new challenges to the US unilateral predilection. Clinton had spoken clearly before the UN General Assembly in 1994 against the continuing use of antipersonnel landmines. But his administration boycotted the subsequent Ottawa Process and introduced, at the Oslo Conference of 1997, eleventh-hour exceptions to accommodate the 'unique responsibilities' of the US while acting for the UN in Korea. It also insisted on the option of withdrawal and an added delay of nine years before treaty implementation. As such these demands failed, but the effort succeeded in providing reasons for Washington not to adhere while clouding the prospect of compliance by others. The Pentagon and Joint Chiefs of Staff prevailed with a US Commander-in-Chief who had conspicuously not served militarily.[112]

As another multilateral process proceeded through Berlin, Bonn and Kyoto, domestic pressures limited a US commitment to cut the emission of effluents contributing to the global greenhouse effect. Far from the bold stand called for earlier by Senator (and presidential candidate) Al Gore,[113] to some environmentalists the Clinton administration seemed to be leading the world toward further threatening climate change. Meanwhile, another multilateral initiative to forbid children as soldiers took shape, notwithstanding earlier US efforts to discourage such conventional action. With regard both to quasi-military multilateral operations and to multilateral agreements, US legislators stressed the need for a clear 'exit strategy' before going forward in the first place.[114]

Unsettled US conduct has nonetheless heartened students of multilateralism to address intergovernmental organizations as such.[115] Less uniformly are organizations marginalized in deference to the unwalled institutions favoured for some time by American practice and scholarship. Moreover, problems of organized multilateralism once again are defined, diagnosed, and prescribed for with alacrity.[116] Achievements and opportunities draw resumed attention.[117] Human rights have received especially cogent analysis; today, furthermore, rights often are examined in multilateral context rather than solely in relation to US foreign policy.[118] Indeed, with regard to human rights, scholarly output far exceeds that of enabling efforts by the US government, as measured by the latter's record of ratifying multilateral human rights treaties. The concern with environmental ills that had mounted discernibly in recent decades has begun, at least, to find published expression regarding one phase of multilateral treatment, conventional law, though less palpably regarding the review, through organized intergovernmental oversight, of agreements' implementation.[119]

Literature on *reform* has flourished. Here a few further general observations must suffice. 'Reform' implies change from the status quo, but this term bears many meanings. To reform an institution may imply the taking of measures that restore the existing institution to a yearned-for bygone state. Alternatively, reform may mean starting with a clean slate and fresh foundation on which like-minded successor founders re-form a new institution to replace the one targeted for extinction. Again, reform may connote the further development of an institution toward enhanced effectiveness, improved accountability, increased efficiency, or other values. Reform may even signify the determination to get out of an institution, thereby reforming one's own earlier decision to join it and justifying this retreat with a stated hope that one's exit will chasten and brace remaining participants to institute salutary change. Thus reformist language can even cover the threadbare probity of disengagement.[120] In principle, reform can rather mean upgraded commitment in an institutionally-engaged participant's own behaviour, implying a regimen for this participant to shape itself up voluntarily. But reform without qualification signifies change without determinacy.

'Reform' suffers further as a vehicle for communicating definite meaning because of its useful ambiguity for purveying political rhetoric. Within the United States, 'reform' is the senior member in a family of vague terms with a common prefix: renew, restructure, re-energize, re-engineer, reinvent, even redeem and resurrect. As counters in political discourse these words serve often to substitute for more precise specification of what, beyond election day or its equivalent, may be intended, let alone actually forthcoming. Reformist writings thus warrant care in reading. True, estimable proposals for change are sometimes advanced in writings on reform;[121] moreover, meritorious reformist elements appear in American writings that eschew reformist aims. Prudent winnowing yields valuable ideas. To this observer the literature on reform seems now less inclined than earlier to long for an erstwhile golden age with its once and future system, to replace existing institutions, or to withdraw, and more inclined to build upon the modest success of the living United Nations.[122]

Support for American studies of multilateralism has grown in recent years. The Academic Council on the United Nations System (ACUNS) includes scholars, state and non-state practitioners, independent observers from many countries besides the US, and even an occasional journalist among its members. ACUNS organizes programmes, prepares aids to teaching, and facilitates access to research opportunities. The Ford Foundation extended financial assistance to ACUNS; other American and international sources followed. *Global Governance*, a refereed journal distributed to ACUNS members, began publication in 1995.

Conclusions

This study of US scholarship on multilateralism stresses American enthrallment with solitary leadership in a changing world. The chapter now lists summarily some matters that American scholars have not yet much attended. It closes by welcoming the promise of recent multilateral studies.

The difficult logical accommodation between world leadership and unilateral action has merely been probed here.[123] One clue to their *psycho*logical accommodation may lie in the American tendency to define today's world as a single-superpower or unipolar system, not one featuring more than one great power. Far less does this system become defined as one comprising numerous noteworthy states, inter-state institutions and non-state entities. As testament to the unipolar conception, few American writings even contemplate a concert of great powers guided by the US to provide multilateral direction and stability.[124] For reasons argued throughout this chapter, few American academic writers ask seriously what conditions would relieve the US of hegemonic stresses by producing strengthened intergovernmental institutions.[125] Beyond consideration of their effectiveness, few analyze what conditions would make strengthened intergovernmental institutions more *accountable* to what the UN Charter calls 'the peoples of the United Nations'.[126] No studies of which I am aware inquire as to how the general standards already set for labour, environmental protection and human rights might actually be implemented, thereby soothing the quixotic passion to exact American expectations under pain of US sanctions in showdowns with individual trade partners.[127] Finally, few American reformist writings today consider improving the quality of US participation as an important part of reforming the United Nations system.

Nonetheless, American scholarly writings about multilateralism once again appear at a wholesome rate. New inquiries address organized internationalism while maintaining a clinical perspective on organizers, including the US, and organizations alike. Feminist contributions now abound, opening new dimensions of multilateralism while forging solidarities that depreciate national boundaries. Critical feminist scholarship also challenges established views of the state (by treating it as a gendered, patriarchal construct ripe for deconstruction) and security (by privatizing, personalizing and sharing the experience of insecurity).[128] Some American scholars have taken cues from the French epistemological revolutionaries Michel Foucault and Jacques Derrida. Postmodernist critiques joggle encrusted verities, destabilize traditional vantage points, and open space for alternatives. Such alternatives do not necessarily entail multilateralism, but the fresh waves of postmodernist writings generate healthy uncertainty and undermine foregone conclusions during times at once conditional and promising.[129] The conceptual adoption of 'multilateralism',[130] however, most clearly indicates a shift by American academics, if only for a multilateralist moment.

Notes

1   Here, as in chapters on the literature by other authors, 'multilateralism' encompasses generally the practice and study of multi-participant institutions and organizing processes. Such relaxed usage is necessary, not least in the present chapter, in order to include writings germane to multilateralism that take no explicit account of the concept.

2   The unmasking of ideology exercises scholars across the social sciences. A note of self-critical caution adapted from anthropologist Clifford Geertz on the universal tendency to exempt one's own abstractions from critical observation surely invites iteration here: '*I* create theories of international relations; *you* hold opinions about foreign policy; *s/he* ideologizes'.

3   Notably the writings of Robert W. Cox, Robert Gilpin and Susan Strange.

4   Recall that security/military exigency historically vies with economic bases for explaining outcomes. ('Spades shape life, but clubs trump spades.') Some

would classify advancing technology and its offspring as irresistible auto-nomous factors molding political decisions. ('Invention is the mother of necessity.') Surely the information revolution, including the transnational outreach of mass media, unleashes forces that governments try to control with decreasing success. For instance, persons not physically upon the scene now commit locally-defined crime. Visual communications thrust Ethiopia, Somalia, Rwanda and parts of former Yugoslavia on to the global agenda, signifying the dynamism of civil society. Of enduring cogency on the integral relationship between information and political economy is A.J. Liebling's dictum that freedom of the press belongs to those who own one – or, it might be added, more than one. The literature on political choices structured by the information revolution will no doubt continue to grow despite the difficulties of establishing causality.

5   Georg Schwarzenberger describes 'hegemony' as 'imperialism with good manners'. Hedley Bull, *The Anarchical Society*, London: Macmillan, 1977, p. 216. The 'good' in 'good manners' probably resides inescapably in the eye of the beholder. 'Manners' perhaps translates as principles, norms, rules, and decision-making procedures. See Stephen D. Krasner, 'Structural Causes and Regime Consequences: Regimes as Intervening Variables', in Krasner, ed., *International Regimes*, Ithaca: Cornell University Press, 1983, p. 1. See also Krasner, *Structural Conflict: The Third World Against Global Liberalism*, Berkeley: University of California Press, 1985. Krasner, pp. 62ff, says that the US used postwar intergovernmental organizations to veil its domination. See also Stephen Gill, *American Hegemony and the Trilateral Commission*, Cambridge: Cambridge University Press, 1989.

6   The almighty quality of hegemony proves clearer when looking at many patterns of political economy than for instance at institutions mandated to facilitate mutual understanding among different cultures or at processes authorizing peacekeeping operations.

7   See Townsend Hoopes and Douglas Brinkley, *FDR and the Creation of the U.N.*, New Haven: Yale University Press, 1997.

8   Michael H. Hunt, *Ideology and U.S. Foreign Policy*, New Haven: Yale University Press, 1987, ch. 2.

9   The quest for a new peer enemy or face-off partner to replace the USSR in a replicated two-power global struggle has been noted by various observers. Some, though certainly not US presidents, script China as a candidate. Iraq among others has played the part of a lesser villain providing focus to US foreign policy and its domestic support. Alternatively, militant Islam serves as a possible supra-state foe or even a competing civilization. On the pattern of finding enemies, see Perry McC. Smith, *The Air Force Plans for Peace, 1943–1945*, Ann Arbor: UMI, 1991, and Michael Klare, *Rogue States and Nuclear Outlaws: America's Search for a New Foreign Policy*, New York: Hill and Wang, 1995.

10 A telling debate has exchanged reflections about how long the United States may remain the greatest power of them all. Paul Kennedy's *Rise and Fall of the Great Powers: Economic Change and Military Conflict from 1500 to 2000*, New York: Random House, 1987 rapidly achieved bestseller status in the US; it aroused a series of rebuttals. See for instance Samuel P. Huntington, 'The U.S. – Decline or Renewal?', *Foreign Affairs*, 67, Winter 1988–89; Henry Nau, *The*

Myth of America's Decline: Leading the World Economy into the 1990s, New York: Oxford University Press, 1990; Joseph S. Nye, Jr., *Bound to Lead: The Changing Nature of American Power*, New York: Basic Books, 1990. The debate did not begin with Kennedy's book; see sources cited in David P. Rapkin, 'The Contested Concept of Hegemonic Leadership', in Rapkin, ed., *World Leadership and Hegemony*, Boulder: Lynne Rienner, 1990. See also Richard M. Nixon, *Beyond Peace*, New York: Random House, 1994, pp. 29–39. Nor has the discussion ended. See Lea Brilmayer, *American Hegemony: Political Morality in a One-Superpower World*, New Haven: Yale University Press, 1994 and Ronald Steel, *Temptations of a Superpower*, Cambridge: Harvard University Press, 1995. In *False Dawn: The Delusions of Global Capitalism*, New York: New Press, 1999, John Gray casts Burkean doubt upon the benefits for liberal civilization of unregulated markets opened by American supremacy. To imply that American exultation in US leadership bridges partisan and other divides does not mean that governmental institutions serve to optimize this leadership. Legislative permission denied for executives effectively to negotiate trade agreements, budgetary wrangles that fail to honour UN dues, accumulating multilateral treaties signed but unratified, and other congressional efforts to micromanage that shackle presidents must perplex observers in other polities, not least those who enjoy a pattern of majority governments held responsible for operating parliamentary systems.

11 'The idea that American prosperity depends upon a world order imposed by the United States has extremely unsettling implications.... As long as U.S. interests are defined in terms of world order, Bosnias will be like buses:... – there will always be another one coming down the street.' Christopher Layne and Benjamin Schwarz, 'American Hegemony: Without an Enemy', *Foreign Policy*, 92, Fall 1993, pp. 11–12, 15–16. Compare Ted Galen Carpenter, *Beyond NATO: Staying Out of Europe's Wars*, Washington: Cato Institute, 1994.

12 'Who Now Cares About NATO?', *Wall Street Journal*, 6 February 1995, as cited by Martin Walker, 'A New American Isolationism?', *International Journal*, 52, Summer 1997, p. 395. Kristol's problems are Mexico, China and 'fundamentalist Islam in north Africa and the Middle East'.

13 'Too Many Arms to Twist', *New York Times*, 22 March 1998. Notwithstanding such debates as those sampled here, within official US circles NATO remains a multilateral institution favoured much more widely than the United Nations.

14 *Temptations of a Superpower*, Cambridge: Harvard University Press, 1995, pp. 135–7.

15 US National Public Radio, 'All Things Considered', 29 January 1998.

16 Haass, *The Reluctant Sheriff: The United States After the Cold War*, New York: Council on Foreign Relations, 1997. The rallying of made-to-order instant coalitions for confronting emergent crises Haass poses, oddly, as an alternative to the fitful, ad hoc, reactive foreign policy emblematic of unilateralism. Madeleine Albright enterprised a variant of the Haass approach by shuttling an ersatz Security Council around several European capitals in an effort to address difficulties with Slobodan Milosevic while minimizing Russian resistance and circumventing Chinese opposition. NATO's air campaign against Serbia and the nation-building exercise in Kosovo showed the alliance's capacity for mission spillover. But NATO leaders long remained

reluctant to perform the sheriff's task of apprehending top indicted war criminals in Bosnia, let alone in Serbia.

17   In announcing his fateful 1968 bid for the presidency, US Senator Robert F. Kennedy held at stake 'our right to the moral leadership of this planet'. US Senate minority leader Robert Dole stated in May 1994 that 'We're not France. We're not Great Britain. We're the United States of America, and we've had moral authority in this world for a long time, and moral leadership in this world for a long time, and the people of the world look to us for leadership.' A more recent variant of the theme of world leadership is the insistence by members of the Clinton administration that America is the 'indispensable nation'.

18   Compare Robert W. Gregg, *About Face? The United States and the United Nations*, Boulder: Lynne Rienner, 1993, p. 73. Fouad Ajami takes the vehicle to sea, calling multilateralism a 'flag of convenience' for US foreign policy. Public Broadcasting System, 'McNeil–Lehrer NewsHour', 29 August 1995.

19   Sewell, 'Congenital Unilateralism and the Adaptation of American Academics', paper presented at American Political Science Association annual meeting, August, 1986, Washington, DC. Though none bears any responsibility for the outcome, the author acknowledges gratefully the suggestions of fellow panelists Alan L. Keyes, Edward C. Luck, Gene M. Lyons and Charles William Maynes.

20   See Holbrooke, *To End a War: From Sarajevo to Dayton and Beyond*, New York: Random House, 1998.

21   Joseph J. Ellis, *American Sphinx: The Character of Thomas Jefferson*, New York: Alfred A. Knopf, 1997, pp. 124, 181. 'Independence forever': Daniel Webster voiced this sentiment in 1826 by quoting John Adams' day-of-death utterance.

22   In offering a somewhat different interpretation regarding an 'auxiliary role' of America's relating internationally, Inis L. Claude Jr. emphasizes 'uncommittedness', *American Approaches to World Affairs*, Lanham, MD: University Press of America, 1986, pp. 5–8. Given this characteristic of uncommittedness, the propensity to concoct 'contact groups' and 'regimes' in preference to working through established UN bodies proceeds plausibly. The fashioning of noncommittal multilateral arrangements to suit unilateral taste the argument elaborates later in this chapter.

23   Note that the belief in a free hand for making foreign policy does not neatly fit practice. Glorification of free agency tends to devalue the need for empirical investigation into the complex permutations of free agency. To exaggerate *actual* autonomy and not merely to exalt the *value* of autonomy contributes to the discouragement of inquiries into the co-determination of US foreign policy. Scholarly American studies rarely examine how individuals acting on behalf of friendly nations lead from the superpower's shadow through the subtle art of influencing the composition and choices of its executive and legislature. The alleged involvement in American politics by agents for China has however spurred intense distress. More broadly, Ronald Steel has observed that 'The more...Washington speaks in the world's name and demands the world's endorsement of its actions, the less freedom of action it enjoys.' 'Lonely At The Top', *New York Times*, 1 March 1998.

24 With respect to the living legacy of American isolationism, see Bruce M. Russett, *No Clear and Present Danger: A Skeptical View of the United States Entry into World War II*, New York: Harper Torchbooks, 1972. James Chace and Caleb Carr emphasize the requisite of *solitude* over isolationism in America's historic search for invulnerability: 'Statesmen have only two basic tools at their disposal when pursuing the national interest – diplomatic negotiation and military force. But negotiation – and this point has never been lost on America's leaders – implies compromise. Absolute security, on the other hand, cannot be negotiated; it can only be won. This is especially true when the nation that seeks it acts in solitude.' *America Invulnerable: The Quest for Absolute Security from 1812 to Star Wars*, New York: Summit, 1988, p. 13. The Strategic Defense Initiative (SDI) and its successor proposals epitomize unilateralism, not merely solitude.

25 A self-appointed spokesman for the armed separatist Republic of Texas suggested in April 1997 that any clash with federal forces or those of Texas Governor George W. Bush could 'set off the liberation of America from the New World Order tyranny'.

26 Charles William Maynes points out that during the last year of the Bush administration, Republicans in the US House of Representatives supported the President on UN matters about 25 per cent of the time. They did not give President Clinton a single supportive vote on similar matters for the first two years of the successor administration, 'and we're talking about the two years before the 1994 revolution' wrought by the Republican takeover of Congress. US National Public Radio, 'Weekend Edition', 9 November 1996.

27 'Not since President [Woodrow] Wilson helped to create the League of Nations and then was denied American membership in it by the [US] Senate has it been easy to sell Americans on the idea of international organization.' Daniel Schorr, 'All Things Considered', 24 September 1996. The film 'Wilson' (1944), awarded five Oscars, proved a box-office disappointment and nowadays rarely regains exposure through television reruns. On the American people's preference for unilateralism over multilateralism see further, for example, Catherine Kelleher, 'Soldiering On: US Public Opinion on the Use of Force', *Brookings Review*, Spring 1994.

28 Television pontificators and inquisitors raise the immediate domestic political cost of cooperating multilaterally well above that of operating unilaterally.

29 Though surely an extreme example, the position bluntly enunciated by former Assistant Secretary of Defense Richard Perle does demonstrate this tendency: 'One of the advantages of winning the cold war is that we no longer have to show the regard we once did for Russian sentiment.' 'All Things Considered', 17 February 1998.

30 William T.R. Fox, *The Super-Powers*, New York: Harcourt, 1944. Fox's superpowers included Great Britain along with the US and the USSR.

31 Compare Robert Latham, *The Liberal Moment: Modernity, Security, and the Making of Postwar International Order*, New York: Columbia University Press, 1997.

32 Goodrich, Edvard Hambro and Anne Patricia Simons, *Charter of the United Nations: Commentary and Documents*, Boston: World Peace Foundation, 1946. This book's 1969 third edition was published by Columbia University Press.

33   For instance, *Field Administration in the United Nations System: The Conduct of International Economic and Social Programs*, New York: Praeger, 1961.

34   *United States Representation in the United Nations*, New York: Carnegie Endowment for International Peace, 1961.

35   'We cannot explain what we have not first described.' John Gerard Ruggie, 'Multilateralism: The Anatomy of an Institution', *International Organization*, 46, Summer 1992, p. 598.

36   On the triumph of behaviouralism and how it came to prevail, see Robert A. Dahl, 'The Behavioral Approach in Political Science: Epitaph for a Monument to a Successful Protest', *American Political Science Review*, 55, December 1961, pp. 763–72. Dahl warns, p. 772, that 'unless the study of politics generates and is guided by broad, bold, even if highly vulnerable general theories, it is headed for the ultimate disaster of triviality'.

37   For instance, Evan Luard, *A History of the United Nations*, New York: St. Martin's, 1982, pp. 3ff. A succinct survey of British scholarly work on international organization is A.J.R. Groom, Paul Taylor and Andrew Williams, *The Study of International Organisation: British Experiences*, Hanover, NH: Academic Council on the United Nations System, 1990. For an American's review of British scholarship on international relations, see Gene M. Lyons, 'The Study of International Relations in Great Britain: Further Connections', *World Politics*, 38, July 1986, pp. 626–45. Various insights as to commonalities and especially differences in British and American styles are addressed in Steve Smith, ed., *International Relations: British and American Perspectives*, New York: Basil Blackwell, 1985. See especially ch. 10 by David Armstrong on international organization. In his introduction, Smith contrasts Britain's extended experience as a great power in a multipolar 'world' with US confirming experience in a bipolar one. He also contrasts the social science milieu that gives rise to the study of international relations in the US with the philosophical, legal and historical roots of its study in Britain, pp. xi, xiii. Both polities' approaches to foreign affairs seem to be coloured by their sense of insularity to decadence across the water.

38   Practitioners led the way. For executive and congressional expressions during 1945, see Thomas M. Franck, *Nation Against Nation: What Happened to the U.N. Dream and What the U.S. Can Do About It*, New York: Oxford University Press, 1985, pp. 14–16. Franck tags this a 'consanguinity trip'.

39   'One should not confuse the moon with the finger that is pointing at the moon', counsels an Asian proverb, for which I am grateful to Don Nakanishi. The first postwar generation of American scholars focused upon the moon, rarely upon a gestalt encompassing the moon and the observer directing attention to it, never upon the pointing finger.

40   Inis L. Claude, Jr., *Swords Into Plowshares: The Problems and Progress of International Organization*, New York: Random House, 1956, 1959, 1964, 1971.

41   As a noted American political scientist once confided, the more whatever might happen regarding international organization could be accounted for by factors other than politics, the more it suited him. Another noted scholar, Harold D. Lasswell, offered complementary advice in a collaborative quest to improve (for instance) 'the organization of the United Nations and other official agencies' and introduce 'a current of salutary transformations wherever policy is made'. Lasswell counseled careful language to further such

aims: ' "policy" is free of many of the undesirable connotations clustered about the word *political*, which is often believed to imply "partisanship" or "corruption" '. Lasswell, 'The Policy Orientation', in Daniel Lerner and Lasswell, *et al.*, eds., *The Policy Sciences: Recent Developments in Scope and Method*, Stanford: Stanford University Press, 1951, pp. 12, 5.

42   The reader may in any event gain added understanding of plenary politics or multilateral diplomacy from some combination of the following: Thomas Hovet, Jr., *Bloc Politics in the United Nations*, Cambridge: MIT Press, 1958; Robert E. Riggs, *Politics in the United Nations: A Study of United States Influence in the General Assembly*, Urbana: University of Illinois Press, 1958; Conor Cruise O'Brien, *To Katanga and Back: A UN Case History*, New York: Simon and Schuster, 1962, ch. 1; Hayward R. Alker, Jr. and Bruce M. Russett, *World Politics in the General Assembly*, New Haven: Yale University Press, 1965; Soo Yeon Kim and Russett, 'The New Politics of Voting Alignments in the General Assembly', in Russett, ed., *The Once and Future Security Council*, New York: St. Martin's Press, 1997.

43   Exemplary studies of domestic US politics and foreign policy include Charles W. Whalen, Jr., *The House and Foreign Policy*, Chapel Hill: University of North Carolina Press, 1982, especially pp. 78–128; Franck, *Nation Against Nation*; David P. Forsythe, *Human Rights and U.S. Foreign Policy: Congress Reconsidered*, Gainesville: University of Florida Press, 1988; Natalie Hevener Kaufman, *Human Rights Treaties and the Senate: A History of Opposition*, Chapel Hill: University of North Carolina Press, 1990; Lawrence J. LeBlanc, *The United States and the Genocide Convention*, Durham: Duke University Press, 1991; Gregg, *About Face?*

44   'Detachment – or, at the most, rare moments of engagement – is America's natural state.' Philip L. Geyelin, 'The Adams Doctrine and the Dream of Disengagement', in Sanford J. Ungar, ed., *Estrangement: America and the World*, New York: Oxford University Press, 1985, p. 197, as quoted by Gregg, *About Face?*, p. 17.

45   Truman's Point Four initiative, leading quickly to expanded technical assistance through the UN, likewise prompted academic efforts. Joseph M. Jones, *The Fifteen Weeks*, New York: Viking, 1955, conveys the spirit and recounts significant events during US mobilization for assistance to Europe in 1947. Dean Acheson, *Present at the Creation: My Years in the State Department*, New York: Norton, 1969, pp. 276–86, offers this US Secretary of State's account of formative events. On the origins of NATO, however, contrast Canadian and British accounts, including Escott Reid, *Time of Fear and Hope*, Toronto: McClelland and Stewart, 1977; James G. Eayrs, *In Defence of Canada: Growing Up Allied*, Vol. IV, Toronto: University of Toronto Press, 1965, ch. 2; John W. Holmes, *The Shaping of Peace: Canada and the Search for World Order, 1943–1957*, Vol. II, Toronto: University of Toronto Press, 1982, chs. 6, 10; Sir Nicholas Henderson, *The Birth of NATO*, Boulder: Westview, 1983. Elsewhere Reid remarks wryly that 'Dean Acheson was present only on the sixth day of the creation of the treaty': see 'The Creation of the North Atlantic Alliance, 1948–1949', in J. L. Granatstein, ed., *Canadian Foreign Policy: Historical Readings*, Toronto: Copp Clark Pitman, 1986, p. 180. A scholarly study of NATO that recognizes the 'O' or organizational effect upon the US is William T.R. Fox and Annette Baker Fox, *NATO and the*

Range of American Choice, New York: Columbia University, 1967. Policy-oriented studies of NATO and of other collective self-defence 'regional' organizations outside Europe are too numerous to sample fairly within present confines. These how-to offerings do further illustrate the relationship – during this period the direct as well as organic relationship – between exigency, practice and theory. Joseph S. Nye, Jr., *Peace in Parts: Integration and Conflict in Regional Organizations*, Boston: Little, Brown, 1971, provides a succinct overview and thoughtful exploration of assorted particular-membership intergovernmental organizations.

46   See especially Ernst B. Haas, *The Uniting of Europe*, Stanford: Stanford University Press, 1958. Karl W. Deutsch capped a collaborative research effort with *Political Community and the North Atlantic Area*, Princeton: Princeton University Press, 1957.

47   For instance Leon N. Lindberg, *The Political Dynamics of European Economic Integration*, Stanford: Stanford University Press, 1963; Lindberg and Stuart A. Scheingold, *Europe's Would-Be Polity: Patterns of Change in the European Community*, Englewood Cliffs: Prentice-Hall, 1970; Bruce M. Russett, *International Regions and the International System: A Study in Political Ecology*, Chicago: Rand, McNally, 1967. On issues of 'science' and methodology prompted by the latter, see Oran R. Young, 'Professor Russett: Industrious Tailor to a Naked Emperor', *World Politics*, 21, April 1969, pp. 486–511; Russett, 'The Young Science of International Politics', *World Politics*, 21, October 1969, pp. 87–94.

48   Though palpably less enamored of an automaticity of integration processes than other scholars, Stanley Hoffmann continued to elucidate the newly emerging Europe.

49   London: Royal Institute of International Affairs, 1943. Several mostly British intellectual currents drawn on by Mitrany are explored in David Long, 'International Functionalism and the Politics of Forgetting', *International Journal*, 48, Spring 1993, pp. 355–79. See also Ashworth and Long, eds., *New Perspectives on International Functionalism*.

50   *Beyond the Nation-State: Functionalism and International Organization*, Stanford: Stanford University Press, 1964.

51   Sewell, *Functionalism and World Politics: A Study Based on United Nations Programs Financing Economic Development*, Princeton: Princeton University, 1966.

52   A brief litany of reborn concepts, along with a critical appreciation of Mitrany as a man for his century, is in Sewell, 'The Functional Approach, the Charter, and New Challenges for the United Nations', Klaus Hüfner, ed., *Agenda for Change: New Tasks for the United Nations*, Opladen: Leske & Budrich, 1995, pp. 39–48.

53   Douglas G. Anglin, as quoted by A.J. Miller, 'The Functional Principle in Canada's External Relations', *International Journal*, 35, Spring 1980, pp. 310–1. The Miller article, pp. 309–28, offers an informative account of the functional principle's evolution within the Canadian context.

54   On Canadian functionalism and the functional principle of representation, see Holmes, *The Shaping of Peace: Canada and the Search for World Order, 1943–1957*, Toronto: University of Toronto Press, 1979, Vol. I, especially pp. 72–3, 235–8. On Article 2 of the NATO Charter, see *ibid.*, Volume II, pp. 112–17. Other sources helpful for understanding Canadian perspectives on multilateralism include Holmes, *Life With Uncle: The Canadian-American Relation-*

ship, Toronto: University of Toronto Press, 1981; Holmes, *et al.*, *No Other Way: Canada and International Security Institutions*, Toronto: University of Toronto Press, 1986; Holmes and John Kirton, eds., *Canada and the New Internationalism*, Toronto: University of Toronto Press, 1988; Holmes, *Looking Backward and Forward*, Hanover: Academic Council on the United Nations System, 1988. Curiously, Dean Acheson, who initially disparaged the 'Canadian article' in NATO's Charter, was, by January 1951, briefing Dwight D. Eisenhower that the North Atlantic treaty offered 'a means and a vehicle for closer political, economic and security cooperation'. Reid, 'The Creation of the North Atlantic Alliance', p. 182.

55 Among noteworthy multilateralist books by proteges and legatees of John Holmes, space permits only a sample: Denis Stairs, *The Diplomacy of Constraint: Canada, the Korean War and the United States*, Toronto: University of Toronto Press, 1974; Douglas A. Ross, *In the Interests of Peace: Canada and Vietnam, 1954–1973*, Toronto: University of Toronto Press, 1984; Kim Richard Nossal, ed., *An Acceptance of Paradox: Essays on Canadian Diplomacy in Honour of John W. Holmes*, Toronto: Canadian Institute of International Affairs, 1982; Margaret P. Doxey, *International Sanctions in Contemporary Perspective*, London: Macmillan, 1987; Doxey, *The Commonwealth Secretariat and the Contemporary Commonwealth*, New York: St. Martin's, 1989; Elizabeth Riddell-Dixon, *Canada and the International Seabed: Domestic Interests and External Constraints*, Kingston: McGill–Queen's University Press, 1989; John English, *Shadow of Heaven: The Life of Lester Pearson, Volume One: 1897–1948*, Toronto: Lester & Orpen Dennys, 1989; Tom Keating, *Canada and World Order: The Multilateralist Tradition in Canadian Foreign Policy*, Toronto: McClelland and Stewart, 1993; Andrew F. Cooper, Richard A. Higgott, and Nossal, *Relocating Middle Powers: Australia and Canada in a Changing World Order*, Vancouver: University of British Columbia Press, 1993; Nossal, *Rain Dancing: Sanctions in Canadian and Australian Foreign Policy*, Toronto: University of Toronto Press, 1994. Canadian scholar Sandra Whitworth devotes extensive attention to public and private forms of multilateralism in *Feminism and International Relations: Towards a Political Economy of Gender in Interstate and Non-Governmental Institutions*, 2nd ed., New York: St. Martin's, 1997.

56 Quoted by Keating, *Canada and World Order*, p. 9. Multilateralism also proves a fitting strategic response to Canada's enduring geopolitical predicament. Lester B. Pearson remembers that 'in one form or another, . . . there was always security in numbers. We did not want to be alone with our close friend and neighbour.' Escott Reid, who quotes this comment from Pearson's memoirs, endorses Arnold Toynbee's judgment that within a 'semi-parliamentary international forum' such as NATO, 'the political experience, maturity, and moderation of [other] countries . . . will weigh heavily in the balance . . . . In a pure power-politics world, on the other hand, these highly civilized but materially less powerful states will count for nothing compared with the United States and the Soviet Union.' Reid and others 'believed that the North Atlantic alliance provided a check and balance on the United States'. 'The Creation of the North Atlantic Alliance', pp. 171, 166, 182; Reid, *Radical Mandarin: The Memoirs of Escott Reid*, Toronto: University of Toronto Press, 1989, pp. 222–40.

57 Dates offer dubious guidance to the onset of this hunker-down sort of uni-lateralism. Toward UNESCO, for instance, the US began damage-control measures in the early 1950s. Sewell, 'UNESCO: Pluralism Rampant', in Robert W. Cox and Harold K. Jacobson, *et al.*, *The Anatomy of Influence: Decision Making in International Organization*, New Haven: Yale University Press, 1973, pp. 162ff; Sewell, *UNESCO and World Politics: Engaging in International Relations*, Princeton: Princeton University Press, 1975, pp. 325–6.

58 On the US, the UN and Vietnam, see Lincoln P. Bloomfield, *The U.N. and Vietnam*, New York: Carnegie Endowment for International Peace, 1968; Franck, *Nation Against Nation*, pp. 155–8; Max Harrelson, *Fires All Around the Horizon*, New York: Praeger, 1989, pp. 157–66. Neither decolonization in Indochina nor the wars that attended decolonization had been brought before the United Nations.

59 For a luminous treatment of practitioners' working assumptions regarding US influence in the UN, at least until the middle 1960s, see Conor Cruise O'Brien, *Writers and Politics*, New York: Random House, 1965, pp. 197ff. After the Assembly legitimated the Beijing Chinese, Senator and former presidential candidate Barry Goldwater among others called on the US to get out of the UN and to get the UN out of the US. Harrelson, *Fires All Around the Horizon*, pp. 215–6.

60 Seymour Maxwell Finger, *Your Man at the UN*, New York: New York University Press, 1980, p. 231.

61 The Carter administration left ILO in 1977. Walter Galenson, *The International Labor Organization: An American View*, Madison: University of Wisconsin Press, 1981, pp. 111–38.

62 Jimmy Carter, *Keeping Faith: Memoirs of a President*, New York: Bantam, 1982, pp. 273–429. US governments long sought to act in a singular if not a monopoly position as Middle East mediator. For instance the Clinton administration appropriated direction of a 'process' following the peace agreement brokered between Israel and the Palestinians by Norwegian foreign minister Johan J. Holst. As ex-President, Carter continued to personify the international role of splendid loner by freelancing his private initiatives, for instance in North Korea with Kim Il Sung during June 1994. See Don Oberdorfer, *The Two Koreas: A Contemporary History*, Reading, MA: Addison Wesley, 1997, pp. 326–36.

63 Compare Cyrus R. Vance, 'The Human Rights Imperative', *Foreign Policy*, 63, Summer 1986, pp. 3–19. Congress subsequently introduced the unilateral device of certifying or decertifying governments, including that of Mexico, as sufficiently or insufficiently vigilant in fighting America's war on drugs to warrant US financial assistance.

64 Abraham Yeselson and Anthony Gaglione, *A Dangerous Place: The United Nations as a Weapon in World Politics*, New York: Grossman, 1974; Daniel Patrick Moynihan, with Suzanne Weaver, *A Dangerous Place*, Boston: Little, Brown, 1978. Moynihan attributes the phrase 'a place where lies are told' to Israeli Ambassador Chaim Herzog; Franck, *Nation Against Nation*, pp. 206–10.

65 On the US these included William A. Scott and Stephen B. Withey, *The United States and the United Nations: The Public View, 1945–55*, New York: Carnegie Endowment for International Peace/Manhattan, 1958; Louis K. Hyde, Jr., *The United States and the United Nations: Promoting the Public Welfare, 1945–55*,

New York: Carnegie Endowment for International Peace/Manhattan, 1960; and Lawrence D. Weiler and Anne Patricia Simons, *The United States and the United Nations: The Search for International Peace and Security*, New York: Manhattan, 1967.

66 For instance, Daniel G. Partan, *Documentary Study of the Politicization of UNESCO*, Boston: American Academy of Arts and Sciences, 1975; Mark F. Imber, *The U.S.A., ILO, UNESCO & IAEA: Politicization & Withdrawal in the Specialized Agencies*, New York: St. Martin's, 1990. Clare Wells' *The UN, UNESCO and the Politics of Knowledge, 1945–82*, New York: St. Martin's, 1987, affords illuminating perspective on 'politicization'.

67 An early prescription: United Nations, *A Study of the Capacity of the United Nations Development System*, Geneva: United Nations, 1969, known also as the Jackson Report.

68 One person's reformation may become another person's deformation. I consider 'reform' additionally later in this chapter and in concluding Chapter 11.

69 *The Anatomy of Influence: Decision Making in International Organization.*

70 Christine Sylvester, quoting from Wendy Brown's 'Feminist Hesitations, Postmodern Exposures', calls on theorists to 'take on everyday people and their international politics, and sceptics who hole-up in a nearly peopleless (though not genderless) International Relations, as partners in a "political conversation oriented towards diversity and the common. . . ."' 'The Contributions of Feminist Theory to International Relations', in Steve Smith, Ken Booth and Marysia Zalewski, eds., *International Theory: Positivism and Beyond*, Cambridge: Cambridge University Press, 1996, p. 272.

71 William J. Dixon, 'Research on Research Revisited: Another Half Decade of Quantitative and Field Research on International Organizations', as conveyed in J. Martin Rochester, 'The Rise and Fall of International Organization as a Field of Study', *International Organization*, 40, Autumn 1986, p. 795. Rochester notes the discontinuation of the journal's section recounting activities of intergovernmental organizations in 1970, and reports continuation of the trend in reduction of articles on global and regional organizations during the 1980s (pp. 795, 801).

72 Robert O. Keohane (1969) and Philippe Schmitter (1971), respectively, according to Rochester, *ibid.*, p. 795.

73 Robert O. Keohane, editor's note, *International Organization*, 33, Summer 1979.

74 The Reaganesque image harmonizes remarkably with Richard Ashley's sketch of today's scholars in motion across the fields of International Relations, conveyed from the rendition of an academic colleague. To Ashley she observes that 'you boys always talk as if you're out there on the plains somewhere, on horseback, galloping alone'. Ashley's colleague notes an IR preoccupation with questions of strategy and a tendency, in Ashley's words, 'to hightail it across the surfaces of historical experience, a stranger to every place, seldom pausing to dismount and explore any locale, eschewing all commitments, always moving as if chasing some fast-retreating end or fleeing just ahead of the grasp of some relentless pursuer'. Ashley proceeds to embroider this picture in a telling and amusing manner. 'The Achievements of Post-Structuralism', in Smith, *et al.*, eds., *International Theory*, p. 240f.

75   Louis Henkin, *et al.*, *Right v. Might*, New York: Council on Foreign Relations, 1989. For reflections on several legal issues of the period under review see also David P. Forsythe, *The Politics of International Law: U.S. Foreign Policy Reconsidered*, Boulder: Lynne Rienner, 1990. On Grenada, see Robert J. Beck, *The Grenada Invasion: Politics, Law and Foreign Policy*, Boulder: Westview, 1993.

76   Contrast the assessments of two US delegation leaders: Leigh S. Ratiner, 'The Law of the Sea: A Crossroads for American Foreign Policy', *Foreign Affairs*, 60, Summer 1982, pp. 1006–1021, and James L. Malone, 'Who Needs the Sea Treaty?', *Foreign Policy*, 54, Spring 1984, pp. 44–63. Compare James B. Morell, *The Law of the Sea: An Historical Analysis of the 1982 Treaty and Its Rejection by the United States*, Jefferson, N.C.: McFarland, 1992. For American participation in preparing the law of the sea convention prior to the Reagan administration, see Ann L. Hollick, *U.S. Foreign Policy and the Law of the Sea*, Princeton: Princeton University Press, 1981.

77   On use of the financial weapon during the Reagan years, see *About Face?*, pp. 59–92. The Reagan administration remained divided over whether to impose a further unilateral limitation on the US percentage of financial obligations. To do so would reduce American control, it was maintained by certain White House staffers. This legacy of indecisiveness apparently continues.

78   Roger A. Coate, *Unilateralism, Ideology, and U.S. Foreign Policy: The United States In and Out of UNESCO*, Boulder: Lynne Rienner, 1988; William Preston, Jr., Edward S. Herman, and Herbert I. Schiller, *Hope & Folly: The United States and UNESCO, 1945–1985*, Minneapolis: University of Minnesota Press, 1989. South Africa had preceded the US by withdrawing from UNESCO some years earlier. The United Kingdom and Singapore followed the US.

79   *About Face?*, p. 68.

80   For instance, Juliana Geran Pilon, 'Through the Looking Glass: The Political Culture of the UN' (1982); Pilon, 'The United Nations' Campaign Against Israel', 1983; Burton Yale Pines, ed., *A World Without a U.N.*, 1984.

81   For instance, Jeane J. Kirkpatrick, *The Reagan Phenomenon and Other Speeches*, Washington: American Enterprise Institute for Public Policy Research, 1983; Alexander M. Haig, Jr., *Caveat: Realism, Reagan, and Foreign Policy*, New York: Macmillan, 1984, notably p. 270; Alan L. Keyes, 'Fixing the United Nations', *National Interest*, Summer 1986, pp. 12–23; Allan Gerson, 'The United Nations and Racism: The Case of the Zionism as Racism Resolution as Progenitor', *Israel Yearbook on Human Rights*, 1987; Gerson, *The Kirkpatrick Mission: Diplomacy Without Apology, America at the United Nations, 1981–1985*, New York: Free Press, 1991; Richard S. Williamson, *The United Nations: A Place of Promise and of Mischief*, Lanham, MD: University Press of America, 1991.

82   For instance, Moynihan, 'Joining the Jackals: The U.S. at the United Nations, 1977–80', *Commentary*, February 1981, pp. 23–31; Gerald Clark, 'Canada Still Says Yes to the U.N.', *Readers Digest*, 1985, pp. 135–42; Charles Krauthammer, 'Let It [the UN] Sink', *New Republic*, 24 August 1987, pp. 18–23; Thomas Mallon, 'The People Next Door', *American Spectator*, December 1989, pp. 22–6.

83   *Managing the Risks of International Agreement*, Madison: University of Wisconsin Press, 1981.

84   *Networks of Interdependence: International Organizations and the Global Political System*, 2nd ed., New York: Knopf, 1984, p. 392.

85 *The General Assembly in World Politics*, Boston: Allen & Unwin, 1986. Robert E. Riggs' *Politics in the United Nations* was reprinted in 1984.

86 Fasulo, *Representing America: Experiences of U.S. Diplomats at the UN*, New York: Praeger, 1984; Finger, *American Ambassadors at the UN*, New York: Holmes & Meier, 1987.

87 *Politics in the United Nations System*, Durham: Duke University Press, 1988.

88 New York: Praeger, 1983. Jackson's book includes an excellent bibliography on non-alignment, pp. 267–74.

89 *States and the Global System: Politics, Law, and Organization*, New York: St. Martin's, 1988.

90 Rochester, 'The Rise and Fall of International Organization as a Field of Study', p. 801.

91 'International Organization: A State of the Art on an Art of the State', *International Organization*, 40, Autumn 1986, p. 753. Of course one can imagine other analogues. Harold Lasswell fancies the thinker acting as a 'maternity hospital for the delivery of a historically viable policy proposal', *The Policy Sciences: Recent Developments in Scope and Method*, p. 12.

92 For instance, J.P. Chamberlain, *The Regime of the International Rivers: Danube and Rhine*, New York: Columbia University Press, 1923.

93 An example of a regimen: Alger's *United States Representation in the United Nations*.

94 Krasner, in *International Regimes*, p. 1.

95 Compare Thomas M. Franck and Edward Weisband, *Word Politics: Verbal Strategy Among the Superpowers*, New York: Oxford University Press, 1972; Paul Keal, *Unspoken Rules and Superpower Dominance*, New York: St. Martin's, 1983; G. John Ikenberry and Charles A. Kupchan, 'The Legitimation of Hegemonic Power', in Rapkin, ed., *World Leadership and Hegemony*, pp. 49–69. If regimes are like sectoral spheres of influence, they might be referred to as *scopes of influence* and subjected to realistic comparative analysis alongside geopolitical spheres of influence.

96 Compare Andrew Fenton Cooper, Richard A. Higgott and Kim Richard Nossal, 'Bound to Follow? Leadership and Followership in the Gulf Conflict', *Political Science Quarterly*, 106, No. 3, 1991, pp. 391–410.

97 Hence we should not be surprised to witness manifestations of regime theorizing and similar justifications of hegemony on behalf of stronger states within 'regional' contexts such as Europe.

98 See Susan Strange, '*Cave! hic dragones*: A Critique of Regime Analysis', *International Organization*, 36, Spring 1982, pp. 479–96. On academic ideologizing, see Hans J. Morgenthau, 'The Commitments of Political Science', in Morgenthau, *Dilemmas of Politics*, Chicago: University of Chicago Press, 1958. Cox, *Neorealism and Its Critics*, p. 207, presents a cautionary note with more general applicability in an oft-quoted passage: 'Theory is always *for* someone and *for* some purpose.... There is, accordingly, no such thing as theory in itself, divorced from a standpoint in time and space. When any theory so represents itself, it is the more important to examine it as ideology, and to lay bare its concealed perspective.'

99 A practitioner's book aids understanding of these developments: Cameron R. Hume, *The United Nations, Iran, and Iraq: How Peacemaking Changed*, Bloomington: Indiana University Press, 1994. Further on evolution of the Club of

Five (C-5) permanent members of the UN Security Council, see James Jonah, *Differing State Perspectives on the United Nations in the Post-Cold War World*, Providence: Academic Council on the United Nations System, 1993.

100   Also as an extragovernmental multilateral technique evidently adapted to the financial exigencies of the Democratic Party in gearing up for the 1996 presidential election. The sobriquet 'Cash-register Coalition' which some Arab commentators dubbed the Gulf action of 1991 appeals as a generic phrase referring to financial consortia as one form of multilateralism constituted momentarily of contributors with wildly discrepant intentions and expectations.

101   Secretary of State Madeleine Albright said on the eve of her early 1998 departure for overseas representations to friendly governments concerning Iraq that 'It is our preference, as it is in all conditions, to...do everything multilaterally, and to...act in concert with others. But I am not going anywhere to...seek support. I am going to explain our position... .' 'All Things Considered', 28 January 1998. Cooked consensus on behalf of the international community proceeded from successive one-on-one briefings, followed in each case by reiteration of a predetermined position, then fed back to attentive publics through such media as CNN.

102   On Public Broadcasting System, 'MacNeil–Lehrer NewsHour', 30 August 1993, and National Broadcasting Corporation, 'Meet the Press', 13 February 1994. In a debate of sorts with Jeane Kirkpatrick before the Council on Foreign Relations, Albright sought to assuage critics in her immediate audience while ladling scorn on to American militiamen: 'The UN is no threat to our sovereignty. It cannot override US law or the Constitution. It has no power to tax us. It has no authority to entangle us in foreign conflicts. And it's not going to descend upon us in black helicopters in the middle of the night to steal our lawn furniture.' US National Public Radio, 'Morning Edition', 17 September 1996.

103   Presidential Decision Directive 25.

104   The catchall phrase 'the UN' diffuses if it does not displace the responsibility of individual participating governments. References to 'New York' promote these effects by attributing responsibility to UN headquarters and headquarters staffers. 'New York' might advance understanding if its evocation also serves as a reminder of the site of Security Council deliberations and the usual venue for consultations of the Council's Club of Five (C-5) permanent members – the first five declared and continuing nuclear powers, who also lead the world in arms exports. Conflation holds a place in the study of multilateralism; disaggregation deserves one. On indifference to Rwanda, see Philip Gourevitch, 'Annals of Diplomacy: The Genocide Fax', *The New Yorker*, 74, 11 May 1998, pp. 42–4, 46. See also 'Frontline: The Triumph of Evil', *http://www.pbs.org/wgbh/pages/frontline/shows/evil* on the Internet. The general shortfall of governments' political will frequently bemoaned by UN officials Gourevitch finds more pointed in the comment by one of them: ' "You do understand, I hope, that when we are talking about Rwanda and we speak of member states, we are speaking in particular about Washington" ' – another conflation. East Timor coverage opens yet another window on the phenomenon of displacement.

105   Daniel Schorr, 'All Things Considered', 17 February 1994; *ibid.*, 24 September 1996.

106 David E. Sanger, 'Talk Multilaterally, Hit Allies With Stick', *New York Times*, 21 July 1996. The Clinton administration did initially oppose another extraterritorial legislative sally by threatening to veto a UN and IMF funding bill because attached to it as a rider was language preventing overseas organizations that receive US family planning funds from counselling on abortion as an alternative.

107 No doubt the anticipated electoral effect of additional tough acts undertaken against popularly-defined US enemies beckoned by suggesting domestic political gains. More specifically, Clinton surely recognized that major electoral battleground states Florida and New Jersey held sizeable numbers of Cuban-American voters, and that other potent constituencies remained exceedingly sensitive to threats seen from Iran and Libya.

108 Elaine Sciolino, 'Dole's Foreign Policy Record: It's Hard to Read', *New York Times*, 28 April 1996.

109 'Talk Multilaterally, Hit Allies With Stick'.

110 Typifying the unilateralist paradigm, Senator Ted Stevens of Alaska described the proposed expansion of NATO as 'just another...chink out of the [US] armour'. 'All Things Considered', 21 October 1997.

111 'The Law of the Sea: A Crossroads for American Foreign Policy', p. 1021. I remain indebted to John W. Holmes for this reference.

112 From her home near Putney, Vermont, anti-landmine campaign coordinator and newly acclaimed Nobel Peace Prize co-winner Jody Williams decried Clinton's desertion of foreign-policy responsibility and her country's failure of leadership by 'not moving with the tide of history on this issue'. Paul Knox, 'Antimine Fight Gets Double Boost', Toronto *Globe and Mail*, 11 October 1997. Apparently the US military does not stand alone in opposing the multilateral effort against landmines. Earlier, Human Rights Watch asked some seventeen US-based corporations making landmine components to renounce future involvement. Some firms did so, but nine, including General Electric and Lockheed Martin, refused. Prudential Securities Social Investment Research Service, with thanks to Douglas Goold.

113 *Earth in the Balance*, New York: Houghton Mifflin, 1992.

114 An exception during the anti-landmines campaign was Senator Patrick Leahy of Vermont. He chided the Clinton administration for coming only reluctantly to the Ottawa Process after 'a hundred other countries' had done so, for taking 'almost a take-it-or-leave-it attitude' and saying in effect 'do it our way or don't do it any way' at Oslo. Then Leahy set out to prepare legislative action that would augment his earlier co-sponsored law to prohibit US exports of landmines.

115 For instance, Donald J. Puchala and Roger A. Coate, *The State of the United Nations, 1988*, Hanover, NH: Academic Council on the United Nations System, 1988. David P. Forsythe edited a collection of essays on international organization: *The United Nations in the World Political Economy: Essays in Honour of Leon Gordenker*, New York: St. Martin's Press, 1989. Margaret P. Karns and Karen A. Mingst edited a collaborative effort to account for evolving US participation in a number of intergovernmental organizations: *The United States and Multilateral Institutions: Patterns of Changing Instrumentality and Influence*, Boston: Unwin Hyman, 1990. Established textbooks for use with university courses reappeared in updated versions as

the pace of change quickened; for instance, Robert E. Riggs and Jack C. Plano's *United Nations: International Organization and World Politics*, Belmont, MA: Wadsworth, 1994 appeared in a revised edition. Teachers also appreciated two additional textbooks, Thomas G. Weiss, David P. Forsythe and Roger A. Coate, *The United Nations and Changing World Politics*, Boulder: Westview, 1994, and Karen A. Mingst and Margaret P. Karns, *The United Nations in the Post-Cold War Era*, Boulder: Westview, 1995. John Gerard Ruggie published a lively interpretation of the US within a multilateral context, *Winning the Peace: America and World Order in the New Era*, New York Columbia University Press, 1996. Two volumes on the new peacekeeping operations emerged: Steven R. Ratner, *The New UN Peacekeeping: Building Peace in Lands of Conflict After the Cold War*, New York: St. Martin's, 1995, and William J. Durch, ed., *UN Peacekeeping, American Policy, and the Uncivil Wars of the 1990s*, New York: St. Martin's, 1996.

116   For instance, Puchala and Coate, *The Challenge of Relevance: The United Nations in a Changing World Environment*, Hanover, NH: Academic Council on the United Nations System, 1989; George Sherry, *The United Nations Reborn: Conflict Control in the Post-Cold War World*, New York: Council on Foreign Relations, 1990; Thomas G. Weiss and Larry Minear, eds., *Humanitarianism Across Borders: Sustaining Civilians in Times of War*, Boulder: Lynne Rienner, 1993; Weiss, ed., *Collective Security in a Changing World*, Boulder: Lynne Rienner, 1993; Durch, ed., *The Evolution of United Nations Peacekeeping*, New York: St. Martin's Press, 1993; Benjamin Rivlin and Leon Gordenker, eds., *The Challenging Role of the UN Secretary-General: Making 'The Most Impossible Job in the World' Possible*, Westport: Praeger, 1993.

117   For instance, Benjamin Rivlin, ed., *Ralph Bunche: The Man and His Times*, New York: Holmes & Meier, 1990; Sidney Samuel Dell, *The United Nations and International Business*, Durham: Duke University Press, 1990; Bartlett C. Jones, *Flawed Triumphs: Andy Young at the United Nations*, Lanham, MD: University Press of America, 1996.

118   David P. Forsythe's books have approached human rights from several illuminating perspectives: *Human Rights and World Politics*, 2nd ed., Lincoln: University of Nebraska Press, 1989; *The Internationalization of Human Rights*, Lexington: Lexington, 1991; *Human Rights and Peace: International and National Dimensions*, Lincoln: University of Nebraska Press, 1993. Jack Donnelly has contributed thoughtful treatments of human rights: *The Concept of Human Rights*, London: Croom Helm, 1985; *Universal Human Rights in Theory and Practice*, Ithaca: Cornell University Press, 1989; *International Human Rights*, Boulder: Westview, 1993. Jessica Mathews of the Council on Foreign Relations calls for debate on when, where and how unilateral pressure can be helpful and decisive, and in what circumstances multilateral pressure is preferable for achieving progress toward human rights. 'Weekend Edition', 28 May 1994.

119   Peter H. Sand, *Lessons Learned in Global Environmental Governance*, New York: World Resources Institute, 1990; Peter M. Haas, *Saving the Mediterranean: The Politics of International Environmental Cooperation*, New York: Columbia University Press, 1992; Lee A. Kimball, with William Boyd, *Forging International Agreement: Strengthening Intergovernmental Institutions for Environment and Development*, Washington: World Resources Institute, 1992; Sand, ed., *The*

Effectiveness of International Environmental Agreements: A Survey of Existing Legal Instruments, Cambridge: Grotius, 1992; Lawrence E. Susskind, *Environmental Diplomacy: Negotiating More Effective Global Agreements*, New York: Oxford University Press, 1993; Oran R. Young, *International Governance: Protecting the Environment in a Stateless Society*, Ithaca: Cornell University Press, 1994.

120   Compare Richard Hoggart, *An Idea and Its Servants: UNESCO From Within*, London: Chatto & Windus, 1978.

121   Useful reviews of reform and its literature include Gene M. Lyons, 'Reforming the United Nations', *International Social Science Journal*, 41, No. 120, 1989, pp. 249–71; John de Gara, *Administrative and Financial Reform of the United Nations: A Documentary Essay*, Hanover: Academic Council on the United Nations System, 1989; Jacques Fomerand, *Strengthening the United Nations Economic and Social Programs: A Documentary Essay*, Hanover: Academic Council on the United Nations System, 1990; Lyons, 'Strengthening the United Nations', *International Journal*, 45, Autumn 1990, pp. 949–58.

122   See for instance two works by Brian Urquhart and Erskine Childers. *Towards a More Effective United Nations*, Uppsala: Dag Hammarskjöld Foundation, 1992 includes two studies, one addressed to reform of the UN Secretariat, the other to strengthening international response to humanitarian emergencies. *Renewing the United Nations System*, Uppsala: Dag Hammarskjöld Foundation, 1994 examines and proposes more generally for the UN system. The continuing series of collaborations between Urquhart and Childers was supported also by the Ford Foundation.

123   Consider Ronald Steel's conundrum: 'A superpower like the United States...can remain a global hegemon...only if it refrains from acting like one.' 'Lonely At The Top.' Former US ambassador to the USSR Jack Matlock warns fellow Americans in 'Too Many Arms to Twist' that 'we can maintain our strength and influence only if we can do so with the support and participation of our friends'.

124   Scholars would have little beyond historical analogue on which to base their studies. Arguably, the government of Iraq has done more to summon a contemporary concert of great powers than has any other government – at least until the nuclear explosions by India and Pakistan. Yet the recalcitrance of Americans to collectivism, even collaboration by a handful of stellar states, still does not augur well for studies that envisage a US-led concert.

125   As we have seen, when Americans write of leadership, they characteristically refer either to US leadership or to the possibility (usually a discounted possibility) of another state, or exceptionally a united Europe, superseding the US as world leader. For Brian Urquhart and Erskine Childers, to the contrary, the want of leadership refers to the UN Secretaryship-General. See *A World in Need of Leadership: Tomorrow's United Nations*, New York and Uppsala: Ford Foundation and Dag Hammarskjöld Foundation, 1990.

126   Some do ask what policies might advance the serial democratizing of individual UN member states so these peoples could better hold accountable their respective governments.

127   History foretells that if interest in such studies should occur, the practitioners would lead the scholars. Research on multilateral implementation of general standards thus may hinge on political leaders' equivalent of a para-

digmatic shift. Presumably such a shift would be prompted by some major exogenous factor.

128   See for instance V. Spike Peterson, ed., *Gendered States: Feminist (Re)Visions of International Relations Theory*, Boulder: Lynne Rienner, 1992; J. Ann Tickner, *Gender in International Relations: Feminist Perspectives on Achieving Global Security*, New York: Columbia University Press, 1992; Peterson and Anne Sisson Runyan, *Global Gender Issues*, Boulder: Westview, 1993; Christine Sylvester, *Feminist Theory and International Relations in a Postmodern Era*, Cambridge: Cambridge University Press, 1994. Some feminist scholars beyond the US develop critiques more explicitly directed to organized multilateralism. See for instance the work of Catherine Hoskyns and Sandra Whitworth as considered by Jacqui True, 'Feminism', in Scott Burchill and Andrew Linklater, *et al.*, *Theories of International Relations*, London: Macmillan, 1996, pp. 219–20, 247. Whitworth's *Feminism and International Relations* combines critical theorizing with substantive treatment of the International Planned Parenthood Federation and the International Labour Organization. Elizabeth Riddell-Dixon illuminates the process of integrating and strengthening the rights of women in 'Mainstreaming Women's Rights: Problems and Prospects Within the Centre for Human Rights', *Global Governance*, 5, No. 2, 1999, pp. 149–71.

129   A useful overview presenting American and non-American postmodernists is Richard Devetak, 'Postmodernism', in Burchill and Linklater, *et al.*, *Theories of International Relations*, pp. 179–209.

130   Compare John Gerard Ruggie, ed., *Multilateralism Matters: The Theory and Praxis of an Institutional Form*, New York: Columbia University Press, 1993. Several essays in this volume appeared previously in *International Organization*.

2
Russian Scholarly Work on Multilateralism

Yevgenia Issraelyan

The apparent end of the cold war and the changing context of international relations have once more put international organization under the microscope. Powerful trends defining the world order include the globalization of political, economic and social problems. Closer interaction of states results in the transformation of relationships, a process of cultural homogenization and the emergence, or awareness, of the global ecosystem.

A crisis of hegemony both at the global level and within most powerful countries, the transformation from a bipolar to a multipolar system, especially after the disintegration of the Soviet Union, as well as the retreat of authoritarian regimes in favour of more democratic forces, also contribute to the changing structure of the world order. The end of the East-West divide and of the military confrontation which characterized Central Europe and the world for the last forty-plus years creates a plethora of new opportunities for the international community. As former UN Secretary-General Boutros Boutros-Ghali put it, 'the immense ideological barrier that for decades gave rise to distrust and hostility – and the terrible tools of destruction that were their inseparable companions – has collapsed. Even as the issues between states North and South grow more acute, and call for attention at the highest levels of government, the improvement in relations between states East and West affords new possibilities, some already realized, to meet successfully threats to common security.'[1]

However, this time of basic changes in the global order is marked by unprecedented contradictory trends. Globalism is threatened by sovereign and nationalistic rivalries, by deep ethnic, religious, social, cultural and linguistic clashes, as well as by the emergence of strong regional centres of power presenting the potential for conflict.

International security is challenged by the proliferation of conventional arms and missile technology, weapons transfers to Third World countries, and armed conflicts. In addition, stability in the world is undermined by new manifestations of discrimination and exclusion, as well as by acts of terrorism. Therefore, the changing world order is characterized at one and the same time by real change, real opportunity, and real uncertainty. The changing context of international relations implies that the problem of international organization will be thoroughly rethought with regard to the future world order.

General review

Such rethinking has been in process within Russia since 1985 as part of a comprehensive, critical examination of theoretical approaches, fundamental assumptions and underlying attitudes in political science, political economy, and all human and social disciplines. New ways of thinking and a retreat from the dogmas of past decades was needed in the perestroika and post-perestroika years to provide the proper backgrounds for transition to a market economy and economic reforms, restructuring of political institutions, and redirection of Soviet and, later, Russian foreign policy. The debate on foreign policy issues intensified after the collapse of the Soviet Union, which had resulted in vital changes in the balance of forces throughout the world and in the geopolitical environment of Russia. The need to design an innovative foreign policy capable of responding to the challenges and commitments of the new global context impelled scholars and politicians to re-examine the lessons of the past and reject many outdated images and beliefs. Ideas, perceptions and attitudes born and initiated in scientific circles affect, influence and, in some cases, determine the policymaking process.

The theory of the class struggle as the background for interstate relationships was challenged and proved inadequate for emergent realities. Similarly, the concept of peaceful coexistence in its interpretation as a form of class struggle was sharply debated. Its fundamental assumption, that the world is divided into two antagonistic, hostile and confronting systems, was abandoned, as was the belief that an 'uncompromising ideological fight' should necessarily accompany peaceful economic, political, and cultural cooperation. Meanwhile, Russia's other principles, such as the renunciation of war as a means of settling interstate disputes, the recognition of the sovereignty and integrity of states, non-interference in the domestic affairs of other countries, and broad business and cultural interaction for mutual benefit, were reconfirmed and given new vigour.

In general, the Soviet and Russian academic communities have developed a new image of the world, viewing it as controversial and diverse, yet integral, interdependent and interrelating. This is how the report 'International Relations in the 1990s and Alternatives of the Soviet Foreign Policy', prepared by the Institute of the USA and Canada of the Russian Academy of Sciences, assessed this dialogue of integration and diversification: 'the world system is sustaining profound changes. Many tendencies and processes which shaped its postwar development are exhausted or vanishing. The split of humanity into two antagonistic systems and two military and political groupings has become a thing of the past. The future world will be much more complicated and diverse and fraught with the opportunities of peaceful co-existence and stable cooperation, mutual rapprochement and enrichment, as well as with the seeds of new confrontation.'[2]

As an integral part of this concept, scholars initiated another essential idea – the 'de-ideologization of Soviet foreign policy' – which signifies renunciation of ideological stereotypes, primarily those of the 'image of the enemy', a retreat from the assessment of world events in the light of the class struggle, and a departure from the practice of imposing Soviet values and principles upon other states. This revised perception of the world led to the review of all attitudes and approaches to international relations. The new concept of international security suggested by military experts and political scientists, and later approved as official Soviet doctrine, reflected the ideas of globalization, reciprocity and multilateralism. It rejected an approach based upon military confrontation of the two superpowers. This recent concept proceeded from the assumption that security can only be universal, and the security of one state can never be achieved at the expense of other states. In addition, it was acknowledged that security can be safeguarded solely by political means.

Among other problems, attitudes to international and regional conflicts were also challenged. In past decades, such conflicts were viewed in the context of contest and rivalry between the two superpowers, and most attention was drawn to the ways of winning, not preventing or settling conflicts. Now the means of easing tensions before they result in clashes, and of resolving their underlying causes by joint international efforts, became the priority for studies of interstate conflicts.

The past and present of the United Nations

The role, activities and evolution of the United Nations were examined in numerous Soviet works. Well-known political scientists, jurists, researchers on international relations, and diplomats (for example Georgii Arbatov, Vladimir Petrovskii, Nicolai Inozemtsev, Georgii Morozov, V. Shkunaev) focused on these issues, aiming to give an unbiased and diversified picture of international organization.

However, many of the scholarly works written in the past proceeded from the confrontational, ideological approach to foreign policy and international relations built on the dogmatic, orthodox assumptions that dominated Soviet political science. The United Nations organization was viewed through the prism of the ideological struggle between 'us' (the Soviet Union and other Socialist countries) and 'them' (meaning western states). As a component of this approach, many scholars gave their unconditional approval and high praise to all Soviet initiatives and undertakings, while western, especially American, attitudes were systematically attacked. The epithets 'hegemony, militarism and adventurism' were broadly applied to American foreign policy, while the Soviet approach, from their perspective, was invariably consistent and aimed at strengthening peace, security and cooperation.

A similar bifurcation was applied to the examination of attitudes of Third World countries in the United Nations. Those who supported and approved Soviet proposals and joined the Socialist countries were referred to as 'progressive' and 'democratic', while those which associated themselves with the western bloc were labelled 'imperialist appendages'.

Tough rhetoric was abandoned in the course of reassessing theoretical approaches to foreign policy issues, especially those works composed after the disintegration of the Soviet Union. Since Russia is successor to the Soviet Union and as such is represented in international organizations, it has committed itself to revise its approach toward the UN system and seek new solutions and opportunities. The resulting search continues.

The works of the late 1980s and 1990s contain more balanced perspectives and images of the world order than did earlier studies. A majority of recent studies are by specialists in international relations, security and disarmament issues, and international law. Considering the United Nations system as a form of multilateralism, they examine its postwar achievements and failures, negotiating and decisionmaking processes, and assess the prospects for future institutional reform. In addition, a group of studies is devoted to the history of the United Nations.[3] As for different functional spheres of multilateralism such as economics, ecology, and disarmament, they too are given attention.[4] Although various matters are considered and different sciences involved, the studies are not interrelated, remaining separated within the framework of their respective disciplines. A multidisciplinary, comprehensive approach to international organization has not yet been formulated.

Analysis of the past and present experience of the United Nations leads most scholars to the conclusion that the United Nations system has a strong potential for guiding the process of global transformation toward desired goals. According to Georgii Morozov, 'multiformity of interstate relations implies an active multilateral diplomacy and broad universal international cooperation, which can solely be provided by the United Nations system'.[5] On the other hand, Dr Vladimir Petrovskii notes that the UN has turned into the 'procurator's tribune', while then-Foreign Affairs Minister Andrei Kosyrev compares it to 'a paper producing factory' and speaks in terms of its 'paralysis'.[6] However, both see possibilities for improvement and are optimistic about the future of this international organization, unlike a small group of scholars who are essentially negative toward the UN. The United Nations, in their view, 'symbolizes and embodies the past and present world, in other words, the world based on force'. They suggest that the United Nations system should be replaced by some other world institution or form of governance meeting the requirements of the changing global order.[7]

Distinct from the scholarship of the past, recent works are critical toward Soviet policy at the United Nations and the conduct of Soviet diplomacy. An emerging generation of scholars concludes that, to a greater or lesser extent, all the states members of the UN, including the Soviet Union, are responsible for its low effectiveness. The main goal of Soviet diplomacy in international organizations, as these studies show, was to propagandize about the 'peace-loving' nature of Soviet foreign policy. Diplomatic speeches showered peaceful phraseology and overloaded with praise the leaders of the State and the Communist Party, while deliberately offering phrases unacceptable to western countries.

In line with this critical approach, Soviet relations with Third World countries within the UN system are re-examined. Specialists acknowledge that the Soviet Union pushed decolonized countries to reject western values and experience, particularly in the field of market economy and political institutions, which they badly needed. Both – the western states on one hand, and the Soviet Union and the Socialist countries on the other – were guilty of creating extremes in the Non-Aligned Movement by supporting individual states militarily and financially. Summarizing the consequences of this paired strategy, Andrei Kozyrev writes that the Third World countries who were striving for economic assistance got used to manipulating skilfully the ideological confrontation of the two blocs and tried to profit from 'selling' their support to one or the other.[8]

The majority of specialists share the view that a potential turning point in regard to international organization has been reached. What are the forces impelling innovation in the UN? Primarily, the redirection of Russian foreign policy, as scholars see it, gives hope for new opportunities in cooperation at the UN. Secondly, the changing attitudes of many western countries eager to respond adequately to the challenges of globalization, and guided by common sense and rationality, suggests a pivotal change. Thirdly, the positions of Third World countries, still diffuse and diverse, yet to a certain extent relieved from the two blocs' rivalry, promises further innovation. These states are expected to increase their influence on UN undertakings. Finally, the democratic movements, particularly the peace movement, will have an impact on creating a more democratic form of institutionalized world order. A complicated, contradictory, interactive and interdependent relationship among these components will determine changes in the United Nations system.[9]

Proceeding from the Marxist-Leninist conception of interstate relations, most Soviet scholars disagreed with western approaches to international organization. Among others, the monograph by Vladimir Fedorov, *The UN and Problems of War and Peace*, presents a critical survey of western scholarship on the UN system. In particular, he is negative about the 'functional approach', which holds that the most desirable route to international community-building proceeds gradually from initial transnational cooperation in the solution of common problems.[10] To the contrary, he considers that this concept provides background for the attempts to depoliticize the United Nations and to reduce its role to that of an ordinary international institution which concentrates on technical and economic issues. The focus of the UN should be, according to Fedorov, disarmament and security affairs. Similarly, he challenges western scholars' views which have implied, as this author affirms, the extension of authority of the UN General Assembly at the expense of the Security Council, the increase in power of the UN Secretary-General, and some other western theories.[11]

Multilateral diplomacy and the negotiating process

Apart from works on international organization, the United Nations performance is examined in other studies of multilateral diplomacy and the negotiating process. The transformation of the world order toward globalization, the collapse of the bipolar system of international relations, and the end of the cold war impelled Soviet and Russian scholars to review the potential, capacities and opportunities for multilateral diplomacy in the changing global context. Scholars comprising this group share the view that the globalization of international problems, such as environmental protection, security, the growing disparity between rich and poor, common diseases, and drug addiction, reconfirm and make even more urgent the importance, indeed the indispensability, of multilateral activities through joint efforts by the world community. The diplomatic approach widely practised toward international organizations in the past, an approach aimed at achieving unilateral benefits, had been challenged and found inadequate for new realities.

According to the former head of the Soviet delegation at the Geneva Conference on Disarmament and author of the book *Diplomats: Face to Face*, the term 'multilateral diplomacy' implies joint consideration of international issues of mutual interest, by many or several states, with the purpose of finding mutually acceptable solutions.[12] Multilateral diplomacy does not challenge bilateral diplomacy and is not an alternative to it. On the contrary, these two may be combined as a means of preventing or resolving conflicts and designing institutional processes.

The diplomacy of groups is a specific form of multilateral diplomacy that is broadly implemented at the United Nations. These groups, diverse in their composition, aims and nature, represent one of the peculiarities of the UN system. In examining the relationship of groups to multilateral diplomacy in the UN, Regina Solovieva singles out different types of groups involved in multilateral diplomacy: geographic groups shaping the formal structure of the United Nations, voting blocs, groups of common interests, ad hoc groups, factions, and others. Groups complicate the picture of multilateral interaction within the UN and lend it a multifaceted texture by combining interests, lobbying, and pursuing other tactics that may modify the parts played by official actors. UN group diplomacy may affect bilateral interstate relations and even to some extent the foreign policy of a state.[13]

Multilateral diplomacy may be employed through conferences, within international institutions, at meetings, by mail, and increasingly by other means of communication. In some cases, multilateral diplomacy paves the way for convening an international conference, and it may well be an integral part of the preparatory process. Alternatively, in such cases as preparation of multilateral initiatives on disarmament and security matters, multilateral diplomacy may not necessarily foretell a conference. Actually, the participants in multilateral processes may not be brought together, but instead express their views in bilateral consultations (for example, American 'shuttle diplomacy' in the Middle East) and by correspondence. Thus multilateral diplomacy has a broader meaning than conference diplomacy.

Specialists point out that multilateral diplomacy has a promising future. The arrival of new members in the United Nations, closer interdependence and interaction of states along with the globalization of international problems, and growing participation of the general public in international fora combine to yield an upgraded role for multilateral diplomacy.

What are the tasks, means and instruments of multilateral diplomacy, and how should the negotiating process in this context be pursued? These issues were debated in the Soviet and Russian academic communities in the late 1980s and 1990s. Along with scholars from the disciplines traditionally concerned with diplomacy (political science, international relations and law) others from the fields of psychology, linguistics and philosophy joined this discourse. As Deputy Director of the Institute of USA and Canada Victor Kremeniuk suggested, it is vitally important to bring together different diplomatic styles and develop a 'universal culture of diplomatic behaviour' based on cooperation, partnership and mutual understanding. The priority task of multilateral diplomacy is to clarify and then coordinate the common interests of states. Moreover, diplomacy must provide all relevant information on changes needed in order to insure cooperation by the academic and political communities of its home country. Finally, diplomacy should engage in setting up negotiating machinery that meets the requirements of this cooperation.[14]

Commitment to maximum participation in dialogue is the foremost and guiding principle of the contemporary negotiating process, points out psychologist Marina Lebedeva.[15] This commitment implies the desire to view and assess the problem from one's partner's perspective – or from others' perspectives in multilateral contexts – and to search, through this means of comprehension, for mutually acceptable decisions. This quest for the reconciliation of interests is, according to her classification, the second principle of the negotiating process. To these two principles Lebedeva adds the necessity of skilful combinations and applications of various diplomatic instruments and methods.

In his monograph, Victor Issraelyan gives recommendations and advice to those learning the art of negotiations. To be successful, negotiators should meet five main requirements. They should enjoy the very process of negotiation, notwithstanding its complications and propensity to exhaust the negotiator. They should possess a perfect knowledge of the subject of the negotiations. They should be aware of the position of their counterpart and understand it. They should proceed from the assumption that their interlocutor is not an adversary or opponent, but a partner. Finally, trust and honesty should underlie any negotiating process.[16]

Although the UN system is the main focus of multilateralism in Russian studies, the relationship between regionalism and multilateralism is touched on in some works.[17] These authors presume that regional arrangements and organizations can render great service if their activities are undertaken in a manner consistent with the UN Charter, and if their relationship with the UN is governed by the Charter's guiding principles. However, the constitutional acts of the regional organizations and the provisions of the UN Charter give grounds for various interpretations. This causes difficulties for effective settlement of conflicts and needs alleviative measures.

V. Emin considers that an international convention on conflict settlement would be helpful.[18] Such a convention would imply that its parties accept mediatory missions in the event of conflict. Mediatory missions might be undertaken by authority of the UN Security Council or initially by authority of regional organizations. If efforts of the mediatory mission do not provide effective results, the UN Secretary-General could set up a commission with an investigative mediatory and reconciliatory assignment. The parties to the convention would also be committed to accept this assistance. Similarly, bilateral agreements may also serve to provide regional organizations with peacemaking and preventive diplomacy functions on behalf of and under the authority of the United Nations.

Future of the United Nations

What kind of international organization could respond to the challenges of the changing world order? In the course of the debate, the ideas of world government and world confederation of states were re-examined and revised. One of the advocates of these concepts,

Academician Andrei Sakharov, believed that the UN, UNESCO and other international organizations should compose a rudimentary world government based exclusively on human values.[19] This aim has since been revitalized and found some supporters among Russian scholars.

By contrast, two scholars from the Institute of World Economy and International Relations, Elgiz Pozdniakov and Irina Shadrina, are mostly critical of the UN system. They call for abandoning it. The outlook for a world confederation of states as a form of world government should not be regarded as completely utopian in relation to the changing world order.[20] In their view, the interaction of two dynamics sustains the plausibility of this concept. Emerging economic and political entities such as what has become the European Union can provide prototypes for the new world governance. At the same time, convergence in modes of thought and practice as a result of rapidly growing commercial, cultural and political contacts leads to democratization of the global society. From their perspective, globalization of the economy and of comprehension creates the need for a new form of world governance while providing a possible foundation for a world confederation of states.

However, the majority of scholars contest this theory. Doctors Aleksandr Veber, Andrei Kozyrev and Vladimir Petrovskii do not believe that such a confederation can be founded or that the United Nations may turn in the future into a supra-national structure or super-administrative body, primarily because the world is far from the ideals and fundamental principles of the United Nations. Furthermore, such governance would conflict with the principle of state sovereignty. They foresee that in the period ahead the United Nations will remain devoted to the objectives highlighted in the Charter, as a multilateral and universal organization providing the key international instrument of coordination while balancing the need for good governance with the requirements of an ever more interdependent world.[21]

However, the UN system needs improvement and innovation aimed at fostering its creative and responsive potential. Andrei Kozyrev identifies three groups of alternative solutions offered by the members of the United Nations. The first one, 'conservative' in Kozyrev's terminology, represented by France and some other states, essentially welcomes and appreciates the activities of the United Nations while opposing any fundamental changes in its machinery and procedures. The second group, including the US and some other countries, whose approach is referred to as 'reformatory and conservative', is discontented with some UN mechanisms and activities, primarily in administrative and financial matters, and seeks to reform them. A third group, 'states-reformers and schemers', proposes a radical transformation of the world system and international organization. Their concepts and initiatives usually outstrip the realities of the contemporary world. These proposals are congenial to some Third World countries which strive to profit from their quantitative advantages at the United Nations and to some of the 'regional superpowers' which seek permanent seats on the UN Security Council.

As for the Soviet Union, its attitude represented a combination of the three approaches. Kozyrev is critical of the Soviet Union's 'reorganizational itch' in the perestroika years; he cites the Soviet proposal on the World Space Organization, approached rather as a long-term goal or prospect than as a practical solution. He writes that 'new structures and machineries should be established only after the old ones are exhausted'.[22]

Kozyrev examines what should be done in order to evoke adaptive capability and effective innovation in the UN system. Improvement of coordination within the UN should become one of the essential goals of these reforms, which would imply, in his view, a more accurate definition of its priorities, avoidance of overlapping and duplicative programmes, and a more efficient division of functions between different components of the UN system. A centralized assessment of the programmes under the supervision of the Secretary-General is urgently needed. In addition, he proposes to set up a proper, well-established machinery of interaction and cooperation among the UN agencies. Finally, the purposes and capacities of the UN programmes for economic assistance should be reevaluated and alternative measures should be worked out. He also strongly supports employment of preventive diplomacy as offering a valid contribution toward securing peace in the spirit of the Charter.

An article by jurists Galina Dmitrieva and Igor Lukashuk holds it evident that the principles of democracy must be more consistently and broadly applied within the international organization. One way to do this is to establish a parliamentary assembly based on the proportional representation of population. They also call for the fullest consultation, participation and engagement of all states in the work of the UN system.[23] Among other patterns, questions of procedure are under review as well. Some authors criticize the principle of consensus which, in their view, is sometimes employed by the state members to block the decisionmaking process. To this end, they recommend the reassessment of the status, role and application of consensus practice.[24]

*   *   *

The world is no longer the same place it was before the 1990s. Neither is Russia. This country enters a time of global transition to a new world order with many problems: a devastated economy, the absence of a relevant Constitution and legitimate political institutions, and a public sceptical of the proposed means to solve these problems. At the same time, Russia exists in a geopolitical environment challenged by brutal ethnic conflicts. Will it be able to meet the new economic and political realities? Does it have the potential and capacity to claim the status of a great power and to succeed that of the Soviet Union? What are the priorities and directions of the international activity of new Russia in the changing world and domestic context? All these issues are being debated in the process of shaping Russian foreign policy. Although many outdated orthodox perceptions and attitudes have been abandoned, the search for new approaches and solutions has not yet been completed. This search is likely to be a continuing and time-consuming process.

However, it is apparent that multilateralism and the UN system will remain one of the foundations of Russian external activity. This foundation demands the formulation of a new and systematic approach to Russian policy concerning the United Nations. Therefore, there remains the expectation that international organizations will persist on the agenda of Russian scholarship in years to come.

Notes

1   *An Agenda for Peace*, New York: United Nations, 1992, p. 5.
2   *USA: Economics, Politics, Ideology*, No. 12, 1991, p. 4.
3   See, for example, A. Roschin, 'The Roots of the United Nations', in *International Affairs* [Moscow], No. 7, 1992, pp. 125–33.
4   See, for example, D. Smyslov, 'International Monetary Fund in Contemporary World and the Interests of the Soviet Union', in *USA: Economics, Politics, Ideology*, No. 6, 1991, pp. 20–28; G. Morozov, *Global Ecological Problem*, Moscow: International Relations, 1988; T. Dmitrichev, *The Geneva Forums on Disarmament, 1945–1987*, Moscow: International Relations, 1988.
5   Morozov, *World Community: Utopia or Reality?*, Moscow: Information Agency Novosti, 1987, p. 26.
6   Petrovskii, *et al.*, *International Organization of the UN System*, Moscow: International Relations, p. 4; Kosyrev, *The United Nations Organization: Structure and Activities*, Moscow: Academy of Pedagogical Science, 1991, pp. 19–20.
7   *Journal of World Economy and International Relations*, No. 4, 1989, p. 27.
8   Kozyrev, *We and the World in the Mirror of UN*, Moscow: International Relations, p. 24.
9   Regina Solovieva, *The United Nations: Distribution of Forces and Diplomacy in the 1980s*, Moscow: Science, 1990, p. 176.
10 James P. Sewell, *Functionalism and World Politics*, Princeton: Princeton University Press, 1966, p. 3.

11 Fedorov, *United Nations and the Problems of War and Peace*, Moscow: International Relations, 1988.
12 Victor Issraelyan, *Diplomats: Face to Face*, Moscow: International Relations, 1990, p. 16.
13 *The United Nations: Distribution of Forces and Diplomacy in the 1980s*, pp. 16–17.
14 *USA: Economics, Politics, Ideology*, No. 11, 1991, p. 53.
15 Lebedeva, *You Are Facing Talks*, Moscow: International Relations, 1993.
16 *Diplomats: Face to Face*, pp. 344–5.
17 Among them are the dissertation by B. Bazilevskii, 'International and Judicial Dimensions of Regional Security', defended in 1984; the dissertation by A. Gromyko-Piradov, defended in 1991; works by A.F. Vysotskii that develop a theoretical approach to regionalism and universalism in maritime law, for instance *Maritime Regionalism: Issues of International Law in Regional Cooperation*, Kiev, 1986; the monograph by V. Emin, *Regional Conflicts and International Organizations*, Moscow, 1991.
18 Emin, *Regional Conflicts and International Organizations*, Moscow: Feniks, 1991.
19 Sakharov, *Concern and Hope*, Moscow, 1990, p. 76.
20 *Journal of World Economy and International Relations*, No. 4, 1989, pp. 18–29.
21 *Journal of World Economy and International Relations*, No. 4, 1993, pp. 16–29.
22 *We and the World in the Mirror of UN*, p. 52.
23 *International Affairs*, Nos. 11–12, 1992, pp. 14–22.
24 *International Affairs*, January 1989, pp. 147–57.

3

Chinese Literature on Multilateralism and the United Nations System

Zhang Xinhua

General situation of research on multilateralism and the United Nations system in China

Research on multilateralism and the United Nations system in China is still near its starting point, far from maturity. Evidence of this stage of development follows.

1. **Real interest in and conscious academic endeavours on multilateralism and the UN system has only existed for about a decade.** Some distinguished scholars, most of them international law specialists, have written papers and published articles since the 1950s on the role of the United Nations and certain related major international events and problems, but these writings were in the nature of news commentary, and the issues they focused upon were directly related to China's right and position in the United Nations. Some papers and articles have more intellectual depth and can be regarded as genuine academic endeavours. They were written to concert the current foreign policy and political stand of the Chinese government or directly to serve the policy of the government. The low level of interest can be attributed to the fact that China was then unlawfully expelled from the United Nations and separated from the outside world. It was also closely related to the limited practical needs of the Chinese government. Another important reason for this situation was the macro international environment. Multilateralism had not widely emerged and the United Nations system had not drawn full attention from students of international political economy.

2. **No relatively independent, clear-cut special area of research has yet emerged in China on multilateralism and the UN system.** Scholars have paid increasing attention to the field, and they have achieved some progress in the direction of a distinct research area. Nevertheless,

neither individuals nor institutions in the academic realm have regarded the subject of multilateralism and the UN system as an independent area of research or as an interdisciplinary endeavour. This area has not been regarded as an important academic subject matter. Multilateralism and the UN system are seen as subjects only peripheral or marginal.

3. The research carried out so far is only introductory and cursory. Although some writings have theoretical depth, most fall in the category of textbooks, collections of materials, or briefing information. These do not form any system and lack theoretical principles. Most research utilizes the researcher's empirical judgment. Writings that apply generally accepted theories, perspectives, or methodology and techniques are lacking. Generally speaking, no methodology or technique has developed. But for the fact that certain academic leaders and authorities adorn the field of international law, no leading figure or authority has appeared in the study of multilateralism and the UN system.

4. Research activity and the generation of literature are highly dispersed, as reflected in the multitude of disciplines involved in the study of this subject matter. Analysis of the disciplinary distribution of Chinese authors indicates that research on multilateralism and the UN system has engaged scholars based in many related disciplines including international politics, general political science, economics, international law, administrative management, business management, military science, international finance and trade, and strategic studies. Yet the disciplinary distribution of authors who have written on multilateralism concentrates in the international politics and international law communities. Moreover, this concentration occurs in certain key social science academic institutions. Subjects of international relations such as multilateralism and the UN system have always been the exclusive area of academic endeavour in certain institutions; others either are not interested or do not have this as a responsibility.

5. High dispersion of the generation of literature has two manifestations. One is that, unlike other academic research fields in China, there has so far appeared *no core journal or core periodicals* publishing literature on multilateralism and the UN system. Instead, papers and articles are scattered in about a dozen related journals and periodicals. At present it is hard to judge or foresee which journal(s) will be the major or preferred carrier of this category of literature. Although several law journals are major carriers of literature on multilateralism and the UN system from the perspectives of international law, we cannot predict which journal or what kind of periodical will be the major carrier for papers on non-governmental international and regional organizations and groups. The same is true for literature on reform of the international economic order and on the role and prospect of certain UN agencies.

Another manifestation is the *diversity of literary formats*. Besides textbooks in monograph form and papers and articles published in academic journals, other important formats include dissertations, proceedings of various conferences, collections of special papers, briefing reports, internal documents, working papers, and all kinds of informal publications, including confidential material.

6. **The youthful quality of China's research on multilateralism and the UN system is also reflected in the relatively weak research force, the small number of authors researching collectively, and the narrow coverage of research subjects.** Judging by the literature, a limited number of authors are concentrated in certain limited or similar fields. A large amount of the literature handles almost the same subject and repeats almost the same arguments while totally neglecting many other equally important or more significant matters.

This situation on one hand reflects the immaturity and lack of depth of a Chinese academic endeavor on multilateralism and the UN system. On the other hand, it indicates that this subject requires multidisciplinary research and provides ample room for further exploration and development both in China and the world over.

Research emphasis and methodology

Based on the analysis of available literature, the following research emphases by Chinese scholars writing on multilateralism and the UN system have been identified.

1. **The macro international environment or pattern of international relations wherein multilateralism emerges and the UN system operates is one theme of almost all Chinese university textbooks on international political economy.** This is the most prominent theme of the past decade and in particular of the last few years. It proceeds thus: with the rise of the Third World countries and the strengthening of their role in international arenas, and with the decline in strength of the two superpowers, the international pattern has changed dramatically. This changed pattern constitutes the breeding ground and prerequisite of multilateralism and serves as background against which the United Nations and other forms of multilateral mechanisms operate.

2. **The inequality of the old international economic order and its reform by means of multilateralism is another traditional theme of Chinese literature.** In expounding this argument, many Chinese scholars have expressed dissatisfaction with some of the UN organizations and urged their reform so that a new, equitable order can be established.

3. **The emergence of multilateralism and the functions of different forms of organizing also keynote Chinese literature.** Here regional organizations and groups are focal points. The relationship between their development and the safeguarding of world peace and regional development receive attention. A topic of equal importance is the impact of multilateral organizations on the development of international law.

4. **By far the greatest recent emphasis in Chinese literature is the role and prospect of the UN system, along with revision of the UN Charter and reform of some of its agencies.** This area has been explored chiefly from the perspectives of international law.

Most Chinese writings on methodology are introductory in nature. Some are collections of informative material. Judging by their research or perspectives, in writings on the emergence and mechanism of multilateralism, the structural–functional approach is the main tool of analysis, or at least research efforts on these topics is included in the framework of structuralism-functionalism. In the study of economic order and development problems, Chinese scholars have followed the principles of the underdevelopment theory of Marxism.

Overview of scholarly standpoints

What follows is an overview of the standpoints held by Chinese scholars as revealed in the literature on multilateralism and the UN system.

1. The macro world environment: the change of world order from bipolarity to multipolarity and the evolution of multilateralism

Investigating the change and development of the pattern of international relations has constituted one of the major academic endeavours in the Chinese study of international political economy and international relations in recent years. The general standpoint is that the process of multipolarization is a historical inevitability that is the prerequisite for the emergence of multilateralism, though multilateralism is just one of the manifestations of the process of multipolarization.

As early as 1988, Chinese scholars described the process of world development as a general trend in the shift of bipolarity toward multipolarity marked by the ever-increasing decline of the bipolar system, whereby the bipolars constitute bipolarity within the system of multi-polarity. Gradually a new world relations pattern will take shape and consequently the multipolars will converge after a long historical per-iod, the fruit of changes in international relations since the Second World War. It represents the realignment of the various forces in the international arena since the 1970s and constitutes the new pattern of international politics.[1]

The emergence of this situation has deep-rooted historical reasons. The dramatic change of pattern in international relations since the end of the Second World War is in essence characterized by the development of international society toward multipolarity. The pattern of confronta-tion between the United States and the then Soviet Union during the early postwar period for a short while concealed the trend toward multi-polarity in international relations. However, this temporary bipolarity was only a transient phenomenon wherein the old pattern of Euro-powers governing international relations gradually gave way to a new pattern of multipolarity.

As expounded by a Chinese scholar of international political eco-nomy, the period from the mid 1950s to the end of the 1960s can be regarded as a transient period or turning point wherein the parallel tendencies of independence and self-determination developing both within the Third World and within the two confronting camps of East and West converge into an irrevocable historical torrent and many new global forces become prominent. The dramatic change in the compara-tive strength of these forces in relation to the two superpowers ulti-mately indicate the disintegration of the bipolar pattern and the formation of the multipolar pattern. This is deemed an historical inevit-ability in the development of international relations.

The so-called new pattern began to take shape in the 1970s, when the influence of the United States and the Soviet Union on the international situation decreased. More and more states and groups of states adopted the policy of independence and self-determination and became power-ful global actors exerting their influence on international affairs. The '[i]mportant manifestation of this new pattern of multipolarity is the basic contradiction between the limited strength of the United States and its boundless objectives and the powerful trend of economic and political multilateralism'.[2]

In addition to this historical inevitability, progress in science and technology has been another important force contributing to the for-mation of this new pattern. According to Chinese scholars, the acceler-ated progress of modern science and technology and the rapid development of the economy has promoted world civilization to a completely new stage. Internationalization, diversification, nationalization and individualization have been in parallel operation. The world has become progressively smaller thanks to revolutionary change in information and the means of its communication. Interdependence and mutual complementarity among all countries in politics, economics, science and technology and other fields has made interstate and inter-region relations and contacts ever closer and more regular. No country can achieve development and prosperity by isolating itself from the international family and benefiting itself by sacrificing others. Because of this political and economic interdependence, all countries face the common problem of survival. This trend has provided opportunities to develop their economies rapidly. It has brought the whole world the hope of prosperity and stability, the base of which is universal participation, or maximum and equal participation of all forces in world affairs. Hence multilateralism arises.

For Chinese scholars, the keynote of this multipolar pattern is peace, cooperation and development:

> The various global forces survive and develop in interdependence and mutual confrontation. The content of the international pattern of multipolarity will undergo great changes. With the increase of the strength of the world forces other than the United States and the Soviet Union, more independent centers or players will emerge, resulting in a new multipolar equilibrium world system which will replace the present multipolar system tilting toward the United States and the Soviet Union. The trend toward a more equitable and more progressive international society will be greatly strengthened and world peace will be further guaranteed.[3]

With regard to the effect of this multipolar, multilateral pattern on world peace, Chinese scholars have slightly different perceptions. One position holds that multipolar multilateralism will prevent world war and some of the local strategic moves that prepare world war, as well as functioning to reduce local war and regional conflicts, because

> [t]he growth of the various multipolar forces all represent the formation of certain independent political and economic forces. Peaceful environment is indispensable for the growth of these independent forces. During the process of growth, these forces will mainly concentrate on increasing their political position and economic

strength, not on military build-up or external expansion. Therefore, judging from the overall global strategic relationship, they will stabilize the world situation by way of preventing war.[4]

Others are worried about the negative side of multipolar multilateralism. Typically their concern is that in the multipolar multilateralism pattern, the power of control is decentralized and factors of uncertainty increase, thereby contributing to the occurrence of accidental incidents. Endless conflicts and wars in different parts of the world invite intervention by the more powerful. Yet some maintain that the effects of decentralized power do not matter so much. 'This kind of conflict and war is usually peripheral in nature, and generally speaking will not break the global strategic balance and will not affect the overall situation.'[5]

2. The emergence of multilateralism and its manifestations and functions

As stated above, multipolarity is the prerequisite for the emergence of multilateralism and, in a sense, multilateralism is the manifestation of multipolarity. According to Chinese scholars, multilateralism, or the formation of the various independent political and economic forces, has taken the following forms: (a) interstate and nonstate organizations and groups, including regional as well as international organizations and groups; (b) various international political movements, such as the international non-alliance movement, international peace movement, international environment protection movement, and movement for national independence and self-determination; (c) global and regional party organizations, such as Socialist International, Liberal International, International Democratic Union, Christian Democratic International associations; (d) private multinationals and various economic cooperation organizations.

These multilateral forms include both interstate and nonstate manifestations. Their complementary functioning will realize the process of maximum participation, or non-exclusive participation, of all forces and all peoples in international affairs. By extending access to participate, the functioning of multilateralism promotes the process leading toward universal equality and democracy in global society.

According to the Chinese literature, these various forms of multilateralism have played important roles in safeguarding peace and promoting development. An overview of Chinese arguments concerning the first two categories follows. Limitations of space prevent the inclusion of other forms of multilateralism.

(a)   Flourishing development of multilateral organizations and groups, notably regional formations, along with their functions

Since the end of the Second World War, especially during the past twenty-five years, interstate and nonstate multilateral organizations and groups have mushroomed, constituting a remarkable phenomenon in modern international relations, as well as an important manifestation of multilateralism. In addition to the United Nations and the various UN affiliated organizations, about 4,000 different kinds of comprehensive and specialized organizations and groups that have objectives and activities related to the various fields of international society have appeared.

Among these organizations, the development of *regional* organizations is especially prominent. Chinese scholars regard the emergence and activities of these regional organizations as the most substantial manifestation of multilateralism. Two major reasons explain their rapid development. First, the rise of the Third World countries contributes significantly. They have made great progress in consolidating political independence, developing national economies and safeguarding national rights. But under the conditions of international competition between the United States and the Soviet Union, aggressive expansion of the superpowers, and faced with the situation of control of the world economic order by international monopoly capitalism, they have gradually come to realize that for a single country it is difficult to resist control and domination by big powers. It was imperative that they unite and speak in one voice in international political and economic arenas; this was the only way for them to cast off the control of superpowers and break away from the yoke of the old international economic order. The regional organizations and groups that are mushrooming and growing stronger have increasingly become important channels and mechanisms for strengthening and developing South–South cooperation. Moreover, they are making efforts to secure more equitable and inclusive participation in global institutions.

The second factor is the limitation of the United Nations system in handling international affairs and the corresponding need for regional development and cooperation. Although the United Nations has achieved a lot in safeguarding world peace, the performance of its functions has been severely restrained. People cannot expect the United Nations to solve all the problems facing international society in a world full of complex and intricate contradictions. More and more countries have realized that regional organizations can effectively handle many affairs in their respective regions by following the UN Charter and its principles.

The emergence and development of regional organizations and groups is considered the inevitable manifestation of present-day multilateralism. During recent decades in international affairs they:

(1) Created good conditions for regional stability and peace by promoting solidarity and seeking concord. Regional organizations generally include friendship between neighbouring countries and the realization of regional stability, peace and prosperity as provisions in their constitutions. Their practice testifies that these objectives are being realized to different degrees in various regions.

(2) Adhered to the general orientation of anti-imperialism, anti-hegemony and anti-colonialism, jointly resisting outside threats.

(3) Promoted regional economic cooperation and coordinated social development. Some regional organizations have the revitalization of national economies as their key objective and have been trying to concentrate scattered resources to develop and utilize natural resources and promote and coordinate exchanges in trade and finance within the region.

With the strengthening of regional economic interdependence and the improvement of people's lives, regional as well as global peace can be guaranteed. 'The practice of regional organizations has indicated that the argument held by functionalists that non-political means can be used to prevent war has had its echo in regional situations.'[6]

Chinese scholars believe that the existence and development of regional organizations and groups is in line with historical trends and therefore has undeniable potential. As for their future prospects, they foresee the following:

(1) The cohesive force will surpass the centrifugal force. Most regional organizations were established on the basis of the common interests of their member states. When disagreement occurs, most members will be willing to solve contradictions through patient, repeated consultation to seek common ground while reserving differences.

(2) More attention is being paid to the handling of concrete matters and to flexibility in cooperation and coordination. The most remarkable example is ASEAN's principle of 'five minus one' in safeguarding solidarity and achieving consensus of most of the member states.[7]

Another example is the efforts by the Union of Regional Cooperation for South Asia to stop discussing bilateral and controversial problems and proceed functionally by cooperation on projects of common interest, moving from the easy to the difficult so that suspicion among member states can be reduced and effective cooperation achieved.

(3) Regional organization members are striving for high-level integration. The scope and depth of their functions have developed. Some organizations not only aim at cooperation on trade, finance and industrial and agricultural production, but also encourage states to restructure their respective economies and perform economic reform.

(4) Outward links are closer and closer. Regional organizations have not indulged in narrow, exclusive regionalism. While strengthening internal connections, they have strengthened external links through bilateral and multilateral arrangements. In the future, with the raising of the level of regional integration and the increase in demand for a global exchange of personnel, material, information and capital, regional organizations' outward ties are expected to become closer and more intense.

(b) International political movements: An example

Of the modern international political movements, the peace movement is the mass movement that has lasted longest and spread widest. It has not only profoundly affected the process of development of the world situation, but also the internal policy and social–political development of various countries. Since the 1980s, the international peace movement entered a new stage of development and has become an important form of multilateralism. It has demonstrated the following characteristics or functions:

(1) It has become a global, 'whole people' multilateral movement with wide participation. The large number of participants, the range of membership, the breadth of the affected area and the vigour of the movement are all unprecedented. It has spread to nearly every country. Participants come from nearly all classes and communities, including political, religious, cultural, scientific and technological sectors. World-renowned figures and political leaders take part. Its activities have begun to be combined with other mass activities and have adopted diverse forms.

(2) The trend to neglect ideological difference is increasingly apparent, demonstrating an ever stronger transcending-of-ideology quality.

Some participants believe in Marxism and scientific socialism; some believe in neutralism and pacifism. There are feminists, communists, social democrats, liberals, conservatives, and people with extreme ideological beliefs representative of various religious factions.

(3) Trans-border joint peace action is becoming prevalent. The western Europe peace movement is combining with peace organizations of eastern Europe, and 'West–East' dialogue has appeared.

(4) The peace movement is being combined with other social and mass movements. Movements involving labour, youth and women's organizations and those for national liberation and democracy are working in concert with and support the international peace movement. People have put forward the slogan of 'Peace and Labour'. Western peace organizations are making every effort to seek support from Third World countries.

The international peace movement, representing the increasing wakening of the world's peoples and reflecting their firm determination against war and for peace, plays an important role in developing the world situation. According to Chinese scholars, this role has borne the following consequences:

(1) It served as a check on the arms race between the United States and the Soviet Union.

(2) It generally affects the relationship between the United States and its alliances, and the relationship between alliances. The rise of the international peace movement has exerted influence on the foreign and domestic policies of various countries, especially western European countries.

(3) The rise of the peace movement further strengthened the world peace force and promoted the development of factors preventing war, and is thus of great significance in safeguarding peace.

Chinese scholars also believe that the international peace movement has more far-reaching significance and functions as an important form of multilateralism, because it is deepening. It has become a multilateralism with multiple functions. When first started in western Europe in the 1980s, its spearhead was directed at the nuclear arms race between the two superpowers, but it rapidly expanded all over the world, including Third World countries. Since 1984, the mass movement has looked quieter, but in essence it entered a new stage of deepening development.

The struggle against the nuclear arms race began to broaden to include a struggle against competition for superpower positions. Many peace movement leaders from the Third World stated that all forms of expansionism, colonialism and racism, which increase the possibility of war and tension, must be rejected in order to safeguard peace and development in the world.

Secondly, the struggle for world peace began to be integrated with efforts to solve the South–North contradiction and promote economic development. People have gradually come to realize that to achieve true peace, it is not enough to prevent the nuclear arms race and eliminate nuclear weapons. It is equally or even more important to eliminate poverty, backwardness and the unfair old economic order. A statement by an Italian peace activist has its echo among Chinese scholars: We will not be successful if the peace movement cannot contribute to the establishment of a new international order, the basis of which is justice, the end of exploitation of the underdeveloped 'South' by the 'North', and the right of self-determination enjoyed by the world's peoples.

3 Economic multilateralism and the reform of the world economic order

Another important focus of research by Chinese scholars is the existing international economic order and the need to establish a new order. They are generally critical of the existing international economic order governed by the UN system, believing that with the strengthening of the political role of the Third World countries and the raising of their position in the United Nations, economic multilateralism is on the ascendancy. This situation will surely promote the structural reform of the existing economic order, subsequently making the United Nations and its agencies more suitable to the requirements of the time and better able to promote economic development.

Since the end of the Second World War, many countries have obtained national independence and embarked on the path of national economic development. However, when these Third World or 'developing' countries enter the international family, they find themselves constantly hindered by existing inequitable international economic relations. Within the international economic system, dominated by the developed countries, the economic lifelines of the developing countries are to a large extent controlled by these developed countries. The developing countries are not guaranteed the right to speak and make decisions concerning world economic affairs. This inequitable situation is the inevitable consequence of the existing international economic order within the UN system.

In the Chinese literature, 'international economic order' is defined as an international economic public law system established after the Second World War to govern and adjust interstate economic relations. Through the UN, this public law framework became a kind of system mechanism. The foundation of this system is the three agencies loosely affiliated with the UN and established by agreements concluded in 1944 and thereafter by countries headed by the United States and the United Kingdom – the International Monetary Fund (IMF), the International Bank for Reconstruction and Development (IBRD), and the General Agreement on Tariffs and Trade (GATT). Because interstate economic relations generally are either monetary and financial relations, investment relations, or tariff and trade relations, the three agreements and the institutions they underpin have in reality decided and adjusted all interstate economic relations. Since the agreements stipulated the economic rights and obligations of the signatory parties, and the behaviour stipulated by the agreements must be observed by all the signing countries and their respective governments, they become the international convention for the establishment of an economic order for the whole international society, which is why some western scholars regard them as the major legal documents governing the establishment of the international economic order.

How can this order endanger the economic interest of the Third World countries? Chinese scholars have made probing analyses in order to answer this question. They state that, in the so-called free international market, all economic activities (monetary, financial, investment and trade) of a country are controlled and restrained by the three organizations once it joins them. All trans-border economic activities performed by an individual (legal person or natural person) are indirectly controlled and adjusted on a macro scale by these agreements because the country has committed to the obligations stipulated by the agreements. Therefore, the market is no longer free and the international economic order is by no means free.

The dangers of this mechanism can be seen in the three agreements. The IMF agreement sets up an international monetary system and provides for its structure; it also sets up an International Monetary Fund responsible for establishing such a monetary system. This organization, like IBRD, adopted an organizational form resembling western shareholding private corporations, with member states subscribing shares. Those with more shares have more votes. In this way, international economic organization falls into the hands of a few large shareholders. 'The International Monetary Fund so organized set the worst precedent in the history of international public law.'[8] The consequence is an international monetary system with the US dollar as the standard unit, and the United States the dominator of an international economic order benefitting only it and a few other developed countries.

The International Bank is an international corporation involved in the organizing and operating of international investment. It plays the role of director for investment throughout the world. The IBRD agreement specified the orientation for international investment, to invest in advanced industrialized countries in order to restore and revitalize their industrial production, and in less developed (or underdeveloped) countries in order to develop their resources.

The International Bank and its two fellow Bank Group agencies, the International Finance Corporation (IFC) and the International Development Association (IDA) are the sponsors and organizers for the raising of investment capital from the capitalist world to invest in developing countries. They have exerted great influence on the direction and flow of investment capital all over the world. In this sense, implementation of the International Bank agreement has established the international investment order. The investment practice of all capital-export countries indicates that they have followed this direction.

The International Bank along with IFC and IDA provide low interest loans to Third World countries and raise capital for their development. But the International Bank is only interested in developing their resources so these countries can be turned into raw material and energy production bases for the advanced industrialized countries. Greater and greater supplies of raw material, energy and agricultural products keeps the price for these low. As supply bases of cheap raw materials and energy, the Third World countries will remain in poverty forever.

The General Agreement on Tariffs and Trade established the international trade order after the Second World War. Under conditions whereby developed countries export industrial goods to Third World countries, while the latter mainly purchase these goods with exports of cheap raw materials and energy, the principles of GATT can only help curtail the development of national economies in Third World countries while benefiting developed countries. At present it is not clear whether this situation will be changed by the World Trade Organization (WTO).

Together, the three original agreements helped establish a one-way flow macro cycle in global society wherein developed countries export industrial manufactured goods to Third World countries while the latter supply energy and raw materials. This legal framework was entrenched as the international economic order. Because the order benefits advanced industrial countries, they do their best to protect it.

Faced with this situation, the developing countries have come to realize that the key for them to achieve smooth development of their national economies lies in the reform of this unjust, inequitable old order. They have learned that it is imperative to make structural reform of the old system if they are to be treated on equitable terms in international transactions. According to Chinese scholars, this structural reform includes:

(a) Reforming the pattern of international production, consumption and trade, changing the present inequitable pattern of international division of labour between developing and developed countries. This reform may include the setting up of fair prices for primary resource products, solving the problems of money supply for development funds, increasing the transfer of technology, and allowing Third World products to enter the world market where this has not been the case.

(b) Insuring that the developing countries enjoy full and permanent sovereignty over their respective natural resources, have effective control over the development of their resources, and restrain and supervise the activities of multinationals according to the principle of sovereignty.

(c) Changing the present situation of a powerless position for Third World countries in international economic affairs by making necessary adjustments to the system and regulations of the existing international organizations, including IMF, IBRD and GATT, so that the developing countries can have full and equitable participation in the decision process regarding international economic affairs.

The South–North dialogue designed to address these objectives is the manifestation of economic multilateralism within the framework of the UN system. Third World countries are making wide-ranging efforts through the 'Group of 77'. The resulting activities form a powerful historical torrent to develop and reform the UN system.

4 Role and position of the UN system and recommendations for its improvement

The role and position of the UN system has always been an academic concern of Chinese scholars, but real, objective and rational thinking on their part only appeared in recent years. The general consensus is that the United Nations has played and still plays an irreplaceable role, although its path of development has been problematic. The United Nations as a multilateral systemic mechanism has performed the following functions:

(a) As the most active component of international relations behaviour, it has been a place where multilateral diplomacy has been mostly concentrated. It has provided a world-wide tribunal for politicians of various countries to propagate their respective foreign policies and discuss major international problems.
(b) It has provided a place for negotiation.
(c) It has been an institution for the world's peoples to mediate various kinds of international conflicts.
(d) It has been an active force to promote international economic and social cooperation.

As such an institution, the United Nations has displayed durable vitality and has obtained great achievements:

(a) Contributed to the safeguarding of world peace, mitigation of international conflicts and peaceful solution of disputes;
(b) Upheld the struggle against imperialism, colonialism and hegemonism, and speeded up the disintegration of the old colonial system. It has also made the principle of self-determination, which respects the equal right of all countries regardless of their size, universally accepted;
(c) Endeavoured to put an end to the arms race and realize nuclear disarmament and elimination of large-scale destructive weapons;
(d) Encouraged and promoted respect for human rights and basic freedom of the whole of mankind, along with the ultimate burial of race discrimination;
(e) Contributed greatly to the opening of new prospects of international economic and social cooperation and the gradual establishment of a new international economic order.

Despite these achievements, it is still a far cry from the aspirations and aims set forth by its Charter and expected by the world's peoples. According to Chinese scholars, the problems with the United Nations are twofold, the limitations of its organizational system and mechanism, and the macro international environment. With regard to the latter, the United Nations itself is an epitome of the contradiction between different political forces in the international arena, therefore fierce struggle always exists in its practice. Member states tend to place hopes in the UN to provide their respective benefits, while ignoring consensus and common interests. Member states try to take what they need or demand from the resolutions of the Security Council while at the same time not respecting or cooperating in implementing resolutions, so that many resolutions cannot be implemented. Added to this, a large number of historical problems were inherited from the era of colonial rule, a legacy that presented infinite areas of trouble. This made the problems facing the United Nations all the more complex and intricate when big power control and interference is involved.

The limitation of the UN system has several facets. First, the mechanism of the Security Council and the abuse of veto power always prevents the United Nations playing any substantial role in matters of great international significance. Second, some of its agencies and organizations – for instance the International Court of Justice – are only consultative or coordinative institutions without any comprehensive authority and therefore make it very difficult to achieve anything. Third, the establishment of many of its agencies and their constitution and organization are representative of the old order and embody the will of the old power politics along with the guiding principle of big power control. It is difficult or impossible for these agencies to play any fair and authoritative role within the new world situation. The United Nations has become a 'town council with the whole world participating'.[9]

Despite these limitations, Chinese scholars still believe that 'the role of the United Nations is becoming increasingly important. The question at present is not to weaken it, but actively to solve the problems of its organizational structure. . . . The world needs the existence of the United Nations, and the United Nations needs the support of the world's people and the world's states. The historical mission shouldered by the United Nations and its influence on the world is not eliminable nor replaceable.'[10]

In order further to improve and give strength to its functions, Chinese scholars propose to make efforts in two directions. One is to urge that all member states 'be committed to the moral obligations and responsibilities specified by the UN Charter so that the functions of the United Nations can be strengthened and its system be perfected'.[11] The other is to reform and revise the UN system and its Charter. The latter direction has always been the emphasis of concern and study among Chinese scholars.

With regard to the revision of the UN Charter, their arguments are as follows. The UN Charter was drafted immediately before the end of the Second World War and is the product of the contemporary historical conditions. Compared with the convention of the League of Nations, it contains some basic changes. It is fundamentally a real record of the victory of democratic over anti-democratic forces, of the world's peoples against fascism. However, just because it is the result of the prevailing historical conditions, the Charter can only reflect the power relationship of the contemporary international political struggle. Some provisions inevitably run contrary to the purpose and objectives of the Charter.

During the years since the founding of the United Nations, the balance of power both within and outside the UN has undergone tremendous change, as has the international situation. It is apparent that the original UN Charter and certain mechanisms and agencies cannot meet the requirements of the present situation. 'Certain aspects of the stipulations contained in the Charter are obviously either not equitable or obsolete. Out of the 110 provisions of the Charter, 20 odd have been completely or partially distorted, or put aside as nominal.' [12]

The provisions about the Security Council mechanism and the use of veto power, about the role and operation of the Trusteeship Council, and the decolonization system all need to be reexamined and revised or totally cast off. The Trusteeship system, for example, is the direct result of the international struggle at the end of the Second World War and reflects only this previous power relationship. Some of its stipulations are against the principle of democracy and national self-determination. With the rise and deepening of the national liberation movements, this system is becoming more and more counter-revolutionary and has lost grounds for further existence.

UN special organizations such as the International Bank and International Monetary Fund represent and protect the interest of a few big and rich powers to the detriment of the vast realm of developing countries. Because of this Chinese scholars believe 'it is completely reasonable and legal for the vast number of developing countries to demand ... reexamination and revision of the Charter so as to make it reflect the present world situation'.[13] 'As the Charter was drafted jointly by the then member states, it can be examined and revised jointly according to the requirements of the member states now.' [14] Revision of the Charter, of course, must be carried out with the reform of the system. With respect to such changes, some Chinese scholars publish books and put forward concrete recommendations.

Finally, many Chinese scholars have pointed out that the United Nations now faces new challenges as well as new areas in which to play even greater roles. At the initial stage, such global problems as world population growth, environmental pollution and desertification were not imminent and did not arouse any serious attention. Now they have proved to be challenges to the international society and have come onto the UN agenda. This new situation also requires the improvement of the UN system and more fully multilateralized mechanisms for their solution.

5   Multilateralism and the development of international law

With the development of its activities and the strengthening of the role of the United Nations as the most important and most representative multilateral institution, with the rise of other forms of multilateralism, especially the emergence and ever-increasing activities of regional organizations and groups, the problem of 'gradual development and codification' of international law has aroused much interest and attention among Chinese scholars, especially in the international law community. Their efforts concentrate on two challenges, one the casting off of old obsolete international law principles and the development of new principles, which is closely related to the International Law Commission of the United Nations, the other the push of international organizations and groups in developing international law. What follows is an overview of the Chinese arguments in meeting these two challenges.

In order to maintain the old international political and economic order, those who practise imperialism and colonialism have always tried to maintain the old international law with the characteristics of the old power politics. However, with the rise of newly independent countries and the change in international relations, the old international law should not be continually applied without any revision. The principles and systems which are in conformity with sovereignty and independence and beneficial to world peace and security can continue to be applied, even strengthened. But to adapt to the development and change of international relations, certain old principles and systems of international law should be abrogated or revised. Meanwhile, new principles and systems will inevitably emerge. At present, international law is in transition from the old law to the new modern international law.

The task of codifying and developing international law is shouldered by the UN International Law Commission, according to the UN Charter.

However, the practice of the International Law Commission since its founding has proved that this Commission has been long under the control of certain western countries. Through their representatives in the Commission, these countries tend to force their traditional standpoints as the common regulations of international law and codify them as such so as to maintain the old international order. Its influence cannot be overlooked even to this day.[15]

The International Law Commission has completed the drafting of a series of provisions and has obtained some achievements in the development and codification of international law by following its special working procedure. But its work is not adequate to meet the demands of international exchange and a new world order because of its low efficiency. Certain traditional perceptions held by western countries concerning international law, which represent the interests of imperialism and colonialism, are still influential in this field. Thus the UN's work in this field does not meet the requirements of developing countries, which must change detrimental influences so that international law meets the change in international relations. As pointed out by some international law scholars, the traditional western international law is in a 'floating state' and needs to be reassessed in order to become 'fixed'. In this process, developing countries must participate in the making of international law and will not agree to let part of the countries who have among themselves a common ideology and identical social–economic interests make law for the whole international society. This has become an irresistible historical wave in the field of gradual development and codification of international law.

In this respect, Chinese scholars foresee very complex difficulties that face the UN Commission which must be included on its future agenda. These include international economic development, seabed resources, decolonization, racial discrimination, the human environment, space and outer space, and the peaceful solution of disputes. 'Can the drafts of law which the International Law Commission has completed be revised according to the present situation and become formal conventions? Can the provisions which are now being drafted be completed smoothly to suit the historical trend of development? To what extent can the items on future agendas be accomplished?...These problems will pose a severe test to the performance and effectiveness of the International Law Commission of the United Nations.'[16]

The development and activities of all kinds of international and regional organizations and groups have brought about profound changes to modern international relations. Accompanying these changes are important effects on the development of international law. Chinese scholars have identified the following:

(a) The emergence and increase in the numbers of multilateral organizations and groups poses some urgent questions for modern international law. Among these are the legal position of multilateral organizations and groups; the legal person position of their members; the force, interpretation and revision of basic documents; contracting rights, privileges and exemptions of multilateral organizations and groups; and interorganizational relations.

(b) The scope of modern international law has been expanded by multilateral organizations, especially intergovernmental organizations. Multilateral organizations are not states, hence they differ from the ordinary legal persons and subjects of international law. An intergovernmental organization is in essence a group of states. The wills of the various contracting states are coordinated in the basic documents constituting the origanization and originating this organization's power. Yet the organization has itself to some degree acquired an international personality and become an entity of international law. This changes the situation wherein international law only accepted states as entities. Meanwhile, in addition to interstate relations, state–international organization relations and interorganizational relations have opened a new category of international relations, adding new rules to modern international law.

(c) The development of multilateral organizations and groups has expanded the scope of origins of international law. Traditional sources of international law include international conventions, international practice, general legal principles, law cases (legal precedents), and theories. Early international law was mainly based on common law. The emergence and increase in membership of multilateral organizations has brought about a large number of international treaties. These treaties tend to supplant other sources of international law. In reality, any treaty is a source of law to its signatory states.

(d) The basic documents constituting an international organization tend to determine the general rules and regulations that the international society must observe. With wider ratification of the basic documents, these rules and regulations will be universally accepted and thereby come into force as general international law. And this, in turn, will promote the future development of international law.

Notes

1 Feng Tejun, *Modern World Political Economy and International Relations*, The People's University Publishing House, 1988, p. 56.

2 Yu Zhengliang, 'On the Bipolar and Multipolar Pattern of Modern International Relations', in *Exploration of Peace*, Shanghai Academy of Social Sciences Publishing House, 1988, p. 133.

3 *Ibid.*, p. 138.

4 Pan Guang, 'Effect of Multipolarization of World Pattern on the Peace-maintaining Cause of the Mankind', in *Exploration of Peace*, pp. 55–56, 52.

5 Yu Zhengliang, 'On the Bipolar and Multipolar Pattern of Modern International Relations', *Exploration of Peace*, p. 136.

6 Yang Yuguang, 'The Development of Regional International Organization and World Peace', *Exploration of Peace*, p. 38.

7 [Editor's note, with gratitude to Pierre Lizée: The original five members of the Association of Southeast Asian Nations – Indonesia, Malaysia, the Philippines, Singapore and Thailand – sought from ASEAN's inception to provide themselves with a mechanism for discussion and concerted action that respected the autonomy of each. In this spirit, it was understood that decisions would be reached through consensus rather than majority voting. The need to act nonetheless led to the principle of five minus one: if only one member stands in the way of a consensus, the consensus is deemed to stand.]

8 Li Zerui, 'On the Legal Mechanism of International Economic Order', in *Management World*, 1989, p. 120.

9 Jiang Shikui, *Modern World Political Economy and International Relations*, Guangxi Teachers University Publishers, 1989, p. 353.

10 Bian Pengfei, *Modern World Political Economy and International Relations*, Zhejiang University Publishing House, 1988, p. 266; Jiang Shikui, *Modern World Political Economy and International Relations*, p. 353.

11 *Ibid.*

12 Zhao Lihai, *On the Revision of the United Nations Charter*, Beijing University Publishing House, 1982, p. 1.

13 *Ibid.*

14 *Ibid.*

15 Liang Xi, 'The UN International Law Commission and the Development of International Law', in *Papers of International Law*, Law Journal Publishing House, 1981, p. 114.

16 *Ibid.*

4

L'alternative Francophone: A Distinct Approach to International Relations and Multilateralism*

Jean-Philippe Thérien

This chapter analyzes the contribution of francophone literature to the study of international organizations and multilateralism. On the face of it, this task seems very ambitious; indeed, to the best of existing knowledge, no such effort has heretofore been undertaken. Considering the volume of documentation to be accounted for, it would be misleading to imply that this work will be comprehensive. Thus I begin by defining the scope of the chapter.

The body of literature examined essentially consists of writings published in the developed francophone countries: France, Belgium, Switzerland and Canada. This choice means putting aside studies from the developing countries. To do so narrows the range of sources as measured against the total of some forty states throughout the world that are members of *la Francophonie*.[1] Yet this focus is justifiable in several respects. Above all, the countries whose literature will be studied produce the vast majority of monographs and articles in French dealing with international organizations. One can also argue that due to the particularity of its contents, the literature produced in the developing countries has little in common with that published in the developed countries and therefore merits separate analysis. This said, the following analysis will not entirely exclude the contribution made by francophone intellectuals from the Third World since, as expatriates living in countries of the North, they publish a substantial portion of the research originating from these developed countries.

---
* I am grateful to Stéphane Lutard for his research assistance in the preparation of this chapter.

Clearly, to speak of francophone literature on international organizations is to speak first and foremost of studies produced in France.[2] The space of the francophone culture is in many respects just as centralized as is that of France the state. Thus I will often be led to make generalizations based on the experience of this country. The French have always exerted a great influence over francophone intellectuals. This influence can be explained above all by the sheer weight of numbers: more than half the world's French-speakers are French.[3] What is more, the status that French society accords intellectuals predisposes them to play a role as global *avant-garde*.

Even beyond these considerations I must concentrate my inquiry because the literature on international organizations is so vast. Hence I focus upon that segment of research which, from an empirical or theoretical point of view, addresses intergovernmental organizations with a universal domain. Special attention will be given to the various institutions of the UN, with correspondingly less attention paid to regional bodies such as the EU and NATO and to interregional organizations such as *la Francophonie*. Likewise, little consideration will be given to private international organizations such as multinational corporations and non-governmental organizations. This focus is justified firstly because the UN is the topic which has attracted the most attention by francophone specialists on international organizations, and secondly because the United Nations system represents the most highly developed form of international multilateralism. In chronological terms, this study will emphasize works produced since the early 1980s. At times, however, it will be useful to draw on earlier texts in order to situate current discussions within an historical context.

Of course, the francophone literature on international organizations is not a homogeneous, perfectly integrated whole. It would be erroneous to suppose that the francophone literature on international organizations has an identity of its own, an identity quite distinct from the literature produced in other languages. While lines of demarcation may be drawn between texts written in French and those written in English, it would be much more difficult to specify precisely how the francophone literature differs from that in Spanish or Italian.[4] These qualifications highlight the rough-and-ready quality of the study's procedure. It cannot be stressed enough that it is impossible to take account of all the different approaches and viewpoints reflected in the francophone literature on international organizations. Put in more modest terms, the aim of this contribution is to identify some of the major tendencies in the subject matter, tendencies which will emerge most clearly from a comparison of literature on international organizations and multilateralism published in French with the larger corpus published in English.

Two leading ideas frame this study. The first contends that the francophone literature on international organizations is in many ways 'underdeveloped'. The second maintains that notwithstanding its inadequacies, francophone literature on international organizations makes a substantial contribution to universal knowledge of the subject. Recalling that *more* does not necessarily mean *better*, I seek to show that the contradiction between the two theses propounded is more apparent than real.

An underdeveloped field of study

a. International organizations and international relations

An assessment of francophone literature on international organizations and multilateralism requires first a closer look, in the broadest sense, at the developmental level of francophone research in the field of international relations. Since the study of international organizations is in all respects a subset of the study of international relations, the underdeveloped status of francophone literature on international organizations appears in no small way to be a consequence of the underdeveloped status of francophone literature on international relations.

To speak of underdevelopment is of course to make a judgment that has meaning only in a comparative sense. For instance, the underdevelopment of francophone literature on international relations can be readily understood by comparing it to francophone literature in other areas. The study of international relations is certainly less rich than other fields in the francophone universe of social sciences. Inspired by a long tradition of research on the state and the Third World, political sociology and the sociology of development in the francophone world seem to present research fields more mature than that of international relations.

Here it appears pertinent to observe that the international relations literature published in French is relatively meagre when compared to that published in English. For diverse reasons that French authors were among the first to point out, international relations remains until this day a specialty of the Americans.[5] Quantitatively, the output of monographs and articles in English probably exceeds tenfold that in French. Francophone specialists in this field command considerably smaller financial and institutional resources than do their anglophone colleagues. While a large number of universities in the US have research centres devoted specifically to international affairs, only a handful of comparable institutes are found in the francophone world: the *Institut français des relations internationales* and the *Centre d'études et de recherches internationales* in France, the *Institut royal des relations internationales* in Belgium, the *Institut universitaire de hautes études internationales* in Switzerland, and the *Institut québécois des hautes études internationales* in Canada.[6] Moreover, francophone journals devoted to international relations are fewer and less specialized than their anglophone counterparts. Some of the better known titles are the *Annuaire français de droit international*, *Défense nationale*, *Etudes internationales*, *Politique étrangère*, *Politique internationale*, *Revue générale de droit international public*, and *Studia diplomatica*.

This simple enumeration shows a mixture of genres, with law, history and political science rubbing shoulders. Given a context within which international relations is always in search of objects and methods, it seems highly unlikely that francophones doing research on international organizations will ever have at their disposal a channel for the dissemination of their work as specialized as the American journal *International Organization*. If we add to this the fact that francophone studies on international relations are often descriptive and generally put relatively little emphasis on theory, it is understandable that, apart from the notable exception of the work of Raymond Aron, francophone studies enjoy a relatively small audience abroad and are seldom translated.[7]

The underdeveloped state of francophone research in international relations is well known. It is of more than anecdotal significance that it was a Frenchman by adoption, Stanley Hoffmann, who wrote the article on international relations in the *Traité de science politique* published by Grawitz and Leca in the mid 1980s.[8] Noting the short history of international relations as a field of study in France, some authors have concluded that there is neither a French approach to, nor school of, international relations.[9] To speak of an approach or school peculiar to francophones would be even more inappropriate.

In the francophone world, the underdevelopment of international relations studies is due to the fact that the subject enjoys little autonomy as a discipline in its own right.[10] In other words, international relations has an identity problem. This field of study has not yet succeeded in distinguishing itself from its originators which, as elsewhere, are international law and the history of diplomacy. In France, it has been barely a generation since international relations gained recognition as a valid research area in political science. Contrast this situation with that in the US, where international relations, though remaining close to political science, has gradually progressed to become a key subject whose personality is more and more distinct. Thus the debate on the status of international relations proceeds on entirely different bases in the anglophone and francophone worlds. Moreover, this whole discussion is affected by the lack of any clear definition of the boundaries of international relations as a field. In francophone milieux, international relations continues to be associated extremely closely with regional studies.[11] The latter is a highly dynamic research field since France and Belgium, due to their colonial pasts, boast an impressive number of experts in African and Oriental studies. Yet this success of regional studies casts a shadow upon the study of international relations *stricto sensu*. Finally, we should note that in francophone countries the study of international relations remains a field that is more open than in the United States to the contributions of practitioners.[12] While fostering dialogue between different schools, this situation has probably slowed the emergence of a sense of belonging to a scientific community as integrated as that existing in the US.

b. The paucity of theoretical discussion

The underdevelopment of francophone literature in international relations stems first and foremost from its weakness with regard to theorizing. Commentators have condemned repeatedly the short shrift given by francophone researchers to conceptual frameworks and explanatory models.[13] To this charge Marcel Merle retorted cogently that no approach to problems starts from scratch.[14] He points out that scientific activity always rests upon epistemological assumptions, whether these are explicit or not. The analysis of discourse, pre-eminently a francophone speciality, spotlights the importance of what lies unstated. Thus it would be wrong to assert that francophone literature in international relations is based on no theoretical framework. Nevertheless, the contribution made by francophones to the construction of a general theory in international relations has to date been marginal. On the whole, francophone authors seldom compare their postulates with those of other authors, and when they do, the discussions that follow often focus disproportionately on the work of other francophones.

This general environment weighs heavily upon the development of francophone studies on international organizations and multilateralism. In particular, it explains why, from a theoretical standpoint, the approach such authors most commonly take toward the study of international organizations is the empirico-descriptive approach.[15] Because of the weight of law and of history in the study of international phenomena, this approach has naturally given way to inquiries that emphasize either legal or historical issues.[16] Furthermore, the predominance of the empirico-descriptive approach converges with the educational aims inherent in the production of textbooks.[17] The legal method seeks to dissect the institutional mechanisms and rules of the game in international relations. For its part, the method of diplomatic history tends to stress the actions of major statesmen and to consider events as the product of individual circumstance. Both of these ways of reading reality are useful, and they are not necessarily obsolete simply because they are traditional methods. Each possesses heuristic properties that undoubtedly cast light on the exercise of power and on conflicts of interest. But the empirico-descriptive approach is inherently unconcerned with abstraction. Consequently, it is scarcely if at all prone to facilitate those generalizations and laws without which the formulation of theory is unthinkable.

It is true that the predominance of the empirico-descriptive approach has not prevented the development, in recent years, of a more sociological approach among francophone scholars writing on international relations and international organizations. The leaders of this sociological movement, Marcel Merle and Philippe Braillard, have attempted to show how a systemic approach can offer a useful analytical framework for the interpretation of international phenomena.[18] Regarding international organizations more specifically, the sociological approach has, *inter alia*, pointed up the diversity of functions fulfilled by such institutions in the dynamics of international relations. By regrouping various existing typologies, Marie-Claude Smouts has identified five functions that characterize the operations of all international organizations: legitimation, monitoring, information, socialization and standard-setting.[19] In a wider sense, the sociological approach has succeeded in giving more vigor to francophone thinking on international organizations by presenting these organizations as actors, and by posing questions about their relative autonomy. No definitive answers have yet been reached on this issue but a growing consensus seems to be forming around the idea that 'international organization constitutes a factor that gives structure to the international system ... placing certain limits upon the scope of action by members of this system'.[20] The sociological approach thereby distances itself from the realist school, traditionally dominant in the anglophone world, according to which international relations are ultimately governed by the sovereign ability of states to maximize their power.

Overall, the fact remains that the contribution made by francophone authors to the formulation of a theory of international organizations has been extremely limited.[21] In her assessment of this matter – one of the most comprehensive surveys currently published in French – Smouts cites not one French-language source that has exerted a significant impact on theory beyond the francophone world.[22]

A terminological gulf has hitherto separated the literature on international organizations published in French from that published in English. The growing use of the notion of actor (*acteur*) by francophone authors may perhaps signal a turnaround in this respect. This usage has not only favoured a rapprochement with one segment of the community of American specialists, but without wishing to exaggerate the scale of the movement, one might also suggest that the sharing of this notion has aided a tendency to universalize knowledge relating to international organizations. In any case, it should be pointed out that the formalized nature of some English-language discourse on the subject leaves the majority of the francophone community rather cold. For instance, when francophone authors investigate the relative autonomy of international organizations, very few can identify with formulations that seek to determine whether these institutions are to be classified as independent, dependent or intermediate variables.

The difference between the conceptual reference points in francophone literature and those in English-language literature is one of cardinal importance. First of all, this difference explains why, traditionally, francophone authors rarely cite their anglophone colleagues or enter into their theoretical discussions. It also helps account for why francophone research on international organizations has developed in a vacuum, and why French authors are almost totally unrepresented in English-speaking academic networks. Francophone research on international organizations has gained very little from the process of 'cross-fertilization'. The fact that Americans have an even worse record in this respect constitutes, for francophone researchers, very meagre consolation.

In general, francophone authors make scant use of the methods and theories devised by their anglophone colleagues, and rarely take the time to make critical analyses of them. For example, francophone specialists in the field of international organizations have never shown a great interest in quantitative methods. They have little use for mathematical and statistical tools, and even less for game theory.[23] In all likelihood they will show just as little attraction to the theory of *public choice* which, having become increasingly popular in American political science, has penetrated the field of international organizations.[24] The concept of *regime*, around which so many published English-language efforts have crystallized during the past decade and a half, is also disregarded by francophone authors. This notion has been perceived mostly as a passing fashion, or even as a retrograde step fostering the rise of neorealism.[25] Francophone authors are in a sense so detached from the theoretical controversies that animate English-language literature on international organizations and multilateralism that they have scarcely seen any point in putting forward a systematic alternative.

In the last analysis, the underdevelopment of francophone literature stems in large part from the hold exercised by the juridical tradition. Despite the ever-increasing volume of work on multinational firms and non-governmental organizations,[26] francophone researchers continue to take their cue very much from the institutional approach, which stresses intergovernmental organizations. It is worth recalling that the latter are, along with states, the only subjects recognized by public international law. In the United States, the study of international organizations has gradually metamorphosed, broadening its focus to include all issues of international cooperation. In the francophone world, such a paradigmatic mutation is slow to materialize. The sluggishness of this process is to be explained in part by considerations of a semantic nature. 'International cooperation' does not mean the same in French as in English. In French, it refers more narrowly to the notion of development aid. It is not surprising that while the theme of North–South cooperation has captured the interest of many francophone specialists, relatively little work has been produced on anything relating to North–North cooperation. Ultimately, the more restrictive meaning that attends the French expression *'coopération internationale'* provides a further disincentive to francophone authors to reach beyond international institutions in an attempt to understand institutionalized patterns of international behaviour.[27]

Francophone literature's contribution

a.   A critical and reflective orientation

In spite of its underdevelopment, international organizations research published in French is richly rewarding. Its volume shows a steady growth. Even if the sociological approach is not dominant, it is gaining in popularity. In what follows, the aim will be firstly to demonstrate that, its many lacunae notwithstanding, the theoretical reflection that underlies the francophone literature on international organization is not lacking in interest. Secondly, by taking the crisis of the UN and development as cases in point, we show that francophone authors have enriched the empirical study of significant sectors of the activity of international organizations. This analysis makes evident that francophone literature plays an important role in deepening knowledge about multilateralism. As a corollary, it seems that the profound indifference of English-speaking scholars to such contributions seriously undermines the credibility of their claim to seek the establishment of a *science* of international relations or international organizations worthy of this name.

Whatever may be said of its modest theoretical pretensions, francophone writing on international organizations displays far greater ideological pluralism than its English-language counterpart. On the whole, it is less conservative and more critical of the established political order. Its openness to analyses with Third World and neo-Marxist perspectives illustrates vividly its spirit of pluralism. We will return to examine more closely the nature of the contribution made by *tiers-mondiste* writers. With respect to neo-Marxist inspired analyses, the two textbooks by J.-L. Mathieu and by P.-F. Gonidec and R. Charvin offer good examples of a panoramic review of international relations.[28] Daniel A. Holly's more specialized studies on UNESCO have sought to show how this international organization, understood as a superstructure reflecting economic contradictions, consolidates a world-wide process of capital accumulation and helps to maintain inequalities between rich and poor countries.[29]

It lies beyond the scope of this chapter to judge the explanatory potential of Third World-oriented and neo-Marxist influenced writings. Suffice it to say that they occupy a prominent position in francophone literature on international organizations. Unlike their American colleagues, few francophone authors would venture an appraisal of studies on international organizations without taking account of the contribution of authors from developing countries or from the former Socialist countries. This disposition indicates a less ethnocentric, more universalist vision of the world than is evident in most American writings.

Moreover, the distrust shown by francophone authors toward the excessive theorizing and quantification so prevalent among American writings derives from an epistemological approach that cannot simply be brushed aside. It is clear that most English-language writers on international relations have little concern for the dangers of conceptual reification. In the study of international organizations, the popularity that the concepts of integration, complex interdependence and regime successively have enjoyed in the United States patently acted to stimulate and shape the production of writings on multilateralism. But it is less certain that this succession of concepts has made the theory of international organizations a cumulative process. Francophone authors are more sensitive than their anglophone counterparts to this consideration, since francophone social scientists as a whole have been more distrustful of the positivist and rationalist postulates that American authors frequently accept without questioning their implications. Frederick A. Gareau observes that historically the French have remained unimpressed by a scientism that legitimizes the disciplinary autonomy of international relations *made in the USA*.[30] Without a doubt this explains why, instead of mapping out a possible development of 'the' theory, some specialists prefer to speak simply of a taxonomy of approaches.[31] As it gradually became evident to what extent the actual functioning of international organizations was fraught with confrontation among highly diversified modes of thinking, the scepticism of francophone authors toward excessive theorizing quite naturally strengthened. Above all, their stance draws attention to the fact that the domination of the model devised by English-speaking authors in the analysis of international organizations is geographically limited. In a field of study that, by definition, aspires to produce a scientific discourse with universal validity, one must acknowledge that this presents a serious handicap.

While they have surely provided little grist for the mill of the 'normal science'[32] of international relations, the critical epistemology of French-language authors has nourished the reflection of dissident American scholars concerned with international relations and organizations. Curiously, these dissidents have been inspired less by francophone specialists in international relations than by historians and philosophers. In the 1970s, for instance, the work of Fernand Braudel was extensively drawn on by Immanuel Wallerstein and by all other followers of the world-economy theory.[33] During the past decade, the work of Michel Foucault has probably made the greatest impact of all francophones upon English-speaking specialists on international relations.[34] This phenomenon is all the more astonishing since Foucault has written virtually nothing on the subject! Nonetheless, his influence on the post-positivists is such that every one of the articles published in a recent issue of *International Studies Quarterly* on the theme 'Speaking the Language of Exile: Dissidence in International Studies' makes reference to his work.[35] Foucault has clearly become one of the mentors of the dissident movement that is currently challenging the dominant paradigm in international relations. If for no other reason, we must pause a moment to consider this author's contribution to the study of international organizations.

Foucault is an historian of ideas whose method could be described as structuralist. His work consists of showing that, as a social practice, the production of knowledge is an historical process framed by a particular culture and discourse. To each historical period there corresponds, he would claim, a power/knowledge configuration defining the conditions that govern the production of ideas. Since it is predicated on a profoundly relativistic epistemology, Foucault's thinking encourages a tendency to call into question the existence of such eternal truths as (for example) those that, it is claimed, underpin the realist view of international relations. Moreover, by insisting that social institutions are largely fashioned by a given body of knowledge and a specific discourse, Foucault has also provided ammunition for the opponents of realism, who believe that the exercise of power cannot be reduced to the material categories of might and money.

Foucault's writings have encouraged the emergence of a highly dynamic cognitive current in the study of international regimes.[36] It is well known that the analysis of regimes is dominated by neorealist theory, the epistemology of which is fundamentally positivist. However, a growing number of researchers deem this approach to reality unsatisfactory because it fails to take note of the inter-subjective dimension of principles and norms that form the very architecture of regimes. Foucault inspires these scholars and stimulates inquiry on the manner in which the principles and norms underpinning regimes are internalized and invested with distinct meanings for different international actors. Reworking some of the basic concepts offered by Foucault, James F. Keeley for instance has defined regimes as sets of discourses and disciplines.[37] In all this discussion, Foucault's contribution ultimately concerns the responses that may be found to problems raised less than the way these problems are envisaged. In the same context, this seminal author's shadow looms behind the recent emergence of the notion of *epistemic community* in analyzing the processes of international cooperation.[38] The research programme to which this idea of epistemic community is geared attempts to show how international cooperation is structured on the basis of consensus formed within a community of experts. It finds support in the Foucauldian method in that Foucault seeks to establish a connection between the formulation of discourse and the construction of reality. In the present state of research, it would be extremely rash to predict where the Foucault effect in international relations will stop. Since francophone intellectuals have often been accused of lagging behind the fashions set by their English-speaking colleagues, it is somewhat ironic to find American internationalists discovering after his death such a monumental French author.

To be sure, francophone writers on international relations do not share the infatuation of their English-speaking colleagues with Foucault. All the same, Philippe Hugon has usefully reminded us that the whole cultural background to francophone thinking has been influenced by those authors who, like Bachelard and Lévi-Strauss before Foucault, gave pride of place to meaning and tended to distrust empiricism.[39] Such a context makes it easier to understand why francophone research on international relations and international organizations has a strong anthropological bent. This bent is frequently reflected in a concern to highlight the role of culture and cultural differences in the analysis of social processes. Such a perspective leads authors to assign great significance to values, ideologies and world visions as axes structuring international political and economic relations.[40] Francophone literature has notably helped draw attention to the extent to which the project for an international society underpinning the mandate of the UN and its specialized institutions is predicated on liberal individualism and on a western, unilinear conception of progress.[41]

b. The UN crisis and development: focal subjects

In terms of research fields, francophone authors have over the years addressed virtually the entire spectrum of international organizations' activities and all facets of multilateralism. Of course subjects have not received equal attention. Some matters, such as multilateral trade negotiations, the specialized technical agencies and the growing realm of environmental issues, have received less attention from francophone authors than from their English-language counterparts.[42] By contrast, other issues have received considerable attention. Paramount among these are two subjects: the intertwined issues of crisis/reform with respect to the UN system, and development.

Francophone authors have subjected to particularly close scrutiny the UN system's tendency to drift off course throughout the first half of the 1980s. Their analyses make it clear first of all that this tendency, which since 1987 has gradually abated, previously applied globally. Thus francophone literature has insisted that even though the crisis was felt more acutely in certain specialized agencies such as UNESCO and ILO, this crisis affected the entire UN structure and thereby the very logic of multilateralism. Francophone specialists have also pointed up the diversity of symptoms marking the deterioration in the UN's functioning during the early 1980s. The main parameters of their diagnosis may be outlined as follows.[43]

On the operational level, the UN's leadership totally failed to function in the face of the rekindling cold war, the worsening of regional conflicts, the failure of global North–South negotiations, and the explosion of Third World debt. On the administrative level, the extensive fragmentation of the UN system made planning of activities progressively more difficult, and the lack of coordination within the organization favoured bureaucratization and duplication. Finally, on the financial level, the UN had to cope with serious budget restrictions following a unilateral decision on the part of the United States, the organization's principal financial backer, to reduce the proportion of its contribution. Francophone authors did not, however, confine themselves to simple description of the institutional stalemate; they proceeded to seek the social and political factors that might explain the shift away from multilateralism.

Given what was said earlier about the impact of the historical perspective upon the francophone literature on international relations, it is not surprising that such authors should have stressed that the UN crisis did not come about, as if by the wave of a magic wand, in the aftermath of some particular event, such as the hike in crude oil prices or Ronald Reagan's election as President of the United States.[44] Rather the tendency has been to stress that the so-called crisis stemmed from a profoundly conflict-ridden structure of international power and from a growing polarization of state interests.[45] The North–South cleavage activated spiraling tensions as this cleavage superseded East–West confrontation. Thus the systematic opposition between the will of the developing countries to convert their automatic majority into political authority and the ability of the developed countries to resist this pressure stands out in francophone analyses.

Moreover, francophone authors have given great prominence to the ideological dimension of the UN crisis. They support the idea that the North–South confrontation masked a conflict of values without historical precedent. Victor-Yves Ghébali quite rightly points out that politicization has always been a feature of the international system, and that what has changed since the early 1970s has been the tendency for such politicization to operate in favour of a new majority.[46] In short, the South's strategy has been to derive the greatest gain possible from those western values that benefit them and to denounce those that do not.

This atmosphere of tension reached its culmination at UNESCO, from which the US and the United Kingdom respectively withdrew in 1984 and 1985. Thus it is perfectly natural that francophone authors should have written so extensively on this organization and the troubled period it went through during the early 1980s.[47] Their analyses make it clear that the crisis of UNESCO, characterized by its administrative and budgetary problems, arose essentially from political factors. Indisputably, the adoption of many excommunicative resolutions beyond its mandate, as well as the debate on the New World Information and Communications Order (NWICO), led to serious reassessment of the institution's objectives. Francophone authors have attributed the erosion of UNESCO's capacity for action above all to the failure of the universalization of those liberal principles enshrined within its Constitution in 1945. For such authors, the emergence of Third World countries on the international scene has been accompanied by a rejection of the hegemony of western culture and of the development model based on the laws of the market. Given the symbolic importance of UNESCO's cultural mission, the ideological nature of this rejection led to the paralysis of the organization.

It nonetheless deserves emphasizing that francophone specialists have not painted a wholly negative picture of UNESCO's work and that at times they have gone to great lengths to underscore some of its successes in the areas of literacy and the safeguarding of humanity's common heritage.[48] The special attention paid to UNESCO also confirms the importance that francophone authors accord the cultural dimension of international relations.

Francophone authors have also commented abundantly on the reforms that the UN and its specialized agencies have finally undertaken in recent years.[49] One of the most prolific commentators on this process, Maurice Bertrand, was indeed one of the reform's main architects, first as a member of the Joint Inspection Unit and subsequently as a member of the Group of 18. The fact is generally accepted that, from the administrative standpoint, the UN has embarked upon an unprecedented process of self-criticism. Despite their strong emphasis upon problems of planning and management, the recommendations of the Group of 18, it is widely held, led to a political breakthrough by instituting a new procedure based on consensus for approval of the budget.

To be sure, there remains a feeling that the UN's reform has not been completed. And yet, though few studies have so far been made on the subject, the experts seem to see the end of the cold war as a major turning point in the history of the United Nations.[50] This turning point is often depicted as a result of the structural redefinition of East–West relations. With regard to this shift, the episode of American–Soviet collaboration during the Gulf War and the desire expressed by the former USSR to join GATT, the IMF and the World Bank served as major eye openers. It has also been pointed out that the developing countries are now less hostile to liberalism, and that the developed countries are more conscious of the global dimensions of issues confronting the international community.

For many long years the optimistic analyses of the UN were few in number.[51] Today, however, they make up a majority. Francophone authors are by and large convinced that by the end of the 1980s, things had changed for the better in the universe of international organizations.[52] Yet they do anticipate many more challenges on the UN's agenda. Regarding the political level, the inefficacy of the UN's decisionmaking apparatus has been extensively debated.[53] Specialists are far from agreement on the urgency of need for certain changes, though some agree that there exists a growing contradiction between the sclerosis of the decisionmaking procedures and the evolution of the international power structure. Various blueprints for reform have been proposed. Some have suggested enlarging the Security Council to accommodate the emergence of new economic powers and the distinct interests of the Third World.[54] Others have taken up the idea out of America of a 'binding triad', a procedure whereby the decisions of the General Assembly would become obligatory if approved by a two-thirds majority of the members of the General Assembly accounting simultaneously for two-thirds of the world's population and two-thirds of the contributions to the UN's budget.[55] On the economic level, Bertrand's proposals, which have had little impact upon decisionmakers, continue to arouse interest among scholars. Postulating that peace is seriously jeopardized by international disparities of income, and that the international economic institutions are failing to meet the needs of today, Bertrand has proposed setting up an 'economic security council' whose operation would be modelled upon the EU.[56] Adopting an even more *avant-garde* position, some authors have concluded that the management of world affairs can no longer be left to states alone, and that as a consequence the UN should ensure truer representation of the peoples.[57] Marc Nerfin in particular proposes that the UN be restructured around three chambers, the first of which would represent governments, the second businesses and the third non-governmental organizations. It matters little that such a project is for the time being no more than a pipe dream. It further confirms the interest shown by francophone authors to redefine multilateralism and the role of the United Nations.

Along with the profusion of francophone studies on the UN crisis, considerable importance has been accorded the theme of international organizations and development. These two lines of inquiry are obviously not mutually exclusive, since most authors have held that the UN crisis was primarily provoked by the deadlock in the North–South dialogue. But francophone specialists in international organizations have gone much further in their treatment of development issues. The attention paid to these questions stems from two parallel series of factors. On one hand, development is a favourite topic throughout the francophone social science community. It is no coincidence that the concept of Third World (*Tiers Monde*) was invented by a Frenchman, Alfred Sauvy.[58] Furthermore, because of the UN's failure in matters of collective security, the promotion of development gradually became established as that organization's operational priority. R.-J. Dupuy captured this trend in an evocative formula when he asserted that development had become Job One in UN lingo (*le signifiant du langage de l'ONU*).[59]

For quite some time now the development process has prompted a flow of contributions by francophone authors. While it is more and more difficult to speak of a single, homogeneous Third World current, it can fairly be said that various 'Third World sensibilities' have exerted a decisive influence on the orientation of historical, legal, sociological, political, anthropological and economic research produced in French. The reasons for this phenomenon are historical: both France and Belgium were colonial powers, and the trade flows, migratory movements and cultural exchanges between these two countries and their former colonies have always been very substantial. In recent years, francophone research on development has been marked by various changes, the chief of these undoubtedly being the withering away of general theories and the rehabilitation of cultural factors.[60] Although it is passing through a period of radical self-scrutiny, francophone research on development continues full of vitality.

This general interest in development questions is reflected in a variety of ways within francophone research on international organizations. Here we consider two facets of development: the study of *development law* and the study of *multilateral development funding*. In both, francophone authors have made extremely useful contributions to the advancement of knowledge.

The expression 'development law' refers to the body of resolutions and conventions that have been produced, in particular through the UN, for the purpose of establishing a new balance of forces between developed and developing countries. Guy Feuer has gone so far as to assert, in a rather striking formula, that development law is the creation of francophone thinkers.[61] His claim may not be irrefutable, but it is certainly quite compatible with the traditional predominance of the legal approach in the francophone analysis of international relations. In any case, it was a Frenchman, André Philip, who coined the term 'development law' in 1964.[62] An article by Virally published the following year is recognized as having had a decisive impact on the emergence of the concept of 'duality of norms', or dual standards.[63] This concept is the juridical cornerstone on which the developing countries have erected doctrine to legitimize their strategy for establishing a new international economic order (NIEO).

A controversy has raged among francophone authors as to whether or not the new international economic order is dead.[64] Be this as it may, the legal doctrine that gave impetus to the new international economic order, namely development law, is alive and well. This doctrine gives rise to a range of discussions concerning the link between individual and community, also the relative importance of economic rights as against political, social and cultural rights in the dynamic of development. Certain radical Third World commentators have condemned development law, calling it an instrument that serves to maintain the dependency of countries in the South.[65] Following Feuer's lead, the prevailing trend now is to see it instead as a form of 'soft law', occupying an intermediate zone between law and non-law. Given the transformations now taking place in the international system, one may expect that coming years will witness a segmentation of development law that takes greater account of the growing differentiation among Third World countries.[66] And it is most likely that francophone specialists will continue to exert an important influence in the choices made.

Francophone literature on international organizations has also devoted special attention to the multilateral financing of development. While such authors have referred in passing to the UNDP's loss of credibility and the rise of multi-bilateralism,[67] they have inquired more particularly into the role played by the international financial institutions – in particular, the International Monetary Fund and the World Bank – within the Third World. Francophone research on the latter question remains smaller in quantity than that published in English. This said, the 1980s provided francophone authors with an opportunity to interest themselves in financial and monetary issues that had not previously existed. Until this period, the francophone literature on international financial insitutions (IFIs) was made up essentially of textbooks of a rather general nature.[68] The belated interest in the place of IFIs on the part of francophone specialists can be explained largely by developments in the evolving international environment: whereas trade problems drew most attention during the 1960s and 1970s, the debt burden became palpably the main external constraint upon development in the 1980s. Tying in with this major change in the North–South relationship, it is significant that a growing number of francophone research teams are investigating structural adjustment.[69]

Infused with strong Third World preoccupations, francophone research on multilateral development funding has by and large adopted rather critical positions. In her work on the IMF, Marie-France L'Hériteau illustrates this trend particularly well by highlighting the social costs of structural adjustment and showing how the IMF has made itself the promoter of a liberal development model closely geared to economic internationalization.[70] Francophone authors have nevertheless recognized the great difficulty of finding a coherent alternative to the economic theories of the IMF and the World Bank. The approach taken by L'Hériteau, which consists in asking if the rationality of the IMF prevails because of its might (the rationality of the policeman) or because it is right (the rationality of the professor), comes close to the conclusion reached by Zaki Laïdi, for whom the World Bank is 'neither demiurge nor demon'.[71] Laïdi has insisted judiciously on the ability of developing countries to respond each in its own way to the recipes for economic liberalization advocated by the World Bank. In the final analysis, the most solid common denominator among francophone authors on multilateral development funding is their conviction that the IFIs now wield unprecedented power in determining the economic options of Third World countries and in realigning international political relations.

Conclusion

This chapter is very limited in scope, yielding a profile of francophone literature on international organizations that can be no more than an approximation. It nevertheless identifies certain undeniable tendencies. Thus, for instance, it appears that in the francophone community, the study of international organizations has not been clearly defined, straddling as it does several disciplines. Only a fairly limited number of intellectuals regard international organizations as their own distinctive specialty. In spite of all this, because of its ideological openness and the expertise that some researchers have acquired on specific questions, the francophone literature on international organizations constitutes a significant contribution to a universal knowledge about multilateralism.

One of the most distinctive traits of francophone literature is its greater receptivity than its English counterparts to the idea of social change. Rarely have francophone authors made themselves the unconditional defenders of the existing liberal order. The ideology of the American Right, aggressively embodied in the works of the Heritage Foundation,[72] has evoked very little enthusiasm among francophone researchers. Far from being convinced that acquired rights are by definition inalienable, or that the exercise of hegemony is necessarily legitimate, most francophone specialists are more sensitive than their English-speaking colleagues to the urgent need for democratizing international relations. In the final analysis, the difference of focus and tone between the literature on international organizations published in French from that published in English reinforces the view that the interests of the United States do not always accord with those of all the developed countries.

From the epistemological standpoint, the writings of francophone authors fuel both sides of the debate on the nature of the process of producing knowledge relative to international organizations. Sometimes the francophone literature suggests that the study of international organizations is a cumulative process, hardly, if at all, influenced by its social context. This is, for example, what one might deduce from the gradual passage from a legal approach to a sociological approach, a modification that gives greater prominence to the notion of international actor. Indeed, it is noteworthy that francophone jurists themselves see this change as a sign of progress.[73]

By contrast, francophone authors' habitual wariness of the modelling of international processes, particularly if this entails quantification, might lead one to conclude that there exists an unbridgeable paradigmatic chasm between their perspective and that dominant in the English-speaking community. Because it is rooted in a conception of rationality that is more interpretive and less instrumental, the literature of the francophone community reflects a profound scepticism as to the cumulative nature of the process of producing knowledge about international organizations and multilateralism. To cut a long story short, the controversy remains open.

My study tends to corroborate Galtung's view that in the social sciences there exist cultures and styles that cannot be reconciled.[74] This said, even though the gulf remains profound between francophone and anglophone scholars studying international organizations, this does not preclude the possibility of mutual benefit resulting from greater cross-fertilization. Francophone authors could make more use of certain approaches, methods and techniques that have not greatly interested them so far. For their part, English-speaking authors might perhaps come to realize that if their analytical categories have won so little acceptance in the French-speaking world, it is probably because these categories are less universal than they think.

Translated from the French by Gunnar R. Sewell

Notes

1 For a general study of the structures and operation of la Francophonie, see P.-F. Chatton and J. Mazuryk Bapst, *Le défi francophone*, Bruxelles/Paris: Bruylant-L.G.D.J., 1991.

2 Nonetheless, an impressive number of high-quality publications stem from authors in Switzerland. The scale of their contributions doubtless may be explained largely by the special part played by the city of Geneva in the development of modern international organizations.

3 Haut Conseil de la Francophonie, *Etat de la francophonie dans le monde*, Paris: La Documentation française, 1990, p. 17.

4 See Johan Galtung, 'Structure, Culture, and Intellectual Style: An Essay Comparing Saxonic, Teutonic, Gallic and Nipponic Approaches', *Social Science Information*, 20, No. 6, 1981, p. 820.

5 On this subject see Alfred Grosser, 'L'étude des relations internationales, spécialité américaine?', *Revue française de science politique*, 6, No. 3, 1956, pp. 634–51; Bahgat Korany, 'Où en sommes–nous? Au delà de "l'apple pie" anglosaxon', in Korany, ed., *Analyse des relations internationales: approches, concepts et données*, Montreal: Gaëtan Morin, 1987, pp. 297–308. Regarding the literature in English, see in particular K.J. Holsti, *The Dividing Discipline: Hegemony and Diversity in International Theory*, Boston: Allen & Unwin, 1985.

6 Until 1995 the *Centre québécois de relations internationales*.

7 Gene M. Lyons, 'Expanding the Study of International Relations: The French Connection', *World Politics*, 35, No. 6, 1982, p. 135.

8 Stanley Hoffmann, 'L'ordre international', in Madeleine Grawitz and Jean Leca, eds., *Traité de science politique*, 1, Paris: PUF, 1985, pp. 665–98.

9 Marcel Merle, 'Sur la "problématique" de l'étude des relations internationales en France', *Revue française de science politique*, 33, No. 3, 1983, p. 426; Marie-Claude Smouts, 'The Study of International Relations in France', in Hugh C. Dyer and Leon Mangasarian, eds., *The Study of International Relations: The State of the Art*, Basingstoke: Macmillan, 1989, p. 227.

10 Frederick H. Gareau, 'The Discipline of International Relations: A Multi-National Perspective', *Journal of Politics*, 43, No. 3, 1981, p. 790.

11 'The Study of International Relations in France', p. 223.

12 See for example Philippe Moreau-Defarges, *La politique internationale*, Paris: Hachette, 1990; Philippe Moreau-Defarges, *Les relations internationales dans le*

monde d'aujourd'hui: conflits et interdépendances, 3rd ed. Paris: Editions STH, 1987.

13 Dominique Colas, 'La recherche en sciences juridiques et en sciences politique', in Maurice Godelier, *Les sciences de l'Homme et de la société en France: analyse et propositions pour une politique nouvelle*, Paris: La Documentation française, 1982, p. 365.

14 Marcel Merle, 'Sur la "problématique" de l'étude des relations internationales en France', *Revue française de science politique*, p. 405.

15 This term is from Merle, *ibid.*, p. 406.

16 Pierre Gerbet and Michel Virally offer concise illustrations of these two methods. See Gerbet, 'Naissance et développement de l'organisation internationale', in Georges Abi-Saab, ed., *Le concept d'organisation internationale*, Paris: UNESCO, 1980, pp. 29–50; Virally, 'Définition et classification des organisations internationales: approche juridique', *ibid.*, pp. 51–67. For a systematic application of the empirico-descriptive approach, see the voluminous work by Jean-Pierre Cot and Alain Pellet, *La Charte des Nations Unies: commentaire article par article*, Paris/Brussels: Economica–Bruylant, 1985.

17 See for instance Paul Reuter and Jean Combacau, *Institutions et relations internationales*, 4th ed., Paris: PUF, 1988; Alain Gandolfi, *Institutions internationales*, 2nd ed., Paris: Masson, 1984; Jean Charpentier, *Institutions des relations internationales*, Paris: Dalloz, 1985.

18 Merle, *Sociologie des relations internationales*, 4th ed., Paris: Dalloz, 1988; Merle, *Les acteurs dans les relations internationales*, Paris: Economica, 1986; Philippe Braillard, *Théorie des systèmes et relations internationales*, Brussels: Bruylant, 1977.

19 Smouts, 'L'organisation internationale: nouvel acteur sur la scène mondiale?', in Korany, ed., *Analyse des relations internationales: approches, concepts et données*, pp. 164–5. See also Merle, *Sociologie des relations internationales*, pp. 375–9.

20 Braillard and Mohammad-Reza Djalili, *Les relations internationales*, 2nd ed., Paris: PUF, 1990, p. 40. For a different point of view, see Charles Zorgbibe, *Les organisations internationales*, 2nd ed., Paris: PUF, 1991, p. 19.

21 This assertion could be qualified in any number of ways. For example, mention may be made of Panayotis Soldatos' contribution to the formulation of a post-neo-functionalist approach. See in particular Soldatos, *Le système institutionnel et politique des Communautés européennes dans un monde en mutation: théorie et pratique*, Brussels: Bruylant, 1989.

22 'L'organisation internationale: nouvel acteur sur la scène mondiale?', pp. 152–61.

23 See Virally, 'Problématique pour la recherche universitaire sur l'avenir des organisations internationales', in Institut international d'études diplomatiques, *L'avenir des organisations internationales*, Paris: Economica, 1984, p. 182; Braillard, 'Les sciences sociales et l'étude des relations internationales', *Revue internationale des sciences sociales*, 36, No. 102, 1984, p. 669. One may nonetheless find an application of game theory in Pierre Martin, 'L'après-Tokyo Round: la réciprocité spécifique dans la politique commerciale américaine récente', *Etudes internationales*, 21, No. 1, 1990, pp. 5–38.

24 Roland Vaubel and Thomas Willet, eds., *The Political Economy of International Organizations: A Public Choice Approach*, Boulder: Westview, 1991.

25 'L'organisation internationale: nouvel acteur sur la scène mondiale?', pp. 158–9. A rare use of the concept of regime is found in Jean-Philippe Thérien, 'Le Canada et le régime international de l'aide', *Etudes internationales*, 20, No. 2, 1989, pp. 311–40.

26 On these two themes, see C.-A. Michalet, *Le capitalisme mondial*, 2nd ed., Paris: PUF, 1985; Mario Bettati and P.-M. Dupuy, eds., *Les ONG et le droit international*, Paris: Economica, 1986.

27 Friedrich Kratochwil and John Gerard Ruggie, 'International Organization: A State of the Art on an Art of the State', *International Organization*, 40, No. 4, 1986, p. 754.

28 J.L. Mathieu, *Les institutions spécialisées des Nations Unies*, Paris: Masson, 1977; P.F. Gonidec and R. Charvin, *Les relations internationales*, 3rd ed., Paris: Montchrestien, 1984.

29 Daniel A. Holly, *L'UNESCO, le Tiers Monde et l'économie mondiale*, Montreal/ Geneva: Presses de l'Université de Montréal/Institut universitaire des hautes études internationales, 1981.

30 'The Discipline of International Relations: A Multi-National Perspective', p. 791.

31 Braillard, *Théories des relations internationales*, Paris: PUF, 1977, pp. 9–10; Braillard, 'Les sciences sociales et l'étude des relations internationales', p. 673.

32 To borrow the expression coined by Thomas Kuhn in *The Structure of Scientific Revolutions*, 2nd ed., Chicago: University of Chicago Press, 1970.

33 See in particular Immanuel Wallerstein, *The Modern World-System I: Capitalist Agriculture and the Origins of the European World-Economy in the Sixteenth Century*, New York: Academic, 1974, and Wallerstein, *The Modern World-System II: Mercantilism and the Consolidation of the European World-Economy 1600–1750*, New York: Academic, 1980. See also Fernand Braudel, *Civilisation matérielle, économie et capitalisme XVe–XVIIIe siècle*, 3 vols., Paris: A. Colin, 1979.

34 Among his major works, see Michel Foucault, *Les mots et les choses: Une archéologie des sciences humaines*, Paris: Gallimard, 1966; Foucault, *L'archéologie du savoir*, Paris: Gallimard, 1969; Foucault, *Surveiller et punir: Naissance de la prison*, Paris: Gallimard, 1975; Foucault, *Histoire de la sexualité*, 3 vols., Paris: Gallimard, 1976–1984.

35 See Richard K. Ashley and R.J.B. Walker, eds., 'Speaking the Language of Exile: Dissidence in International Studies', special issue of *International Studies Quarterly*, 34, No. 3, 1990. See also James Der Derian and Michael J. Shapiro, eds., *International/Intertextual Relations: Postmodern Readings of World Politics*, Lexington: Lexington, 1989.

36 See Stephan Haggard and Beth A. Simmons, 'Theories of International Regimes', *International Organization*, 41, No. 3, 1987, pp. 509–13; Kratochwil and Ruggie, 'International Organization: A State of the Art on an Art of the State', pp. 753–5; James F. Keeley, 'Toward a Foucauldian Analysis of International Regimes', *International Organization*, 44, No. 1, 1990, pp. 83–105.

37 'Toward a Foucauldian Analysis of International Regimes', p. 92.

38 See Peter M. Haas, ed., 'Knowledge, Power, and International Policy Coordination', special issue of *International Organization*, 46, No. 3, 1992.

39 Philippe Hugon, 'Les trois temps de la pensée francophone en économie du développement', in Cahiers du GEMDEV, *Recherches récentes, en langue française, sur le développement*, No. 18, Paris, 1991, p. 127.

40   Smouts, 'La crise des organisations internationales', *Etudes*, No. 358, 1983, pp. 165–73; Braillard, 'Les sciences sociales et l'étude des relations internationales', pp. 661–76; Jean-Pierre Colin, 'L'espérance en question ou: la crise du système juridique international', *Revue belge de droit international*, 18, No. 1, 1984–5, pp. 776–93; Smouts, 'L'organisation internationale, rose des vents dans l'espace cardinal', *Revue française de science politique*, 36, No. 6, 1986, pp. 752–65; Thérien, *Une voix pour le Sud: Le discours de la CNUCED*, Montréal/ Paris, Presses de l'Université de Montréal-L'Harmattan, 1990.

41   See in particular Pierre de Senarclens, *La crise des Nations Unies*, Paris: PUF, 1988.

42   It should be noted nonetheless that these questions are not wholly absent from the attention of francophone authors. See for example P.M. Dupuy, 'L'action des organisations internationales dans le domaine de la protection de l'environnement', in R.-J. Dupuy, ed., *Manuel sur les organisations internationales*, Dordrecht: Martinus Nijhoff, 1988, pp. 598–624; Monique Benisty, 'Le GATT pour quoi faire', *Politique étrangère*, 52, No. 2, 1987, pp. 425–33; Victor-Yves Ghébali, 'L'UIT et le Rapport de la Commission indépendante pour le développement mondial des Télécommunications', *Annuaire français de droit international 1985*, Vol. 31, pp. 671–85.

43   A good deal has been published in French on the process of crisis and reform in the UN. See in particular Ghébali, *La crise du système des Nations Unies*, Paris: La Documentation française, 1988, and de Senarclens, *La crise des Nations Unies*. See also André Lewin, 'La coordination au sein des Nations Unies: mission impossible?', *Annuaire français de droit international 1983*, Vol. 29, pp. 9–22; Ghébali, 'Réflexions sur les activités opérationnelles des Nations Unies', *Etudes internationales*, Vol. 17, No. 4, 1986, pp. 837–47; Yves Beigbeder, 'La crise financière de l'ONU et le Groupe des 18: Perspectives de réforme?' *Annuaire français de droit international 1986*, Vol. 32, pp. 426–38; Yves Beigbeder, 'Réformes administratives et structurelles des Nations Unies', *Etudes internationales*, 18, No. 2, 1987, pp. 353–70; C.-A. Colliard, 'Quelques aspects des problèmes de financement des organisations internationales', in Société française pour le droit international, *Les organisations internationales contemporaines: crise, mutation, développement*, Paris: Pédone, 1988, pp. 63–84; Paul Tavernier, 'Le processus de réforme des Nations Unies: du rapport Bertrand (1985) au rapport du Groupe des 18 (1986)', *Revue générale de droit international public*, 92, No. 1, 1988, pp. 305–34.

44   See Jean Touscoz, 'L'ONU à refaire', *Etudes*, No. 374, 1991, pp. 437–8.

45   These factors would also explain the failure of the United Nations in matters of collective security. See Virally, 'Le maintien de la paix et de la sécurité internationale', in René-Jean Dupuy, ed., *Manuel sur les organisations internationales*, p. 397–423.

46   Ghébali, 'La politisation des institutions spécialisées des Nations Unies', in Nicolas Jécquier and Franz Muheim, eds., *Les organisations internationles entre l'innovation et la stagnation*, Lausanne: Presses polytechniques romandes, 1985, p. 87.

47   See in particular de Senarclens, *La crise des Nations Unies*, pp. 169–99; Ghébali, *La crise du système des Nations Unies*, pp. 57–76; Maurice Flory, 'La crise de l'UNESCO', *Annuaire français de droit international 1985*, Vol. 31, pp. 653–70; de Senarclens, 'La dérive de l'UNESCO: essai d'analyse psycho-culturelle',

Etudes internationales, 16, No. 4, 1985, pp. 771–93; Ghébali, 'L'évolution de la crise de l'UNESCO', *Défense nationale*, 42, August–September 1986, pp. 87–101.

48 See for example Jean-Pierre Colin, 'L'avenir indécis du système des Nations Unies (l'exemple de l'UNESCO)', *Revue belge de droit international*, 21, No. 1, 1988, p. 20.

49 In addition to the documents mentioned earlier on the crises affecting the UN and UNESCO, see Ghébali, 'Vers la réforme de l'Organisation internationale du travail', *Annuaire français de droit international 1984*, Vol. 30, pp. 649–71; Francis Maupain, 'La réforme de l'Organisation internationale du travail', *Annuaire français de droit international 1987*, Vol. 33, pp. 478–97.

50 See Touscoz, 'L'ONU à refaire', pp. 437–47; Colin, 'L'ONU et les institutions internationales après la guerre du Golfe', *Politique étrangère*, 56, No. 3, 1991, pp. 649–61; Pascal Lorot, 'Organisations économiques internationales: le retournement soviétique', *Politique étrangère*, 54, No. 3, 1989, pp. 469–76.

51 For an example of unshakeable optimism, see Daniel Colard, 'L'ONU a quarante ans: réflexions pour un bilan', *Défense nationale*, 42, February 1986, pp. 67–81.

52 This point of view is clearly formulated in Charles Zorgbibe, *Les organisations internationales*, pp. 33–4. It should be noted, conversely, that the Gulf War has given rise to a new questioning of the legitimacy of the UN's action. See Joe Verhoeven, 'Etats alliés ou Nations Unies? L'ONU face au conflit entre l'Irak et le Koweït', *Annuaire français de droit international 1990*, Vol. 36, pp. 145–94.

53 For a discussion of the decisionmaking machinery of the Security Council, see Smouts, 'Réflexions sur les méthodes de travail du Conseil de sécurité ', *Annuaire français de droit international 1982*, Vol. 28, pp. 601–12.

54 Touscoz, 'L'ONU à refaire', p. 444.

55 André Lewin, 'La triade contraignante, une nouvelle proposition de pondération des votes aux Nations Unies', *Revue générale de droit international public*, 88, No. 2, 1984, pp. 349–59.

56 Maurice Bertrand, *Refaire l'ONU: un programme pour la paix*, Geneva: Editions Zoé, 1986, pp. 92–8.

57 See Marc Nerfin, *IFDA Dossier*, No. 45, January–February 1985, pp. 2, 32; Touscoz, 'L'ONU à refaire', p. 446.

58 Alfred Sauvy, 'Trois Mondes, une planète', *L'Observateur*, 14 August 1952, p. 5.

59 R.J. Dupuy, 'Conclusions générales du colloque', in Société française pour le droit international, *Les Nations Unies et le droit international économique*, Paris: Pédone, 1986, p. 371.

60 Michel Vernières, 'Regards croisés sur la littérature en français consacrée au développement', in Cahiers du GEMDEV, *Recherches récentes, en langue française, sur le développement*, pp. 5–15.

61 Guy Feuer, 'Le droit international du développement. Une création de la pensée francophone', in Cahiers du GEMDEV, *Recherches récentes, en langue française, sur le développement*, pp. 107–15.

62 André Philip, 'Les Nations Unies et les pays en voie de développement', in Société française pour le droit international, *L'adaptation de l'ONU au monde d'aujourd'hui*, Paris: Pédone, 1965, pp. 131–2.

63 Virally, 'Vers un droit international du développement', in Virally, *Le droit international en devenir: essais écrits au fil de ans*, Paris: PUF, 1990, pp. 78–87.

64 See the contradictory statements by Jean Touscoz, 'Préface', in Société française pour le droit international, *Les Nations Unies et le droit international économique*, p.v, and by R.-J. Dupuy, 'Conclusions générales du colloque', *ibid.*, p. 378.

65 Madjid Benchikh, *Droit international du sous–développement. Nouvel ordre dans la dépendance*, Paris: Berger–Levrault, 1983.

66 Feuer, 'Le droit international du développement. Une création de la pensée francophone', pp. 111–15.

67 Ghébali, *La crise du système des Nations Unies*, pp. 80–2.

68 See for example Jacques and Colette Nême, *Organisations économiques internationales*, Paris: PUF, 1972; Jacques Fontanel, *Organisations économiques internationales*, Paris: Masson, 1981. From a comparable standpoint, see the more recent work by Jean-Jacques Rey, *Institutions économiques internationales*, Brussels: Bruylant, 1988.

69 GEMDEV, *Lettre du GEMDEV*, No. 23, May 1992, pp. 5–10.

70 Marie-France L'Hériteau, *Le Fonds monétaire international et les pays du Tiers Monde*, Paris: PUF, 1986. For a technical presentation of IMF activities, see Michel Lelart, *Les opérations du Fonds monétaire international*, 2nd ed., Paris: Economica, 1988.

71 L'Hériteau, *Le Fonds monétaire international et les pays du Tiers Monde*, pp. 221–71; Zaki Laïdi, *Enquête sur la Banque Mondiale*, Paris: Fayard, 1989, p. 341; see also Alain Dauvergne, *Le Fonds monétaire international. Un monde sous influence*, Paris: Alain Moureau, 1988, p. 46–7.

72 Established in 1973, the Heritage Foundation is an American think tank devoted to promoting a conservative ideology. Among its many publications concerning the UN system, see in particular Burton Yale Pines, ed., *A World Without the UN: What Would Happen if the UN Shut Down?*, Washington: Heritage Foundation, 1983; Stanley Michalak, *UNCTAD: An Organization Betraying its Mission*, Washington: Heritage Foundation, 1983; Richard E. Bissell, *The United Nations Development Program. Failing the World's Poor*, Washington: Heritage Foundation, 1985.

73 Virally, 'A propos d'une sociologie des relations internationales', *Revue générale de droit international public* 87, No. 1, 1983, pp. 237–41; Virally, 'Droit international et relations internationales', *Revue générale de droit international public* 91, No. 2, 1987, pp. 670–4.

74 Galtung, 'Structure, Culture, and Intellectual Style: An Essay Comparing Saxonic, Teutonic, Gallic and Nipponic Approaches', pp. 848–9.

5
Multilateralism: the Case of Egypt

Hassan Nafaa

Despite its troubled political history, Egypt, compared to most Third World countries, has been an active as well as long-standing participant in international organization. In 1927 she was solicited to join the International Institute of Intellectual Cooperation (IIIC) and became, in 1937, a full member of the League of Nations. After the Second World War she participated, as a founding member, in the activities of the United Nations and all its specialized agencies. On the regional level Egypt played a leading role in establishing the League of Arab States (1945), the Organization of African Unity (1963), and the Afro-Asian, Non-aligned, and Third World movements. In the process of this active participation in international life, not only has a solid body of work on multilateralism accumulated in Egypt, but also the Egyptian academic community has been able to provide international administrations with some of the highest level international civil servants and experts.[1]

Before investigating materials on 'multilateralism', the concept itself invites clarification. Literature on multilateralism in its broader sense should include all scholarly work dealing with all types of interactions between more than two international actors. If I adopt such a broad definition, the scope of this survey might lose its focus. This is why it will be more appropriate to limit this survey to the literature dealing directly with the institutionalized forms of multilateralism (that is, international organizations).

Preliminary remarks

Historically speaking, 'international organization(s)' appeared as an independent discipline in the Egyptian university curriculum only in the departments of International Law. This is why teaching and research on multilateralism has been for many decades the monopoly of specialists in international law. The establishment of a Faculty of Economics and Political Science at Cairo University, and subsequently the multiplication of independent departments of political science within other Egyptian universities, contributed to the emergence of a new generation of scholars armed with additional tools and methodological approaches and perceiving 'multilateralism' through different perspectives.

The evolution of Egyptian foreign policy helped to enlarge the research scope of multilateralism. In addition to their general and legal preoccupations, Egyptian scholars were focusing on the UN management of specific issues from national perspectives, such as the Egyptian–British dispute, Arab–Israeli conflict, and the Suez Canal affair.[2] But the growing militant Egyptian role in world politics during the 1950s and 1960s, and its increasingly intensive interaction with Arab, Afro-Asian, non-aligned and Islamic countries, brought other issues into focus. Regionalism and regional organizations, problems of development and disarmament attracted increasing numbers of scholars. Moreover, the drastic changes occurring in local and regional politics after the 1967 and the 1973 wars put an end to a romantic–revolutionary era in Egyptian and Arab political life and opened a more pragmatic one. Growing political and economic liberalism created favorable conditions for more realistic and scientific approaches to different research problems. Finally, the multiplication of independent or semi-independent political research centres in Egypt and elsewhere in the Arab World had some positive direct and indirect impact upon literature on multilateralism in this part of the world.

Among these centres, two are of particular interest: the Al-Ahram Center for Political and Strategic Studies, and the Center for Arab Unity Studies. The first was established in 1968 and concentrated its research effort, at an early stage, on Israel and Middle East conflict, before extending its research scope actually to include the study of the international and regional systems, conflict management, and international organizations, among other issues. This centre publishes a quarterly review on international affairs (*Al-Siassa Al-Dawlya*), an annual strategic Arab report, in addition to occasional papers.[3]

The Center for Arab Unity Studies was founded in 1975 by a prominent Iraqi intellectual and former minister. It enjoys a completely independent status and soon became the most prestigious specialized research centre on Arab affairs. Since its foundation, this centre has published around two hundred books, many of them by large-scale collective research projects, in addition to fifteen bibliographical volumes on 'Arab Unity' and a regular monthly review.

Despite the relatively few publications directly related to international organization, there is no doubt that these centers were instrumental in facilitating contacts between different specialists and stimulating multi-disciplinary approaches.[4]

General trends and research issues

There is a traditional school on 'international organization' in Egypt highly influenced by, if not a mere reflection of, the French one. Professors H. Sultan, E. Rateb, H. Ghanem, A. Sarhan, B. Boutros-Ghali and others are generally considered as the 'peres fondateurs' of this school. A middle-aged generation including M. Shehab, S. Abdel Hamid, S. Amer and many others, as well as a younger generation of professors of international law, have contributed to keep the tradition alive and even to rejuvenate it.

Most of the literature produced by this school deals with general theoretical and legal matters. Classification of the types of international organizations, their legal status, structure, membership, voting mechanisms and procedures, voting, sanctions–these are among the main pre-occupations, exposed in detail under the generic title of Theory of International Organization(s). Description of specific organizations in terms of functions, working mechanisms and procedures, and major activities also characterize this literature.

The recent contribution of political scientists has taken the form of investigating new research areas such as the impact of the power structure of world or regional systems on the functioning of international organizations, the formulation of national or regional policies toward or within international organizations, and the application of new approaches and techniques in the analysis of classic or new issues. Economists contribute also to this literature through their analysis of the UN and the international economic organizations, along with the impact of their activities on national policies, on Third World countries, and on the international economic order.

In the following pages we discuss the general trends of the existing literature on the UN system and on regional organizations, and consider this literature's methodological approaches.

Aside from the legal and descriptive modes, one of the constant themes surfacing from time to time in Egyptian literature on international organizations is the idea of world government. In 1957, Boutros-

Ghali, subsequently to serve as Foreign Minister and later as UN Secretary-General, wrote a booklet in which he explained how the idea emerged and was perceived by different schools of thought, considering also the attempts at its implementation through the experience of the League of Nations and the United Nations. After deploring the de facto American and Soviet competing world governments, he concluded by assuring readers that 'the only way [to avoid a total destruction of humankind] is to establish a world government capable of insuring peace and security under the umbrella of law, justice and equality'.[5]

Two decades later, another work was entirely devoted to the consideration of whether the modern world organizations could constitute a step toward a real world government.[6] But while the idea has always been and continues to be a matter of major preoccupation for many Egyptian scholars, it is mostly treated and analyzed indirectly and through various other modes of discourse. The idealistic, even romantic views of Dr. Boutros-Ghali were not commonly shared, and a more realistic tone prevailed. Some tried, through a legalistic approach, to measure the gap between ambition and reality by comparing the theory of collective security to the practices of the Security Council, an exercise leading to the conclusion that the system needs complete reform.[7] The ability of the UN to adapt to changes occurring in the international system, and the impact of this system on the functioning of the UN bodies, retained attention and became subject to many analyses and different points of view.[8] The changes occurring in Eastern Europe and the former Soviet Union raised both fears and hopes.[9]

But the UN management crisis and conflict has not been systematically analyzed in Egyptian literature. Only the crisis in which Egypt or other Arab countries have been implicated retained the attention of scholars. Most of the criticism addressed against the UN system, and more specifically against the composition and voting mechanisms and procedures of the Security Council, came by way of analysis, from national (or even nationalistic) perspectives, of the role played by the UN in these particular crises. Among all these crises the UN management of the Palestinian problem and the Arab–Israeli conflict stimulated and absorbed most of the efforts deployed in this field.[10] More recently the UN management of the Gulf crisis and its impact on the future of the UN collective security system became a matter of serious preoccupation and raises more questions than it answers.[11]

Among all the activities of the UN and its specialized agencies, three issues have held most of the attention of Egyptian scholars: colonialism and apartheid, disarmament, and economic development. For obvious reasons, the literature on colonial issues has been decreasing in volume and in importance. Nevertheless, the Rhodesian and the Namibian questions and the problem of apartheid in South Africa were subjected to intensive investigation and studies to which historians, jurists, and political scientists all contributed. The studies reflect a unanimous appreciation of the UN role and orientation in dealing with all these issues, appraisal of the Third World countries, and criticism of the western position vis-à-vis the sanctions imposed against South Africa (and Rhodesia previously).[12]

UN activities in the field of disarmament are described and analyzed in different essays and PhD theses. But it is generally acknowledged that the destiny of disarmament depends more on the outcome of direct negotiation between nuclear powers than on resolution by the UN.[13]

Literature on the activities of the UN system in the field of development is, to the contrary, much more abundant. The activities of ECOSOC, UNDP, UNCTAD, as well as the efforts of the General Assembly to establish a 'New International Economic Order' are described, analyzed and assessed. The contribution of some economists in this field is remarkable, and jurists became actively interested in analyzing the impact of the normative claims of such activities on the emergence of an 'international law for development'.[14] In this literature the general philosophical and ideological orientation is generally appreciated, but the position of the industrialized countries, the operation of international bureaucracy, and the incoherence of Third World policy receive criticism.

But if this mildly critical stance is clear for the activities of the UN and what might be termed its subsidiary bodies, the IMF and IBRD are generally considered as simple tools in the hands of the capitalist system, despite their legal status as specialized agencies and as parts of the UN system. As a matter of fact, the operational activities of these two IFIs and their impact on the Egyptian and Third World economies have been subject to extensive analysis and scholarly work conducted mainly by economists. The existing literature in this field is dominated by Marxist, neo-Marxist or '*Tiers-mondist*' points of view.[15]

Finally, it may be observed that all the other UN specialized agencies except for UNESCO and FAO have not been given any substantial analysis in the existing Egyptian literature on multilateralism.[16]

Regionalism and regional organization

The study of regionalism and regional organizations has been a matter of theoretical preoccupation for Egyptian scholars. This may be explained in part by the fact that the Arab League was established before the United Nations. The Egyptian representatives at the Conference of San Francisco worked hard to obtain UN recognition of the Arab League, and took a militant stand in favor of regional organizations in the famous debate opposing 'regionalists' to 'universalists'. Given this background, there is no wonder in finding that many of the Egyptian 'old guard' scholars produced theoretical works on regionalism and regional organizations, and that the *problematique* of regionalism versus universalism continues to raise research problems and arouse comparative studies.[17]

Most Egyptian scholars focused their research in this field upon the Arab League and the OAU. The other regional organizations were either treated in a comparative context or almost completely neglected.[18] Literature on the Arab League reflects a clear dichotomy between those who perceive the foundation of an inter-Arab organization, based on voluntary cooperation between sovereign and independent states, as a British conspiracy to contain the rising ambition of Pan-Arabism to achieve complete constitutional unity on the one hand, and those who welcomed it as a step forward to build a solid progressive integration based on clear and acceptable rules on the other. But the failure of Arab unity between Egypt and Syria in 1961, and of the numerous subsequent unionist projects, weakened the romantic–revolutionary approach.[19]

During the last decade, literature on this subject has concentrated on assessing and evaluating the failures and achievements of the Arab League, mainly in conflict management and economic integration, and investigated new ways and methods to overcome the ongoing difficulties. To the old dichotomy a new one, opposing those who advocate substantial constitutional amendments to the Charter of the Arab League and those who see such a step as futile without changing the basis of legitimacy of the Arab regimes, seems to be in process.[20]

Literature on the Organization of African Unity reflects a less passionate debate. In addition to numerous legal and descriptive works on the OAU, two important issues receive much attention from Egyptian scholars: dispute settlement within the OAU, and relations between the OAU and the Arab League.[21] Finally, it is noteworthy that a number of Egyptian scholars are paying increasing attention to the study of inter-Islamic relations. Some of their work deals directly or indirectly with the study of international organization.[22]

Methodology and approaches

Research on international organization in Egypt has been, and remains, largely dominated by specialists in international law, as we have indicated. The contribution of political scientists in this field is still limited. Of interest are the findings of a survey of all the studies published in the Egyptian quarterly *Al-Siassa Al-Dawlya* over a quarter century. According to this survey, only 5.8 per cent of the studies published in this specialized magazine in international affairs were about 'international organization' (as against 45.6 per cent on 'international relations' and 16.9 per cent on 'strategic studies').[23] The limited contribution on multilateralism is due, according to the surveyors, to the fact that the study of international organizations belongs to the law sciences, while the younger generation of political scientists are wishing to dissociate themselves from the jurists.[24]

This remark in itself reflects a state of mind and the persistence of a wrong assumption according to which the study of international organization is by definition a study in international law. But it reflects at the same time a deep feeling that the legalistic approach could not lead, alone, to a comprehensive understanding of international relations phenomena, including the phenomenon of international organizations. As a matter of fact, some of the studies referred to and classified in this survey under the general topic of 'international relations' could be accurately and equally considered as studies on 'multilateralism' or 'international organization' in its broader sense.

The traditional Egyptian School, heavily influenced by the French one, has very much evolved over time. The borders of field investigation between 'law of international organizations' and the study of 'international organizations' as a phenomenon of international relations are getting clearer, and the limitations of a purely legalistic approach in this field are becoming widely recognized. Most of the classic textbooks on 'international organizations' are now published under the modest title 'law of international organization(s)' or 'general theory of law of international organization(s)' instead of 'theory of international organization(s)', as they used to be.

The prevailing dominance of the French influence over the Egyptian literature on 'international organization' does not undermine the recent, but steadily growing, impact of the Anglo-Saxon school on this literature through the contribution of Egyptian political scientists in the field. Some concrete examples illustrate this development.

In his MA thesis 'Egypt in the Arab League: A Study of the Role of the Greater State in Regional Organizations', and more particularly in his PhD thesis 'The Council of the Arab League: A Study of Decisionmaking in a Regional Organization', A. Al-Muwafi attempts to shed some light on different factors shaping the nature of the final outputs of the Arab League.[25] His approach seems to be highly influenced by some of the ideas developed in R.W. Cox and H.K. Jacobson, *et al.*, *The Anatomy of Influence: Decision Making in International Organization.* Different quantitative techniques have also been used recently by increasing numbers of Egyptian scholars to explore or to assess, in a more empirical way, some of the activities of international organizations or the activities of some political groups within these organizations. In an original if controversial study on 'the role of the Arab League in conflict management', M. Selim attempts to measure the efficiency of the Arab League in settling disputes between Arab States.[26] He uses similar indicators to those devised by E. Haas, R. Butterworth and J. Nye for their study of conflict management by international organizations. In a recent PhD thesis on 'Voting Behavior of the Arab Group in the UN General Assembly', H. Salah attempts to analyze the voting patterns of the Arab League and the factors affecting these patterns from 1948 to 1984. She uses quantitative techniques suggested by H. Alker, H. Newcombe (and many others) in several studies. Some of her findings challenge many of the assertions commonly acknowledged though based, in fact, on ideological convictions.[27]

Theories of integration, functionalism and neo-functionalism developed by Mitrany, Deutsch, Haas, Nye and many others are revisited nowadays by Egyptian scholars. The failure of all attempts to achieve constitutional Arab unity, and the establishment of Arab subregional political and economic groups, stimulated research comparing the European and Arab integration experiences, and raised questions about the applicability of the functionalist premises in the Arab context.[28]

Finally, in my own study on Egypt and UNESCO, I have sought to apply a systemic approach in order to analyze the relationship between a member state and an international organization. This relationship was perceived through a cycle of inputs, outputs and feedbacks. The factors influencing the state's demands on the international organization, the process of their conversion within the organization, and the mechanism of state reaction to the outputs of the organization were analyzed through an interdisciplinary approach.[29] The same approach was used to analyze the Arab regional policy within UNESCO.[30]

Conclusion

Without question a solid body of scholarly work on multilateralism and international organization has been accumulating in Egypt over decades. But this work is still dominated by a legalistic approach and highly influenced by the traditional French school. Political scientists are increasingly contributing to this literature by introducing methods, approaches and techniques developed by the Anglo-Saxon school, especially its American wing. The contribution of economists is limited to the technical aspects concerning the activities of some economic international organizations. Despite the existing research capabilities, the absence of specialized research centres or collective research projects on international organization did not enable a systematic and interdisciplinary study programme on 'multilateralism' to emerge in Egypt.

Notes

1 For example, A. Badawi was elected as the first Arab and African member of the ICJ (1946–65), and B. Boutros-Ghali was the first Arab and African elected as Secretary-General of the UN.

2 See *Egypt and the United Nations*, New York: Carnegie Endowment for International Peace/Manhattan, 1957; Youssef Chlale, *et al.*, *Le Probleme Du Canal De Suez*, Alexandria: Société Egyptienne de Droit International, 1957.

3 *Al-Siassa Al-Dawlya* ('International Politics') was founded in 1965 within the *Al-Ahram* daily newspaper and has been administered by the Center for Political and Strategic Studies since 1968. Boutros-Ghali, who proposed and initiated its publication, became its Chief Editor and remained in this post until his nomination as Secretary-General of the UN. The *Arab Strategic Report* was first published in 1986.

4 Complete and interdisciplinary scholarly work on the Arab League can be found in 'The Arab League Between Reality and Ambition' (papers and proceedings of seminar), Beirut, Center for Arab Unity Studies, 1983.

5 Boutros-Ghali, *The World Government*, Cairo: State Information Service, 1957; 2nd ed., Cairo: Dar el-Maarif, 1991, p. 92. See also his 'Democracy: A Newly Recognized Imperative', *Global Governance*, 1, No. 1, 1995, pp. 3–12.

6 M.H. Ebiari, *The Modern World Organizations and the Idea of World Government*, Cairo: General Egyptian Book Organization, 1978.

7 See Ibrahim Shehata, 'The UN Charter between the Text and its Application', *Al-Siassa Al-Dawlya*, 84, April 1967; Mofid Shehab, 'The UN between Collapse and Consolidation', *The Egyptian Review of International Law*, 24, 1968; Mona Mohammad Moustapha, *International Organizations between Theory and Practices*, Cairo: Arab Center for Studies and Publications, 1980.

8 See 'The U.N. in a Changing World', special file of *Al-Siassa Al-Dawlya*, 84 April 1986; Hassan Nafaa, 'The U.N. and the World System', *Al-Siassa Al-Dawlya*, 84, April 1986; Nabil Bishr, 'The Adequacy of the Authority Invested in the Security Council in a Changing World', PhD thesis, Faculty of Law, Alexandria University, 1977.

9 Hassan Nafaa, 'The U.N. at a Cross-roads', *Al-Ahram*, 10 June 1990.

10 Tens (if not hundreds) of studies and essays dealing with various aspects of the UN management of the Palestinian question and the Arab–Israeli conflict are available. The interest in this topic remains remarkable. See, for example, Attya Afandi, 'The UN Security Council and the Middle East Conflict', PhD thesis, Faculty of Economics and Political Science, Cairo University, 1983; Walid Alian, 'The UN Role in the Palestinian Question', PhD thesis, Faculty of Law, University of Alexandria, 1989.

11 Hassan Nafaa, 'The UN Management of the Gulf Crisis: A Case Study on the UN Collective Security System', in Al-Rashidy, ed., *International and Regional Dimensions of the Gulf crisis*, Cairo: Center for Research and Political Studies, Cairo University, 1991.

12 See Shawqi Al-Gamal, *The Rhodesian Question between the UN and the OAU*, Cairo: General Egyptian Book Organization, 1977; A. Al-Rifai, 'The African Problems in the UN', *Al-Siassa Al-Dawlya*, 59, 1980; W. Abdel Meguid, 'The UN and the African Liberation Movements', *Al-Siassa Al-Dawlya*, 84, April 1986; Ahmad Aboul-Enein, 'The UN and Namibia', *Revue Egyptienne de Droit Internationale*, 31, 1975.

13 Abdel Fattah Ismail, 'The UN Efforts in the Field of Disarmament', PhD thesis, Faculty of Law, Cairo University, 1972; Yahya Al-Sheimy, 'The UN and Disarmament', *Al-Siassa Al-Dawlya*, 84, April 1986.

14 See Zaki Shafi, 'The UNCTAD', *Al-Siassa Al-Dawlya*, 1, July 1965; Shafi, 'The "77" Group', *Al-Siassa Al-Dawlya*, 11, January 1968; Hassan Nafaa, 'International Organizations and the Problems of Development in the Third World', *Al-Siassa Al-Dawlya*, 62, October 1980; Ismail Abdalaa, *Toward a New International Economic Order*, Cairo: Egyptian General Book Organization, 1977; Ismail Sabri Al-Arabi, *The United Nations and the Economic Development in the Developing Countries*, Beirut: Dar Al-Thaqafa Al-Gadida, 1972; Ahmad Abdel Wanis Shita, 'The Evolution of the ECOSOC', MA thesis, Faculty of Economics and Political Science, Cairo University, 1981.

15 See Ramzi Zaki, 'The Monetary History of Underdevelopment', *Alam Al-Ma'rifa*, 118, Kuwait, 1987; Zaki, *Crisis of External Debt: A View from the Third World*, Cairo: Egyptian General Book Organization, 1978; Adel Hussein, *The Egyptian Economy: From Independence to Dependence*, 2nd ed. Cairo: Dah Al-Mustaqbal Al-Arabi, 1982, 2 vols.

16 On UNESCO, see Hassan Nafaa, 'L'Egypte et l'UNESCO', these de Doctorat l'Etat en Sciences Politiques, Université de Paris I, Paris: Pantheon–Sorbonne, 1977; Nafaa, 'The UNESCO Crisis', *Al-Siassa Al-Dawlya*, 93, July 1988; Nafaa, 'The Arabs and UNESCO', *'Alam Al-Ma'rifa*, 135, Kuwait, 1989. On the FAO, see Hassanein Ali, 'The Role of the FAO vis-à-vis the Starvation Problem in Africa', MA thesis, Faculty of Economics and Political Science, Cairo University, Cairo, 1989.

17 Boutros-Ghali, *Contribution a l'Etude des Ententes Regionales*, Paris: Edition A. Pedone, 1949; M.II. Ghancm, *The Regional International Communities: A Legal Study on Modern International Coalition Systems*, Cairo: Institute of Arab Studies, 1958; Ahmad Moussa, 'Rapports entre les Nations Unis et la League de Etats Arabes', *Revue Egyptienne de Droit International*, 29, 1973.

18 An example of these comparative studies is Fikry Samy, 'The Role of Regional Organizations and International Peace Keeping: A Comparative Study

between the League of Arab States and the OAS', PhD thesis, Faculty of Economics and Political Science, Cairo University, Cairo, 1980.

19 See 'The Arab League between Ambition and Reality', and the extensive bibliography on the Arab League mentioned in the footnotes of the various contributions in this publication. See also L. Shokier, *The Arab Economic Unity: Experiences and Perspectives*, Beirut: Center for Arab Unity Studies, 1986, 2 vols.

20 See Sayed Yasin, ed., *Perspectives of Inter-Arab Relations in the 1990s*, Amman: Forum of Arab Thought, 1992; M. Said, 'The Future of the Arab System after the Gulf Crisis', *Alam el-Ma'rifa*, 158, Kuwait, February 1992.

21 See Boutros-Ghali, *l'OUA*, Paris: Librairie Armon Colin, 1969; Boutros-Ghali, 'The League of Arab States and the OAU', in *The OAU after Ten Years*, New York: Praeger, 1975; (collective) *The Arabs and Africa*, 2nd ed. Beirut: Center for Arab Unity Studies, 1987; Abdel Malik Auda, 'The Arab League and the Technical Assistance to Africa', *Al-Siassa Al-Dawlya*, 47, January 1977.

22 See M.T. Ghoneimi, *Modern and Islamic Thought in International Organization*, Alexandria: Munshat al-Ma'arif, 1971; A. Al-Ash'al, *The Foundations of International Islamic Organization*, Cairo: Dar al-Nahda al-'Arabiya, 1988; M. Selim, 'The OIC and Dispute Settlement', *Al-Siassa Al-Dawlya*, 105, July 1991.

23 Osama Al-Ghazali and Amr Rabi, 'Field Research of Political Scientists in Egypt: A Content Analysis of *Al-Siassa Al-Dawlya*, 1965–1990, Al-Siassa Al-Dawlya, 100, April 1990, p. 11.

24 *Ibid.*, p. 10.

25 Abdel Hamid Al-Muwafi, *Egypt in the Arab League of States: A Study of the Role of the Greater State in Regional Organizations (1945–1970)*, Cairo: Egyptian General Book Organization, 1983; 'The Council of the Arab League of States: A Study on the Decision-making Process in a Regional Organization', PhD thesis, Faculty of Economics and Political Science, Cairo University, Cairo, 1985.

26 Mohammad Selim, 'The Role of the Arab League in Conflict Management', in *The League of the Arab States between Ambition and Reality*, Beirut: Center for Arab Unity Studies, 1983.

27 Hoda Abdel Aziz Salah, 'Voting Behavior of the Arab Group in the UN General Assembly', PhD thesis, Faculty of Economics and Political Science, Cairo University, Cairo, 1992.

28 See Abdel Moneim Said, *The European Community: The Experience of Integration and Unity*, Beirut: Center for Arab Unity Studies, 1986; Ibrahim Awad, 'Theorie de l'Integration Politique et Application au Monde Arab: L'Etude de deux processus dans une perspective neofontionnelle', *Etudes Politiques du Monde Arabe*, Le Caire: CEDEJ, 1991; Hassan Nafaa, *The Experience of Integration and European Unity: It is applicable to the Arab World*, Political papers, 29, Cairo: Center for Political Research and Studies, 1991.

29 Nafaa, 'l'Egypte et l'UNESCO'. See also the comments of Ch. Zorgbib on this thesis in *Le Monde Diplomatique*, September 1977. Nafaa, 'The Study of Relationships between the International Organization and the Member States: A System Approach', *International Interaction*, 7, No. 4, 1981.

30 Nafaa, 'The Arabs and UNESCO', *'Alam Al-Marifa* 135, March 1989.

6
Survey of Scholarly Work on Multilateralism: The Netherlands

Monique Castermans-Holleman
with contributions by
Peter R. Baehr, Dick A. Leurdijk, Nico J. Schrijver

Dutch foreign policy

In a major speech the Dutch Minister of Foreign Affairs has described Dutch foreign policy as 'nourishing the international legal order' by giving staunch support to the United Nations. A common feeling that peace and security are closely linked to freedom and justice inspires this attitude. In addition, because of growing global interdependence, the Netherlands has more and more to rely on international cooperation for both its military and economic security.[1]

Multilateralism, defined as the way in which significant entities in a world order relate to each other with the aim of cooperative management of common problems and the moderating of conflict,[2] is a basic principle of Dutch foreign policy. This positive Dutch attitude toward multilateralism and the rule of law originates from two longstanding conditions: strong commercial interests and a weak military position. Maintenance of international peace and order, a precondition for intensive commerce, would be guaranteed only by international law. Consequently, the establishment of an international legal order has become a central tenet of Dutch foreign policy. Indeed, the Constitution directs its upholders: 'The Government shall promote the development of the international legal order' (article 90). Along with the belief that rules must underpin peace and commercial progress goes a pragmatic recognition that small states like the Netherlands can only hope to exercise some influence on international politics if they are ready to pool efforts with other states.

For these reasons, politicians and scholars in the Netherlands usually take a firm stand for multilateralism. Historically, the Dutch attempt to play a role in shaping international affairs through three international organizations: the North Atlantic Treaty Organization (NATO), for military security; the European Union (EU) for economic cooperation; and the United Nations. Since 1949, NATO has stood at the very centre of Dutch security concerns. Growing attention has also been paid to the Western European Union (WEU) and the Conference on Security and Cooperation in Europe (now OSCE), given their possibilities for creating and maintaining peace and stability in Europe. Dutch support for the EU is another example of the interest devoted to multilateralism. Today this support aims to bring about a full-fledged union. Dutch foreign policy and the quest for common European stands on external issues constitute an item of continuing discussion.

The third important international organization through which successive Dutch governments work to achieve their goals and objectives is the UN. Despite some criticism as to the functioning of the United Nations, policymakers consider it of vital importance for the creation of a real world order. Consequently, they attempt to strengthen its role in shaping world politics. From the beginning, the Netherlands has played an active role in UN activities, as a member of the Security Council (for instance in 1946; 1951–52; 1965–66; 1983–84); by making large voluntary contributions to UN programmes like the United Nations Development Programme (UNDP) and the United Nations Environment Programme (UNEP); and by taking part in such UN peacekeeping operations as those in Lebanon, Cambodia and the former Yugoslavia.

Dutch studies on multilateralism

Strong and longstanding Dutch support for international organizations, especially the United Nations, explains the great amount of attention paid to the UN in Dutch scholarly literature. The extensive study of Dutch foreign policy by Joris Voorhoeve provides an interesting earlier overview of Dutch mundialist policy in general and intergovernmental organizations in particular.[3] In 1990, a contribution to the conference on the future of the UN, held under the auspices of the Academic Council on the United Nations System (ACUNS), was prepared by a number of Dutch authors. P.R. Baehr and M.C. Castermans-Holleman edited a set of case studies on UN issues with which the Netherlands had been deeply involved.[4]

Studies on multilateralism are usually carried out in universities; most of the researchers on UN matters or multilateralism more generally are affiliated to one of the Dutch university research centres. Important research has also been done by non-university affiliated organizations such as the Netherlands Institute for International Relations

'Clingendael'. Articles on the UN can ordinarily be found in professional journals such as *Transaktie* and the *Internationale Spectator*. Another important source of information on UN issues is a journal called *VN Forum*. This periodical is issued by the Dutch association for the UN; it contains leading articles on the UN system and on pertinent developments, general comments, facts and reports on UN sessions.[5]

Periodically, the Dutch Ministry of Foreign Affairs issues publications on UN sessions (*Uitgaven van ministerie van Buitenlandse zaken*, The Hague, Staatsuitgeverij, 1946–) and meetings in various UN arenas. These publications report proceedings and Dutch activities in particular, including the most important Dutch speeches delivered. Several advisory groups also publish on questions relating to the UN. The Advisory Commission on Human Rights and Foreign Policy issued a report on UN supervisory mechanisms regarding human rights; the Advisory Commission on Peace and Security prepared a report on the UN after the cold war; and the Advisory Commission on International Law, in cooperation with the Advisory Commission on Human Rights and Foreign Policy, came out with an interesting report on humanitarian intervention. Finally, the National Advisory Commission on Development Issues has produced many reports regarding development questions and international economic cooperation.

Outline of this survey

The overview summarizes publications on the functioning of the UN by Dutch authors[6] writing in Dutch and English. These publications fall into eight broad categories, giving an overview of the UN's most important fields of work as these are dealt with by the principal organs of the UN, special programmes and subsidiary organs. Studies on specialized agencies are not included. The following subjects are discussed: 1. general works; 2. peace and security; 3. international economic cooperation; 4. human rights and refugees; 5. the environment; 6. international law; 7. the Dutch position at the UN; 8. miscellaneous. A general overview of the literature is offered with each theme. Obviously it is impossible to deal with each study in detail or even to cite all pertinent works. The focus here is upon studies of a substantial and scholarly character published in or after 1980.

In the conclusion attention is paid to matters such as the disciplinary background of authors, their theoretical approaches, polemics, and structural reform proposals.

Overview of publications

1. General works

On the whole, Dutch authors who contribute to a growing volume of scholarly literature on the UN, while quite aware of the system's short-comings, take a constructive position toward the subject. The United Nations provides the forum needed for international cooperation and negotiations.[7] This basically positive approach applies even to a book entitled *The UN Under Attack*, for on the whole participant authors do not make such an attack.[8] Baehr and Gordenker have written a major affirmative general introduction to the UN. The original is in Dutch; an amended version also is available in English.[9] The authors find every reason to expect that the UN will continue as a serious, indeed indis-pensable factor in the international politics of the twenty-first century.

General works about the UN can be usefully divided into several categories. These are historical accounts, discussions of structural change (including revision of the Charter), surveys of activities and multilateral diplomacy.

Historical accounts

Some books on the development of international relations since 1945 mainly fulfill teaching purposes. As part of his treatment of the role of international organizations, Baehr[10] puts heavy emphasis on the UN as the single international organization with a (nearly) universal member-ship and general purposes. The specialized agencies evince universal membership with more limited purposes. Baehr suggests that the more limited the purposes of an international organization, the greater its chances for success – a conclusion that would seem to hold little pro-mise for the UN as a whole. Works dealing with the UN more specifically are those by Leurdijk[11] and Wellens.[12] The latter emphasizes legal ques-tions. Major developments during the UN's first forty years are discussed in a Dutch Ministry of Foreign Affairs booklet.[13]

Structural change

Over fifty years after the founding of the UN, the question is often raised as to whether the structure of the organization, laid down in the Char-ter, remains adequate. Reform of the UN system, including the question of Charter revision, is a topic regularly discussed in Dutch academic as well as political circles. One author has suggested that the International Court of Justice should be asked to give advisory opinions on the legitimacy of proposed Security Council decisions.[14] G. Ringnalda, a former high official of the Ministry of Foreign Affairs who now chairs the Dutch Association for the United Nations, also considers the need for structural change,[15] arguing in favour of semi-permanent membership on the Security Council for a number of major powers without increasing its overall membership. In addition, he has urged increased powers for the Secretary-General. An entire issue of the journal of the Dutch Association for the United Nations treats the question of Charter reform (*VN Forum*, 1992). There ten experts give their views as to whether the Charter needs to be *amended*.

The discussion of UN reform did not begin recently. J. Berteling[16] considered the subject earlier. Specific attention has been directed to the role of the Secretary-General.[17] The Dutch section of the World Federalists has presented a list of proposals (Wereld Federalisten Beweging Nederland, 1985). Schrijver has written about the revival of the Security Council.[18] The current place of the Security Council in international law is handled by P. Kooijmans.[19] W. de Haar and others consider western and non-western views about the UN.[20] A critical account of international decisionmaking is provided by Schrijver.[21]

Surveys of activities and multilateral diplomacy

ACUNS publishes an annual report on the United Nations. It offers a continuing review of major changes in the UN system and the role of international organizations in world politics. Two reports have been prepared by a Dutch team. The 1990 report (Johan Kaufmann, Schrijver and Leurdijk) deals with the original design of the UN, economic issues, development and the environment, peacekeeping, and provides case studies following other matters. Its successor report of 1991 (Kaufmann, Leurdijk and Schrijver) examines the Gulf crisis, conflict resolution, peacekeeping and arms control, human rights, the environment, development and trade, the European Community and the UN, and development toward a new world order.

Kaufmann, who is a scholar as well as an experienced former diplomat, has written a classic on conference diplomacy[22] that draws heavily upon his experience as Dutch representative at the UN and other international organizations. Conference diplomacy he defines as 'that part of the management of the relations between governments and of relations between governments and intergovernmental organizations that takes place in international conferences'. Kaufmann has also edited a book of case studies on conference diplomacy.[23] These essays are written by Dutch as well as foreign scholars and diplomats, and they deal with a great variety of issues negotiated at the UN and beyond.

2. Peace and security

The maintenance of international peace and security is a fundamental concern of Dutch foreign policy. This focus is reflected by the position that the Netherlands has taken through the years within the UN: in its repeated candidacies for a non-permanent seat in the Security Council; in its position on general questions concerning the system of collective security, including issues of arms control and disarmament, and pleas for fact-finding; and in its willingness to participate in Dutch academic circles, suggesting a relationship between Dutch UN policies and Dutch research topics. A similar link can be discerned regarding the increased interest in collective security on policy and academic fronts since the end of the cold war. At that time developments enforced attention by traditional non-UN watchers on the functioning of the UN system of peace and security. This attention paralleled the growing involvement of the Security Council in a spectrum of preventive diplomacy, peacekeeping, peacemaking, peacebuilding, humanitarian intervention, and enforcement measures. Such developments held far-reaching implications for Dutch defence policy in terms of needed adaptation to implement UN tasks. The changed role of the UN, especially the Security Council as central decisionmaking instrument in the sphere of international relations, has also led to a rethinking of the principles of Dutch membership in the UN, in both policy and academic circles, giving a strong impetus to efforts for a redefinition of Dutch interests in the functioning of a UN system of collective security.

Main foci

Four foci emerge from a review of Dutch literature on questions of international peace and security: the principle of collective security, with emphasis on 'the inherent right of individual or collective self-defence'[24] and economic sanctions; issues of arms control and disarmament; peacekeeping; and fact-finding. In a series of yearbooks on peace and security written by policymakers and academics and published by different universities, special attention has been paid year by year to the role the UN plays in questions of arms control and disarmament, including bans on weapons of mass destruction, non-proliferation issues, and verification. A striking feature of Dutch literature on the UN during the eighties was a strong stress upon the role of the organization in regional conflict resolution (Iran–Iraq, Afghanistan, Namibia, Cyprus, Western Sahara, the peace process in Latin America and Cambodia), with special attention given to the functioning of peacekeeping operations in those situations. Two authors, Leurdijk and R.C.R. Siekmann, have followed developments closely; they have authored the majority of writings on peacekeeping published in the Netherlands.[25] Curiously, reference to the increasing involvement of the UN in the resolution of regional conflicts, especially after the breakthrough in 1987 with Security Council resolution 589 on the war between Iraq and Iran, is almost absent. Finally, through the years, since the Dutch took a General Assembly initiative in 1962 by proposing the establishment of a fact-finding mechanism, attention has been given to this idea in the literature, with criteria specified including its creation under UN auspices and its impartiality in order to prevent or settle international disputes.[26]

Collective security and peacekeeping

The end of the cold war, the Iraqi invasion of Kuwait, the Gulf War and its aftermath, followed by increasing UN Security Council involvement in conflict situations all over the world led to a considerable number of publications raising all kinds of questions concerning the implementation of the principles of collective security contained in the UN Charter. These developments were extensively analyzed by a team of Dutch authors (Kaufmann, Leurdijk, Schrijver) in two Academic Council on the United Nations System annual reports.[27] A great deal of attention was given to the role of the UN in the Gulf War, or the Gulf crisis in more general terms. Relatively little attention has been paid to the consequences of the role the UN has played in implementing Security Council resolutions 678 and 688 within Iraq. The participation of the Netherlands in UN peacekeeping operations in different parts of the world, and the humanitarian relief operation in northern Iraq in the spring of 1991, led policy and academic circles to take increased interest in such issues as peacekeeping.

3.   International economic cooperation

One of the continuities in Dutch foreign policy is international development cooperation. This takes various forms, including the granting of approximately one per cent of Dutch GNP as official development assistance (ODA) to developing countries. Aid is given directly to particular countries (bilateral aid), through international organizations (multilateral assistance), and through NGOs. Both the public and the literature support the principle of international development cooperation. Yet a constant debate proceeds on the modalities of development assistance, including the amount, the choice of the recipient countries and the international organizational means, the choice of channel (bi-, multilateral or through NGOs), and whether or not aid can be tied to spending it, wholly or partly, in the Netherlands, thus serving as an instrument of export promotion. One of the most critical studies on this issue is by P. Hoebink; its title translates as 'To give is to take'.[28]

Proposals for reform

Despite support for development aid, there is widespread conviction that aid alone will not suffice for development. In the literature relating to the UN this is reflected in an extensive series of articles on the need to change the rules of the game in international economic affairs, both at the level of international consultation and decisionmaking and in specific fields. As to consultation and decisionmaking, there is sincere interest in enhancing the participation of developing countries. Nobel laureate Jan Tinbergen[29] and former UN ambassador Kaufmann[30] are among the academics who have put forward interesting proposals for reform of the social and economic sectors of the United Nations, including the establishment of a world treasury and the revitalization of the UN Economic and Social Council (ECOSOC).

International trade issues

As far as specific fields are concerned, substantial attention is paid to international trade issues. Studies include an extensive analysis of the Multi-Fibre Agreement,[31] proposals for merging the General Agreement on Tariffs and Trade (GATT) and the UN Conference on Trade and Development (UNCTAD) into an International Trade Organization that would operate on equal footing with the International Monetary Fund (IMF) and the World Bank (IBRD) as a specialized agency of the UN,[32] and a series of articles on the accomplishments and failures of UNCTAD.[33] The latter discuss both UNCTAD's role in the global North–South dialogue and in specific fields such as commodity trade regulation. Some articles discuss in a more general analytical context the evolution of the 'development ideology' of the United Nations as reflected in major UN policy statements such as the UN development decade resolutions.[34] Finally, reference should be made to the Dutch academic interest in the issue of international regulation of transnational corporations. Various articles review the state of affairs with respect to the draft code of conduct on transnational corporations.[35]

Dutch position in international economic consultations

Public support for international development cooperation is palpably reflected in Dutch literature. A lot of sympathy exists for 'going multilateral', whether the issue concerns the granting of development aid or the regulating of foreign investment. While this could be seen as natural for a small country, it is a little disappointing that the multi-lateralist sentiment is hardly linked interpretively to observations on the relatively strong position of the Netherlands in international economic consultation as a member of the EU, the Group of 10 and the executive boards of the IMF and the World Bank. This disconnect is even more striking if we note that attention has been paid to economic issues as far as the allocation of competencies within the Netherlands between various cabinet ministers (Finance, Foreign Affairs, Development Cooperation, Agriculture) and such governmental agencies as the Central Bank are concerned.[36] In the same vein, international economic cooperation in the context of the EU and its impact on the Dutch stand in the UN has been somewhat neglected during the period under review. However, the Maastricht Treaty, providing for more extensive European cooperation in this field, is undoubtedly bringing change both in practice and in theory.

4.   Human rights and refugees

During the last several decades, human rights have become one of the central tenets of Dutch foreign policy. This subject can count on strong public support. Consequently, a great volume of literature exists on the promotion and protection of human rights in the UN framework. One can distinguish four broad categories within the field of human rights literature.

Human rights bodies

In the first category are many works dealing either with the activities of a particular human rights body, like the UN Commission on Human Rights or the Human Rights Committee, or with special procedures or working methods of UN bodies. One book treats procedures developed within the UN to deal with petitions or communications from individuals and private organizations complaining about violations of human rights by particular governments.[37] Substantial articles have been devoted to the thematic procedures of the Human Rights Commission as well as to country-oriented approaches.[38] Each of the two authors cited calls the procedure he describes more effective than others.

With regard to the functioning of particular bodies, one can distinguish between articles dealing with a particular body and articles dealing with the functioning of a body at a special session or time. General articles deal with the Human Rights Committee and its procedures[39] and the Commission on Human Rights. Kamminga[40] concludes that the importance of the Commission can only be measured in political terms. Several articles deal with particular sessions of the Commission and the problems that originated and decisions taken at that particular session.[41] Furthermore, much attention has been paid to the functioning of the Subcommission and the turning of the Commission 'into a full-fledged human rights forum with political overtones'.[42] Finally, attention is paid to activities of particular treaty-bodies like the Committee against Torture and the UN committee entrusted with monitoring the Convention on Economic, Social and Cultural Rights.[43]

Human rights themes

The second broad category is related to writings on special human rights themes. In the first place, much attention is given to torture in the broadest sense, including medical ethics in relation to the treatment of prisoners. Baehr[44] has written on the creation of the UN Convention against Torture, including the role of the Netherlands in drafting this convention. A handbook and article under other authorship address the same subject.[45] Another theme that is dealt with in several articles is the question of involuntary disappearances.[46] Articles have been published on violations in several countries and the UN reaction thereto; examples include Chile, China and Poland.[47] Other works deal with standard-setting with respect to the independence of judges and lawyers, the rights of children, and the rights of women.[48] In addition, many articles heed the role of NGOs in monitoring UN activities in the field of human rights.[49]

Effectiveness

The third category contains articles treating questions on the effectiveness and usefulness of UN activities in the field of human rights. Most of these writings offer a broad overview of developments regarding the protection and promotion of human rights since the creation of the UN and the Human Rights Commission in particular. Attention is paid to the changing notion of sovereignty and the development of human rights law as an obligation *erga omnes*. Most authors are of the opinion that in the field of standard-setting, most of the work has been done. In the phase of implementation, however, a lot of work remains.[50]

Refugees

The last category, dealing with refugees, has been meagre during the period under review. Two books describe the problems of refugees in a general way, giving some attention to UN activities.[51] However, no work examining UN refugee activities in a substantial manner is available.

The only exception is an article on the fortieth anniversary of the UN High Commission on Refugees.[52]

5. The environment

Through the early 1990s, Dutch literature on the environment was dominated by articles on the United Nations Conference on Environment and Development (UNCED), which took place in Rio de Janeiro in June 1992. Before the General Assembly took the decision to hold this international conference, hardly any literature was devoted to the environment or to UN activities in the field. There are, however, a few exceptions. M. Couwenbergh and H. Siepel wrote an article on UNEP[53] to illuminate the question of politicization of UN organs and specialized agencies. They argue that followers of the functionalist theory criticize the politicization of UN organs because they think that a distinction must be made within the UN between political issues to be dealt with by the General Assembly or the Security Council on one hand, and economic and technical issues to be dealt with by alternative organs on the other. When a process of politicization takes place, this distinction disappears. They contend that in the 1970s, UNEP became politicized: more and more attention was paid to the relationship between environment and economic development, whereas unfair international economic relationships were seen as one of the main causes of the bad economic position of many Third World countries. By the 1980s, however, the western countries succeeded in pushing into the background the social side of the environmental question, handling it as a purely technical issue. From the point of view of conflict theory this has to do, according to the authors, with safeguarding the interests of the dominating western countries.

F. Schlingemann[54] gives an overview of the development of the environmental issue as an international problem. In the 1950s, production and growth increased greatly. Only in the 1960s did the other side of this development become clear: issues of pollution, urbanization and the limits of natural resources came to the fore. At that time, the UN began to pay attention to questions concerning the environment, resulting in the first United Nations Conference on the Human Environment, which took place in Stockholm in 1972. Other Dutch articles on the environment are linked to the UNCED conference. They are discussed below.

UNCED

Some writings heed the development of UN environment policy from Founex/Stockholm to Rio; others concentrate on the preparation for the

Rio conference. M. Hooghe[55] describes the Stockholm conference and its corollary, the establishment of a small secretariat dealing with environmental questions, UNEP. He argues that the division between North and South constituted a serious obstacle to the practical realization of a vigorous international environment policy. Regarding more recent activities in the field of the environment, Hooghe is somewhat sceptical about the UN; he contends that it is not yet able to play a dominant role in the field of the environment. A. Berghuizen[56] also offers a pessimistic account: UNCED negotiations mainly took care of short-term governmental interests. The forest convention, for example, was not acceptable to many governments, and it was changed into an 'intention'. Most governments seem to be afraid to lose part of their sovereignty. As a result the UN, consisting of sovereign states, is not the appropriate instrument for the fight against pollution.

N. Kramer[57] is more optimistic; he argues that international opinion regarding the importance of the environment has become more positive than ever before. The cold war is over and in its aftermath many people regard the attack on nature as the most important threat to humanity. From this perspective, the UN must play a role.

Institutional proposals

Schrijver[58] and Leurdijk[59] provide an overview of the institutional proposals offered to strengthen UN environmental policy. Leurdijk pleads for the creation of an Ecological Security Council apart from the Security Council. This new council should have competences of its own and act like a crisis center for sustainable development. If necessary, 'green helmets' should be called in case of a crisis or war threatening the environment. Hooghe, on the other hand, makes a plea for broadening UNEP's mandate. UNEP should develop its activities more independently and should be less subject to political interests which have nothing to do with the environment.

Special themes

As a special theme of the UNCED conference, F.A. Nelissen[60] focuses on the protection of the marine environment. Land-based pollution in particular forms a threat to the international environment, he argues. UNCED should be used as a tool to stimulate ratification by all countries in the UN Convention on the Law of the Sea. Furthermore, new impulses should be given to fight this landbased pollution of the oceans through Agenda 21. J.H. Waller-Hunter[61] maintains that the

Netherlands entered the UNCED debate reasonably well prepared at the domestic level: it has accepted sustainable development as part of its own national policy.

Evaluation of UNCED

B. Metz and P. Vellinga[62] were among the earliest to evaluate the Rio Conference. They express mixed feelings: on the one hand, much publicity was given to the subject in order to mobilize public opinion. Moreover, two covenants were adopted. On the other hand, it turned out that the wealthy western countries were not yet ready to pursue an active environmental policy, whereas sustainable development should begin in the West. Furthermore, they deplore the creation of a new commission, functioning under ECOSOC, which threatens to undermine UNEP.

6. International law

For small nations like the Netherlands, the rule of international law performs the function of guidance in a complex world. Sometimes esteem for the role of law stems from a traditional nationalist attitude: How can the law of nations be applied to the benefit of the Netherlands itself? Sometimes the preference is inspired by a community-oriented attitude: How can international law serve the interests of the world community? This distinction was drawn by B.V.A. Rolling in the preface to the third edition of his *Volkenrecht en Vrede*, 1985. It is not surprising that most Dutch authors take an affirmative stand on the role of international law, also on the importance of UN bodies like the International Court of Justice (ICJ) and the International Law Commission (ILC), while formulating proposals for the codification of special rules in fields like the law of the sea.

Regarding the role of international law in general, most authors are fairly hopeful. M. Brus and S. Muller,[63] for example, contend that with the obvious exception of Iraq, during the Gulf crisis the 'most important actors on the world stage ... [tried] to play the game within the limits posed by international law'. A. Eyffinger,[64] head of the ICJ library, sees an increased faith in the Court during the 1980s as well as in the role of international law as such.

Literature in this field can be classified according to three broad themes: the role of the ICJ and other legal institutions such as ILC; special fields of international law such as codification and dispute settlement in the field of space law, the law of the sea and marine fisheries law; and the Decade of International Law.

The International Court of Justice

A Polish–Dutch colloquium on international law was devoted to the functioning of the Court while celebrating the ICJ's fortieth anniversary in 1986. The resulting book contains contributions on many themes.[65] The book's editors state that at a time when some states are more willing than before to submit their disputes to the Court, continuation of the discussion among scholars as well as supportive research are of the utmost importance. De Waart's contribution deals with the question of non-appearance before the Court. De Waart concludes that 'the least the international order can do is prevent offenders from pretending that they are acting legally'. M. Noortman[66] points out that the marginal role played by the Court is only explained by the fact that many states lack the willingness to bring conflicts before it. However, Noortman concludes, more and more non-western states come to the Court and the position of the former Socialist countries develops in a positive direction.

P. Hoefer-Van Dongen[67] assesses the desirability of preliminary rulings by the Court. In theory, this would be very attractive, she argues; in practice, however, it would create many problems. P. Glebbeek[68] considers a specific case before the Court: *The United States v. Nicaragua*. Regarding the codification of international customary law, Siekmann[69] observes that the ILC deals mainly with technical, nonpolitical matters whereas questions of a more political nature, like those related to the law of the sea, are dealt with by special drafting committees of the General Assembly and other UN organs.

Special fields of international law

A study by M. Benkoe, W. De Graaff and G.C.M. Reijnen[70] reflects on the current state of space law within the UN. This book results from a process of co-production; two lawyers and a specialist on solar systems are responsible. H. Van Traa-Engelman[71] focuses on the settlement of space law disputes, concentrating not only upon the draft convention on the settlement of space law disputes, but also on existing methods within the framework of particular regulations like the Moon Treaty. A. Broches[72] addresses the historical development of UN Commission on International Trade Law (UNCITRAL) norms within the UN system and concludes that the UNCITRAL Law on International Commercial Arbitration (1985) meets the basic requirements of modern arbitration law.

With respect to law of the sea, J.A. Walkate,[73] an official in the Dutch Ministry of Foreign Affairs and member of the Prepcom of the International Seabed Authority as well as of the International Tribunal for the Law of the Sea, focuses on chapter XI of the Law of the Sea Convention treating the deep seabed and the elaboration of this part of the convention. E. Hey concentrates on another part of the 1982 Convention: the provisions applicable to transboundary marine fisheries resources. She seeks to answer how the international law of the sea accommodates interests of different states in transboundary stocks after the extension of coastal state jurisdiction.[74]

Decade of International Law

The Decade of International Law receives attention in a special issue of *The Leiden Journal of International Law,* also published as a book.[75] It has contributions from Dutch scholars as well as foreign experts on such questions as the enhancement of international law and the strengthening of international peaceful dispute settlement. Brus and Muller, editors, review the purposes, origin, character and reactions to the Decade. In his contribution, P.H. Kooijmans[76] notes that various procedures for solving disputes between states are rarely used because states do not consider them suitable for political reasons. He pleads for an increased role by individuals and NGOs in order to claim respect for the rule of law.

W.J.M. Van Genugten and Castermans discuss the programme of action for the Decade as adopted by the General Assembly in 1990. They regret that despite many concrete items deserving immediate attention, hardly any suggestion for concrete action was included in this programme of action. The neglect justifies a fear that the Decade of International Law will die without a struggle.[77] Notwithstanding their concerns, most authors in this field see the UN as the most important guardian of the international legal order.

7.   The Dutch position at the UN

In general the Dutch strongly support the United Nations. The Netherlands has used the UN as a forum to achieve results in a number of concrete policy fields. These policy fields, as well as general trends and developments, have been discussed in a number of contributions regarding the Dutch position on the UN. For instance, as noted in the introduction, the Baehr and Castermans-edited volume entitled *The Netherlands and the United Nations* contains writings by experts on a number of issues. Here in brief are several of them.

As part of this collaborative effort, Shrijver examines the Dutch initiative to adopt a Charter of Development. He discusses the functions of the development decades and suggests the revitalization of a Dutch initiative to adopt a Charter of Development as a global framework for international development cooperation, to be combined with the development of so-called 'development contracts'. Siekmann examines how the Netherlands' participation in the UN Interim Force in Lebanon (UNIFIL) came about, what influence the Dutch parliament has on this kind of decision, and why the Netherlands withdrew its units in 1985. He offers recommendations as to the organization and regulation of UN peacekeeping, for example by drafting general guidelines or principles for these operations. An account of Dutch efforts to establish a fact-finding mechanism in the UN is provided by Leurdijk. He concludes that the Dutch initiative in the 1960s came too early. However, the situation more recently seems to confirm that the original intention to underline the importance of fact-finding as a means of solving disputes *has* been honoured, at least on an ad hoc basis. The UN role in disarmament as well as the Dutch points of view and initiatives are discussed by J.T. Hoekema. He concludes that arms transfers, conversion, conventional disarmament and confidence-building measures will be the key policy issues for states in the coming years. It is, however, unclear whether and how the UN could act as a forum for negotiations. Finally, H. Gajentaan pays attention to population policy issues, Dutch initiatives regarding the strengthening of the Population Commission and the UN Fund for Population Activities (UNFPA). The editors conclude this study by discussing four major elements of Dutch foreign policy in the UN that emerge from the cases considered: a strong emphasis on development of international law; a commitment to development issues; a tendency toward 'bridge-building' between North and South, for instance in the realm of population problems; and a concern for the promotion of human rights.

The issues discussed in *The Netherlands and the United Nations* correspond with the majority of the themes discussed in other publications. Below, passing note is made of other publications which focus on the Dutch position or on Dutch initiatives in different fields.

Human rights

In 1984, the General Assembly adopted the Convention against Torture. Baehr[78] describes Dutch activities in bringing about the draft convention, including efforts by experienced and dedicated officials of the Dutch Ministry of Foreign Affairs. He points to the key role played by other small countries like Sweden and some African states in drafting this convention. NGOs also played an important role. Castermans-Holleman[79] describes Dutch contributions to the drafting of the Universal Declaration on Human Rights (1948). Those contributions were rather marginal; it was only in the 1960s that Dutch attention to the promotion of human rights developed. Dutch human rights policy is described extensively in Castermans-Holleman's study dealing with Dutch human rights policy at the UN from 1945 to 1985.[80] The author seeks to gain better insight into the whys and wherefores of Dutch human rights policy and into the factors contributing to the Netherlands being in a position to exert an influence on the international decisionmaking process. Attention is paid to the importance of having a non-official delegation leader and the important role that NGOs can play.

Peace and security

One means to keep the peace consists of participation in UN peacekeeping forces. Especially after the positive response of the Dutch government with regard to the request of the Secretary-General to take part in UNIFIL, many articles were published. M.G. Woerlee[81] assesses UN peacekeeping operations in general, their weak as well as strong dimensions, also the preconditions for a successful peacekeeping operation. In a subsequent article he discusses Dutch participation in UNIFIL and its history. The Netherlands offered troops for peacekeeping as early as the 1960s, though the offer was not accepted until 1978.[82] Woerlee and other authors agree that this reluctance on the part of the UN was caused by Dutch colonial history as well as the close alliance of the Dutch with the United States. Commentators also describe the training of the Dutch UNIFIL battalion, the pressure its dispatch put on the remainder of the Dutch army, and the problems that arise from a force comprised mainly of conscripts.

The discussion on participation in peacekeeping operations culminated when the Dutch government decided to withdraw from UNIFIL in 1985. Siekmann[83] concludes that no official regulation exists regarding withdrawal of contingents either internationally or nationally. In the Dutch parliament an effort was made to formulate some criteria, notably the condition that it is reasonable to expect that the task can be fulfilled. In 1985, the Dutch government referred to these criteria: the UNIFIL mandate could not be fulfilled any longer in a proper way, and the situation became ever more dangerous. Siekmann deplores the Dutch decision; it was announced exactly on the UN's fortieth anniversary, a blunder. Furthermore, the Dutch task had to be taken over by other forces facing the same risks. Finally, he wonders whether this decision would have implications for the future role of the Netherlands as a peacekeeper. Baehr offers this decision as an example of the tension between the theoretical support for the UN in Dutch foreign policy and the practical implementation of this support.[84]

Finally, with respect to efforts to strengthen the peace, Leurdijk[85] criticizes the Dutch government for not being actively involved in the International Year for Peace proclaimed by the UN for 1986. He points out that the Dutch voted in favour of this international year in the General Assembly, but domestically nothing was done to promote it. In this way the Dutch contribute to discounting the credibility of UN-designated international years.

International law

Th. De Bruyn,[86] an official in the Ministry of Foreign Affairs, describes Dutch participation in the drafting of the 1982 Convention on the Law of the Sea. The Netherlands did sign the convention, but ratification would take place only as soon as the effective implementation of the Law of the Sea was insured. By signing the convention, the Netherlands nonetheless tried to exercise influence in the preparatory commission. Regarding the actual situation – the unacceptability of the existing chapter XI to important countries like the US and several western European countries – it would be better to draft a new chapter on deep seabed exploitation, the author concludes.

Examining the case of *UN Council for Namibia v. Urenco, UCN and the State of the Netherlands*, Schrijver points out that one may doubt whether instituting legal action in the Netherlands is the most appropriate method to put an end to the illegal depletion of the natural resources of Namibia. Nevertheless, such public legal proceedings in a constitutional state like the Netherlands will command respect in UN quarters and can constitute a Dutch contribution to the strengthening of the international legal order.[87]

Security Council

A number of authors have sought to assess the weight of Security Council membership in general and the possibilities for the Netherlands in particular. On one hand, the Netherlands is a small country lacking much influence; on the other, the fact that the Netherlands usually takes a fairly independent position, and that the country is not involved in major international disputes, will create fair chances for successful initiatives. H. Scheltema, who was Ambassador of the Netherlands to the UN during part of the period of Dutch membership, is rather sceptical about the possibilities for the Netherlands to exercise any influence at all.[88] In another contribution, Dutch membership in 1983–84 was compared with the membership during the period 1965–66, testing the viewpoint that Dutch influence in international politics is supposed to have decreased in the 1980s.[89] Regarding Security Council membership, this seemed not to be the case. Increased support from the ministry in The Hague as well as a somewhat neutral position regarding various questions seemed to account for the rather successful role the Netherlands played in the Security Council during 1983–84.

Three officials of the Ministry of Foreign Affairs share their points of view regarding Dutch initiatives in the Security Council. E. Craanen discusses Security Council involvement in the conflict in Central America.[90] R.H. Serry describes the rather unsuccessful efforts of the Security Council to solve the problems suffered by Lebanon. When the situation culminated in December 1983, the Dutch presidency of the Security Council tried to renew the efforts to bring the conflict to an end. Unfortunately, these efforts were blocked by the Soviet Union as well as by the United States. The only thing the presidency could accomplish was the evacuation of the PLO and its leader, Yasser Arafat, from the northern Lebanese town of Tripoli, under the UN flag.[91] P.M. Kurpershoek analyzes the Dutch efforts in the Security Council regarding apartheid in South Africa. This was a Dutch initiative taken at the instigation of the Dutch parliament. The author contends that this initiative was only successful because of the deteriorating situation in South Africa, strengthening the need for renewed international action, along with the intensive negotiations conducted by the Dutch delegation.[92]

8. Miscellaneous

One can distinguish several articles dealing with special topics like the problem of drugs or UN activities affecting special groups like women and children. Another group of articles deals with the position that particular countries take toward the UN on one hand, and UN involvement with special countries on the other.

Special topics

Former Dutch Ambassador to the UN in Vienna L.H.J.B. Van Gorkom describes the consensual drafting of the UN Convention against illicit traffic in narcotic drugs and psychotropic substances in terms of approbation. The adoption of this convention in 1988 was an example of the vitality and effectiveness of the UN system of international decisionmaking. It was one of the first times, he points out, that East and West as well as North and South overcame serious legal and political obstacles.[93]

Authors writing on the protection of women and youth are less enthusiastic about the progress made. F. Linden, youth representative in the Dutch delegation to the General Assembly in 1988, suggests that the specialized agencies should better heed the protection of youth.[94] Ph. Weijenberg-Pot, women's representative in the Dutch delegation to the General Assembly in 1989 and 1990, calls for more attention to women outside the Commission on the Status of Women.[95] J. Van Der Linden considers the International Year of the Homeless and the activities of Habitat,[96] and H. Rolfes delves into the International Conference on Children that took place in 1990.[97]

Several authors point to the significance of UN social programmes. It is held of the utmost importance that more attention be paid to the work of the UN in secondary schools. Teachers should not start with the organizational structures of the UN, but with processes in world politics, from there moving to the involvement of the United Nations.[98] The contribution of NGOs to the work of the UN stems from their expertise, their power to increase public involvement, and their resonance in informing public opinion.[99]

Particular countries

In a series of articles, Leurdijk considers that the UN, in the 1980s, went through an exciting and important phase.[100] He points to developments in the United States and the Soviet Union. Several incidents illustrate the fact that the US was unhappy with the way the UN was functioning. One has only to think of its withdrawal from UNESCO, the Kassebaum amendment, the attitude regarding the International Court of Justice, and the delay in paying its regular assessments. The author explains the dissatisfaction with the functioning of the UN as follows: for years the UN was the most important forum for the promotion of American concerns in world politics. With the increasing membership of Third World countries, the American – western – position declined. The US government proposed a system of weighted voting, at least in the field of decisions regarding the UN budget, aimed at re-establishing American leadership in the UN. Leurdijk indicates that at the end of the 1980s, the American position changed again: the US did recognize once more the importance of multilateral diplomacy. Perhaps this had to do with the fact that the position of the Soviet Union, indeed the Soviet Union as such, changed radically.

In 1987, Mikhail Gorbachev published an article in *Pravda* explaining the new Soviet concept of foreign policy. From that moment the USSR would strive for a comprehensive system of international peace and security; the UN should have to play a major role in this system. The Soviet Union would be 'no more Mr. Nyet'; it favoured UN peacekeeping operations, suggested enhancement of the Security Council, and took a radically different position on human rights. Leurdijk stresses that these developments were closely connected with the internal changes in the Soviet Union: the UN should have a central position in the struggle for a stable and safe world, a precondition for the internal – economic – development of the Soviet Union.[101]

Former Dutch Ambassador to the UN in New York R. Van Schaik analyzes the consequences of changes in eastern Europe.[102] Regarding the future of the UN, he is optimistic: he trusts that the UN will respond to evolving needs of the times. Finally, he asks for more attention to pressing problems of a global nature, to the pervasive difficulty of poverty, and to enhancement of legal instruments and mechanisms in the fight against human rights violations.

The evolution of European cooperation has received a great deal of attention in Dutch literature. Generally speaking, authors take a positive stand on the effects of the increased European cooperation within the UN. If the EU members take a common stand at an early stage, they may also influence the positions of other countries. M. Weisglass, however, points out that sometimes it can be more effective for every EPC member to express its point of view individually.[103] On issues such as apartheid, decolonization, the Middle East, disarmament, and budgetary matters, it is difficult to reach a common point of view. With regard to questions dealt with by the Security Council, in which only two EU partners have permanent seats, no coordination takes place.

Other writings examine the policy of the UN regarding specific countries or areas. Leurdijk considers the special position of Switzerland regarding the UN.[104] The peace process in Namibia receives attention by several authors. Siekmann and Leurdijk offer a proposal for the Middle East: an independent Palestinian state should be established; elections should take place under the auspices of the UN; and a UN peacekeeping force should guarantee the security of this new state as well as the security of the neighboring countries. This new Palestinian state should have no army of its own.[105] Leurdijk and Siekmann also commend the UN as promoter of a new universal principle: fair and free elections.[106] The UN no longer simply strengthens the peace by dispatching peacekeeping forces, but also by organizing elections, for instance in Namibia and Nicaragua.

Conclusions

The introduction stated that support for international organizations has been a longstanding feature of Dutch foreign policy. This strong support explains the great amount of interest and attention paid to the UN in Dutch literature. Generally speaking, there has been an increase in publications on the UN in recent years. The growing involvement of the Security Council in basic questions of peace and security increased even further Dutch interest in the functioning of the UN system. If one looks closely at the literature on environmental questions, it turns out that substantial attention has been directed to this subject only in recent years. The advent of UNCED helps to explain the rise in Dutch interest.

In the 1980s, concern with UN human rights activities increased. In addition, much attention to other matters has been noted. On the other hand, it has been pointed out that Dutch policy regarding the UN does not always fit the principle of strengthening the international legal order. The Dutch position when the Indonesian case was discussed at the Security Council, the withdrawal of the Dutch contingent from UNIFIL, slow ratification procedures for important treaties, as well as some organizational changes at the Ministry of Foreign Affairs that imply less interest in international organizations like the UN all illustrate this conclusion.

Character of the studies

Most studies are of an informative, practical and descriptive character. Writings on human rights and the environment make this particularly clear. Scholarship of a more philosophical or theoretical orientation is hardly available. For example it is striking that not a single author turns his or her thoughts to the linkage between peace with security and human rights. In theory, the UN has always recognized this link; in practice, however, this precept has hardly been followed by the Security Council. Southern Rhodesia, South Africa, and 'Kurdish' Council resolution 688 are the main exceptions. In the field of the environment the same holds true. Only two exceptions to this observation can be mentioned: first, the article on politicization in the UN dealing with UNEP activities from a functionalist viewpoint as well as from a conflict theory viewpoint;[107] second, the articles giving an overview of institutional proposals by Schrijver[108] and Leurdijk,[109] which attend to the need to relate environmental questions to the notion of international security and to the question of the limitation of sovereignty through the increasing importance of cooperation on the environment.

In the field of peacekeeping, various articles have been written by members of the military. Usually they focus on the implications of participation for the Dutch army, its individual conscripts and volunteers, and their training. Generally speaking, they pay less attention to implications for the Dutch position as peacekeeper, peacekeeping in general, or the restoration of international peace and security, themes that are being dealt with mainly by academics. In other fields, the majority of writings are prepared by scholars. International law topics are exclusively covered by lawyers. Together with political scientists, historians and economists, they form the bulk of UN watchers. On the environment, few articles are written by ecologists.

Critical notes

A striking difference is observed in the position taken toward the UN by activists, officials and scholars. Activists, usually representatives of NGOs, sometimes have a rather negative view regarding UN activities and possibilities. Officials of the ministries and in particular members of the Dutch delegations to several UN conferences usually offer a somewhat more optimistic assessment. They often point to the importance of UN activities and the Dutch contribution to these activities in particular. Scholars often draw the necessary distinctions. As a matter of fact, most authors take a positive stand on international cooperation. Clearly, all carry the conviction that UN activities are important. Without doubt this relates in some rather direct respect to the theoretical approaches employed. Most authors evince an idealist/institutionalist or pluralist vision of international relations without evident self-consciousness of this perspective. In their opinion the positions of international organizations like the UN are always of enormous importance; these play a major role in international politics. Furthermore, writers take the view that the agenda of international politics is not simply dominated by military and security issues, as a realist perspective would suggest. In order to preserve peace, other matters such as a better social–economic climate and a greater respect for human rights are important as well, they maintain.

Given this orientation, it is not surprising that most authors take a positive stand on the role the UN plays in world politics; they 'believe' in the work of the UN. This is not to say that no adverse comments are made. For example, the growing strength of the Security Council and the implementation of the principles of collective security in actual policy has raised serious reservations among Dutch authors in recent years. These reservations reflect concerns about the dominant position of the United States, or the western powers, in the Security Council, and about implementation of the system of collective security dictated by them. At the same time, doubts are raised about the effectiveness of the traditional doctrine of peacekeeping. With respect to the protection of human rights, one author expresses his concern as follows: 'The UN and human rights: Failure or success? Certainly not a failure, not in the field of normsetting and not even of implementation. However, in a world where victims of serious violations of human rights can be counted by millions, the word "success" sounds odd and out of place. Their suffering can only mean to us that we should do better since their suffering spells the word "failure" life-large.'[110]

Polemics

Authors hardly ever engage in polemics. One exception can be mentioned: no agreement exists when the composition of the Dutch delegation to the General Assembly is under discussion. This delegation consists of officials of the Ministry of Foreign Affairs. Members of parliament as well as representatives of groups like labour organizations, women and youth act as observers. One author questions the need to include members of parliament *and* representatives of groups because only some groups from Dutch society are represented. At the same time, all groups are represented in parliament; and parliament controls the implementation of foreign policy. Therefore it is not necessary to let these groups take part in the Dutch delegation. Another problem has to do with the fact that all members of the delegation must adhere to the directives issued by the Ministry of Foreign Affairs, which may cause problems for non-ministerial representatives. Other authors point to the expertise of these representatives and the experience they receive with respect to the work of the UN.[111]

Structural reform

The question of Charter revision, the composition of the Security Council, the powers of the ICJ and the Secretary-General, and the reform of the socio-economic sectors of the UN receive constant attention. In the field of human rights, most authors urge better supervision mechanisms in general. One pleads for a global country-by-country approach wherever gross and systematic human rights violations occur, comparable to the existing practice of studying the situation in certain countries by country-oriented fact-finding organs like the special rapporteurs and working groups.[112] Both this author and others opposed the appointment of a High Commissioner for Human Rights, arguing that this position has been sliced up already and can hardly work in a more efficient way than existing mechanisms. Radical proposals for reform yield to proposals advanced in order to make better use of existing mechanisms and procedures. Most discussions taking place can be summarized by stating that there is a strong consensus behind strengthening the United Nations. This consensus obtains in policy circles as well as academic circles.

Notes

1 Speech delivered at Leyden University, 17 September 1992.
2 Compare the definition of multilateralism given by Robert W. Cox in 'Globalization, Multilateralism and Democracy', presented to the Inaugural Pan-European Conference, Heidelberg, 16–20 September 1992.
3 *Peace, Profits and Principles: A Study of Dutch Foreign Policy*, Leiden: Martinus Nijhoff, 1979. Useful subsequent overviews and compilations include the product of a working group on Dutch foreign policy: Ph.P. Everts, ed., *The Politics of Persuasion: Implementation of Foreign Policy in the Netherlands*, Aldershot: Avebury, 1989. See also Everts, 'Recent and Current Research on International Affairs in the Netherlands', in *Internationale Spectator*, 43, November 1989, pp. 646–54. And see P.R. Baehr, 'International Relations Research in the Netherlands', in *Orbis*, Summer 1982, pp. 517–24.
4 *The Netherlands and the United Nations: Selected Issues*, The Hague: T.M.C. Asser Instituut, 1990.
5 Regarding sessions of human rights organs, comparable information can be found in a journal issued in English, the *Netherlands Quarterly of Human Rights*.
6 Publications by non-Dutch authors are included when they are written in Dutch or appear in a Dutch publication and are internationally difficult to obtain but important for the discourse in the Netherlands.
7 P.R. Baehr, 'Kan de wereld zonder de Verenigde Naties?', in *Vragen naar de onbekende weg: kernproblemen van de internationale betrekkingen*, S. Rosemond and J.G. Siccama, eds., Assen/Maastricht + Den Haag: Van Gorcum + Instituut Clingendael, 1990, pp. 11–19.
8 J. Harrod and Shrijver, eds., *The UN Under Attack*, Aldershot: Gower, 1988.
9 *De Verenigde Naties: ideaal en werkelijkheid*, 2nd ed. Meppel + Amsterdam: Boom, 1992; *The United Nations in the 1990s*, New York: St. Martin's, 1992.
10 'De rol van internationale organisaties sinds 1945', in *De Wereld na 1945*, D.F.J. Bosscher, H. Renner, R.B. Soetendorp, R. Wagenaar, eds., Utrecht: Het Spectrum, 1992, pp. 37–58.
11 D.A. Leurdijk, 'Het nut van de multilaterale diplomatie: voorzichtig met de VN', in *Intermediair*, 21, 27 September 1985, pp. 15–19.
12 K.C. Wellens, 'The United Nations Forty Years On', in Wellens, ed., *Peace and Security: Justice and Development*, The Hague: T.M.C. Asser Instituut, 1986, pp. 81–99.
13 K.E. Vosskühler, *40 jaar Verenigde Naties*, Den Haag: Ministerie van Buitenlandse Zaken, 1985.

14 A. Bloed, 'Toetsing van besluiten van de Veiligheidsraad', in *NJD 1992*, pp. 661–4.

15 'Herstructurering van de Verenigde Naties', in *Internationale Spectator*, 46, September 1992, pp. 523–31; also in *VN Forum*, 5, 1992, pp. 1–11.

16 'De herziening van de structuur van de Verenigde Naties', *Internationale Spectator*, 34, 1980, pp. 161–9; 'De Verenigde Naties: genezing is moeilijk', *Internationale Spectator*, 41, February 1987, pp. 84–91.

17 J.F. Engers, 'De Secretaris-General van de Verenigde Naties', *Internationale Spectator*, 34, 1980, pp. 266–77; Leurdijk, *Perez de Cuellar en het haperen van de VN*, Den Haag: Nederlands Instituut voor Internationale Betrekkingen 'Clingendael', October 1983.

18 'Commentaar: de "wederopstanding" van de Veiligheidsraad van de Verenigde Naties', *Transaktie*, 19, December 1990, pp. 294–8.

19 'Zwijgt het recht als de Veiligheidsraad spreekt?', *NJB 1992*, pp. 847–52.

20 De Haar, G. Kampman, H. Toelhoek, eds., *De Verenigde Naties in beweging: westerse en niet-westerse visies*, Nijmegen: Studiecentrum voor Vredesvraagstukken, 1990.

21 'International Organization for the Management of Interdependence: Alternative Ideas in Pursuit of Global Decision-making', *Bulletin of Peace Proposals*, 19, 1988, pp. 175–85.

22 *Conference Diplomacy: An Introductory Analysis*, 2nd ed., Dordrecht: Martinus Nijhoff/UNITAR, 1988.

23 *Effective Negotiation: Case Studies in Conference Diplomacy*, Dordrecht: Martinus Nijhoff/UNITAR, 1989. See also an earlier work co-authored with John G. Hadwen: *How United Nations Decisions Are Made*, Leiden: Sijthoff, 1960.

24 J.M.G. Meuffels, *De Verenigde Naties en de handhaving van de vrede: de praktijk van de Verenigde Naties*, Katwijk aan Zee: Albedon Klop, 1980; M.M.M. Van den Bos, 'De Verenigde Naties en het recht tot zelfverdediging van staten', *Internationale Spectator*, 40, February 1986, pp. 114–20.

25 For instance Leurdijk, 'The Expediency and Effectiveness of UN Peacekeeping Operations', in *NILR 1988*; R.C.R. Siekmann, *Basic Documents on United Nations and Related Peace-keeping Forces*, Dordrecht: Nijhoff, 1985; 'The Codification of General Principles for United Nations Peace-Keeping Operations', in *NILR 1988*.

26 G. Walraven, 'A Dutch Initiative in the United Nations: Fact-Finding', in *The Politics of Persuasion*, pp. 231–40; Leurdijk, 'Fact-Finding: A Dutch Initiative in the UN Revitalized', in *The Netherlands and the United Nations*, pp. 45–61.

27 *Changing Global Needs: Expanding Roles for the United Nations System*, Hanover: ACUNS, 1990; *The World in Turmoil: Testing the UN's Capacity*, Hanover: ACUNS, 1991.

28 *Geven is nemen: de Nederlandse ontwikkelingshulp aan Tanzania en Sri Lanka*, Nijmegen, 1988.

29 *Revitalizing the UN System*, Santa Barbara: Santa Barbara Nuclear Peace Institute, 1987.

30 'The Economic and Social Council and the New International Economic Order', in D.P. Forsythe, ed., *The United Nations in the World Political Economy: Essays in Honour of Leon Gordenker*, Basingtoke: Macmillan, 1989, pp. 54–66.

31 N.M. Blokker, *International Regulation of World Trade in Textiles*, Dordrecht: Martinus Nijhoff, 1989.

32 J. Pronk, 'Towards a New International Trade Organization', in *The UN Under Attack*, pp. 71–93.

33 Notably, H.A.J. Coppens, 'UNCTAD-7: consolidatie met vooruitzichten: de collectieve onderhandelingsstrategie van de Derde Wereld', *Internationale Spectator*, 41 September 1987, pp. 433–40.

34 For instance, L. Emmerij, 'De drie panelen van het derde ontwikkelingsdecennium', in *Strategie in ontwikkeling*, ed. M. Sint and W. Verburg, Amsterdam: Intermediair, 1980, pp. 134–58; Schrijver, 'De internationale ontwikkelingsstrategie voor de jaren 1981–1990', *Intermediair*, 17, 6 February 1981, pp. 1–13.

35 M.H. Muller, 'De onzekere toekomst van de gedragscode van de Verenigde Naties voor transnationale onderemingen', *Internationale Spectator*, 40, June 1986, pp. 371–81; R.H. Buikhema, *De multinationale onderneming in juridisch perspectief*, Den Haag: T.M.C. Asser Instituut, 1992.

36 Compare J.W.M. Engels and Schrijver, 'Ontwikkelingssmenwerking en kabinetsformatie 1986: Proeve van een comepetentieregeling', in *Internationale Spectator*, 40, June 1986, pp. 388–93.

37 T.J.M. Zuijdwijk, *Petitioning the United Nations: A Study in Human Rights*, Aldershot: Gower, 1982.

38 M. Kamminga, 'The Thematic Procedures of the United Nations Commission on Human Rights', *NILR 1997*; M. Nowak, 'Country-oriented Human Rights Protection by the UN Commission on Human Rights and its Subcommission', *Netherlands Yearbook of International Law*, 1991, pp. 39–90.

39 H. Koudstaal, 'Het mensenrechtencomité van de Verenigde Naties en klachten van groeperingen', *NJCM–Bulletin*, 12, September 1987, pp. 437–42; T. Zwart, 'De behandeling van individuele klachten door het mensenrechtencomité van de VN', *Recent ontwikkelingen op het gebied van de mensenrechten*, Leiden: Stichting NJCM–Boekerij, 1988, pp. 60–71.

40 'De Commissie voor de Rechten, van de Mens', *VN Forum*, No. 3, 1990, pp. 15–18.

41 Castermans-Holleman and W.J.M. Van Genugten, 'Controversies tijdens de 46ste zitting van de VN-Commissie voor de mensenrechten', *Internationale Spectator*, 44, August 1990, pp. 482–7; K. Davidse, '47ste zitting van de Commissie voor de Rechten van de Mense en toezicht op de naleving van burgerrechten en politieke rechten in het kader van de VN', *NJCM-Bulletin*, July–August 1991.

42 T. Van Boven, 'The United Nations Sub-Commission on Prevention of Discrimination and Protection of Minorities', *NQHR 7–4*, 1989, pp. 464–71; see also C. Flinterman, 'The United Nations Subcommission on Prevention of Discrimination and Protection of Minorities', *NQHR 63*, 1988, pp. 53–7; Van Boven and Flinterman, 'Vijfjaar Subcommissie ter voordoming van discriminatie en bescherming van minderheden', *NJCM-Bulletin* 17–4, 1992, pp. 400–10.

43 Nowak, 'De eerste zitting van het VN-Comite tegen Foltering', *NJCM–Bulletin* 13–5, July–August 1988, pp. 483–7; S. Leckie, 'The Appearance of the Netherlands before the UN Committee on Economic, Social and Cultural Rights', *NQHR 7–3*, 1989, pp. 308–13.

44 'The General Assembly: Negotiating the Convention on Torture', in *The United Nations in the World Political Economy*, pp. 36–53; 'The United Nations Convention Against Torture', in *The Politics of Persuasion*, pp. 296–309.

45 J.H. Burgers and H. Danelius, *The United Nations Convention Against Torture*, Dordrecht: Martinus Nijhoff, 1988; Burgers, 'An Arduous Delivery: The United Nations Convention Against Torture (1984)', in *Effective Negotiation*, pp. 45–53.

46 T. Van Dongen, 'In laatste instantie: verdwijningen en de Verenigde Naties', *Internationale Spectator*, 40, July 1986, pp. 468–78.

47 F. Gruenfeld, 'Human Rights in Chile', in *The Politics of Persuasion*, pp. 269–81; Castermans-Holleman, 'China en de mensenrechten', *VN Forum*, 3, June 1990, pp. 1–4.

48 Leckie, 'The UN and the Independence of Judges and Lawyers', *SIM Newsletter* 17, pp. 13–28; A.J.M. Delissen, 'De rechten van het kind: na 10 jaar voorbereiding nu bij verdrag vastgelegd', *NJCM Bulletin*, 1990, pp. 566–76; L. Lijnzaad, 'Het kussen van een kikker: de werkelijke betekenis van het Vrouwenverdrag', *Nemesis*, March/April 1991, pp. 5–18; H.D. Stout, 'Internationaal vrouwenklachtrecht', *NJB*, 12 September 1987, pp. 999–1000.

49 For instance, P.H. Kooijmans, 'The Non-governmental Organizations and the Monitoring Activities of the United Nations in the Field of Human Rights', in *The Role of Non-governmental Organizations in the Promotion and Protection of Human Rights: Symposium Organized on the Occasion of the Award of the Praemiun Erasmianum to the International Commission of Jurists*, Leiden: Stichting NJCM-Boekerij, 1992, pp. 15–22.

50 Kooijmans, 'Human Rights – Introduction', in *Peace and Security*, pp. 67–73; H. Van Aggelen and Flinterman, 'Het Vnbeleid ter bescherming van de rechten van de mens: de effecten sinds 1945', *VN Forum*, 4, 1991, pp. 23–8.

51 J.A. Hoeksma, *Tussen vrees en vervolging, een inleiding in het vluchtelingenrecht*, Assen: Van Gorcum, 1982; R. Fernhout, *Erkenning en toelating als vluchteling*, Kluwer: Deventer, 1990.

52 R. Vonk, 'Jubilerende vluchtelingenorganisatie onder het mes: 40 jaar Hoge Commissariat voor de Vluchtelingen', *Internationale Samenwerking*, 6, January 1991, pp. 2–5.

53 M. Couwenbergh and H. Siepel, 'Politisering in de Verenigde Naties: naar aanleiding van het United Nations Environment Programme', *Internationale Spectator*, 39, June 1985, pp. 340–6.

54 'Ecologie en milieu', in *De Verenigde Naties in beweging*, pp. 47–53.

55 'The United Nations and the Environment: From Stockholm 1972 to Rio de Janeiro 1992', *Internationale Spectator*, 45, November 1991, pp. 668–73; 'Het milieubeleid van de Verenigde Naties: van Stockholm 1972 tot Rio de Janeiro 1992', in R. Aspeslagh, et al., eds., *De aarde beheren: naar duurzame en ecologische veiligheid*, Assen + Maastricht: Van Gorcum, 1992, pp. 15–23.

56 'De VN hebben geen remedie tegen verdere verzieking van het milieu', *VN Forum*, No. 3/4, 1991, pp. 45–8.

57 'Internationale conferentie over milieu en ontwikkeling: in juni 1992 in Brazilie', *Internationale Samenwerking*, 5, October 1990, pp. 2–3.

58 'International Organization for Environmental Security', *Bulletin of Peace Proposals*, 20, No. 2, 1989, pp. 115–21.

59 'Veiligheid, milieu en de Verenigde Naties: het institutionele vervolg op UNCED', in *De aarde beheren*, pp. 73–90; 'Een Veiligheidsraad voor het milieu?', *VN Forum*, 5, No. 1, 1992, pp. 18–21.

60 'Internationaal milieurecht en de toekomst van het zeemilieu', in *De aarde beheren*, pp. 91–100.

61 'The Netherlands En Route for Rio: A Highly Industrialized Country's Position on Environment and Development', *Internationale Spectator*, 45, November 1991, pp. 718–22; 'Nederland op weg naar Rio', in *De aarde beheren*, pp. 25–32.

62 'Rio: flop of investering?', *Internationale Spectator*, 46, October 1992, pp. 585–90.

63 'The Decade of International Law: Idealist Dream or Realist Perspective?', *LJIL*, 3, 1990, p. 1.

64 'Het Internationaal Gerechtshof in 1991', *VN Forum*, 4, 1991, pp. 11–14.

65 A. Bloed and P. Van Kijk, eds., *Forty Years International Court of Justice: Jurisdiction, Equity and Equality*, Utrecht: Europa Instituut, 1988.

66 'Het ICJ: mogelijkheden en onmogelijkheden', *VN Forum*, 5, 1992, pp. 13–17.

67 'Een nieuwe rol voor het Internationale Gerechtshof?', *NJB*, 43, 5 December 1987, pp. 1390–3.

68 'Het conflict tussen Nicaragua en de VS en de rol van het Internationale Gerechtshof', *Transaktie*, 16, 1987, pp. 146–58.

69 'De International Law Commission', *VN Forum*, 3, 1990, pp. 23–6.

70 *Space Law in the United Nations*, Dordrecht: Nijhoff, 1985.

71 'Settlement of Space Law Disputes', in M. Brus, *et al.*, eds., *The United Nations Decade of International Law: Reflections on International Dispute Settlement*, Dordrecht: Nijhoff, 1991, pp. 139–55.

72 '1985 UNCITRAL Model Law on International Commercial Arbitration: An Exercise in International Legislation', *Netherlands Yearbook of International Law*, 18, Dordrecht: Nijhoff, 1991, pp. 3–67.

73 'Het zeerecht van de sterkste?', *VN Forum*, 1, 1988, pp. 26–30.

74 *The Regime for the Exploitation of Transboundary Marine Fisheries Resources – the United Nations Law of the Sea Convention – Cooperation between States*, Utrecht, 1989.

75 *The Decade of International Law*, Dordrecht: Martinus Nijhoff, 1990.

76 'Inter-state Dispute Settlement in the Field of Human Rights', pp. 87–98.

77 'Een decennium voor het internationale recht', *NJB*, 30 May 1991, pp. 899–902.

78 'Nederland en de totstandkoming van de VN-conventie tegen martelingen', *Internationale Spectator*, 41, November 1987, pp. 549–56.

79 'Veertug jaar Universele Verjklaring van de Rechten van de Mens: een Nederlandse bijdrage aan internationale normering', *Internationale Spectator*, 42, November 1988, pp. 696–702.

80 *Het Nederlands mensenrechtenbeleid in de Verenigde Naties*, Den Haag: T.M.C. Asser Instituut, 1992.

81 'Het Nederlandse VN-contingent in Libanon 1979–1985', *Militaire Spectator*, 158, September 1989, pp. 407–14.

82 'Het Nederlandse VN-contingent in Libanon 1979–1985 (2)', *Militaire Spectator*, 158, October 1989, pp. 448–57. See also H.J. Neuman, 'Wijziging van de Nederlandse bijdrage', VN te velde, Den Haag: NIW, 1980.

83 'De terugtrekking van het Nederlandse contingent uit UNIFIL', *Internationale Spectator*, 40, February 1986, pp. pp. 93–103.

84 'Nederland en de Veiligheidsraad van de Verenigde Naties', *Transaktie*, 15, 1986, pp. 15–24; 'Nederland en de VN: beginsel en praktijk', *VN Forum*, 1988, pp. 5–9.

85 'Nederland en het Internationale Jaar van de Vrede', *Internationale Spectator*, 40, March 1986, pp. 209–14.

86 'Nederland en het VN-verdrag inzake het recht van de zee', *Internationale Spectator*, 39, July 1985, pp. 425–34.

87 'De VN-Raad voor Namibie versus Urenco, UNC en de Staat der Nederlanden', *Internationale Spectator*, 41, December 1987, pp. 657–67; 'The UN Council for Namibia vs Urenco, UCN and the State of the Netherlands', *LJIL*, 1, 1988, pp. 25ff.

88 'The Dutch Role in the Security Council: Working Group 1', in *Peace and Security*, pp. 8–12.

89 M. Holleman, 'Nederland in de Veiligheidsraad: 1965–1966 en 1983–1984', *Internationale Spectator*, 40, July 1986, pp. 460–7.

90 'De Veiligheidsraad en het conflict in Midden-Amerika 1982–1984', *Internationale Spectator*, 39, June 1985, pp. 376–81.

91 'UNIFIL, Nederland en de rol van de Verenigde Naties in Libanon', *Internationale Spectator*, 39, May 1985, pp. 273–80.

92 'Sancties tegen Zuid-Afrika: Nederland in de Veiligheidsraad', *Internationale Spectator*, 39, April 1985, pp. 248–53.

93 'De nieuwe VN-drugsconventie: "the system works"', VN Forum, 2, July 1989, pp. 21–3.

94 'Jongeren en de VN: geen woorden maar daden', *VN Forum*, 1989, pp. 6–10.

95 'Vrouwenbeleid en de VN', *VN Forum*, 1990, pp. 16–19.

96 'Habitat 1987: over de plaats in het beleid voor een plek om te wonen', *Internationale Spectator*, 41, September 1987, pp. 441–7.

97 'VN-topconferentie zet kinderen bovenaan agenda van regeringen', *VN Forum*, Winter 1990/91, pp. 11–14.

98 R. Aspeslagh, ed., *De Verenigde Naties: is daar nog wel les over te geven?*, 's-Gravenhage: Nederlands Instituut voor Internationale Betrekkingen 'Clingendael', 1986.

99 N. Sybesma-Knol, 'De inspraak van NGOs in de VN', *VN Forum*, 1989, pp. 16–23.

100 'De VS en de VN', *Internationale Spectator*, 38, September 1984, pp. 544–53; 'De Verenigde Naties: Amerikaanse vertegenwoordigers', *Studia Diplomatica*, 38, 1985, pp. 747–67; 'Financiële problemen van de Verenigde Naties: Amerikaanse bijdrage ter discussie', *Internationale Spectator*, 40, May 1986, pp. 297–307; 'Het Amerikaanse leiderschap in de Verenigde Naties', *Internationale Spectator*, 43, March 1989, pp. 191–8; *Het Russische VN-beleid onder Gorbatsjov*, Den Haag: Nederlands Instituut voor Internationale Betrekkingen 'Clingendael', September 1989.

101 'Sovjetunie en de VN: "No more Mr. Nyet"', *VN Forum*, December 1988; pp. 21–24; 'Een nieuwe visie op de Verenigde Naties: het Russische beleid onder Gorbatsjov', in *De Verenigde Naties in beweging*, pp. 29–45.

102 'Eastern Europe and the United Nations', in P. De Klerk and L. Van Maare, eds., *Een kwestie van visie, opstellen over politiek, recht en cultuur: liber amicorum voor L.H.J.B. van Gorkom*, Maarssen + 's-Gravenhage: Gary Schwartz + SDU, 1990, pp. 129–44.

103 'De Europese Gemeenschappen in de algemene Vergadering van de Verenigde Naties in 1986', *Nieuw Europa*, 13, March 1987, pp. 17–20.

104 'Zwitserland en de Verenigde Naties', *Intermediair*, 22, 14 March 1986, pp. 155–57.

105 'Vijf-fasenplan voor de Palestijnse kwestie', *VN Forum*, 3, Winter 1990–91, pp. 21–3.

106 'Midden-Amerika, de VN en vrije verkiezingen', *VN Forum*, 2, 1989, pp. 6–9.

107 M. Couwenbergh and H. Siepel, 'Politisering in de Verenigde Naties'.

108 'International Organization for Environmental Security'.

109 'Veiligheid, milieu en de Verenigde Naties'; 'Een Veiligheidsraad voor het milieu?'

110 Kooijmans, 'Human Rights – Introduction'.

111 Baehr, 'Commentaar: waarnemen bij de Verenigde Naties', *Internationale Spectator*, 42, June 1988, pp. 395–6; E.H. Braam, 'Comentaar: parels voor de zwijnen?', p. 395; Leurdijk, 'Commentaar: niet-ambtelijke pottekijkers', *Internationale Spectator*, 42, August 1988, pp. 510–11; Kaufmann, 'Respons: over het nut van niet-ambtelijke conferentiegangers', *Internatonale Spectator*, 43, April 1989, pp. 272–3.

112 M. Nowak, 'Country-oriented Human Rights Protection by the UN Commission on Human Rights and its Subcommission', *Netherlands Yearbook of International Law* (1991), pp. 39–90.

7
Scholarly Work on Multilateralism in Hungary

Károly Nyíri

The idea of multilateralism does not have very deep roots in Hungary. History shows that the Hungarian people and their leaders do not like order forced on them from the outside. This means that Hungarian thinking tended to be unilateral- or autonomy-minded in matters of power and politics for centuries. Democratic thinking was traditionally far from Hungarian society, and it would seem that multilateralism needs a high sense of democracy, not only in theory, but especially in practice.

In her 1100-year history, Hungary never happened to be in an alliance *where she would have realized that common rules serve her interests in the same way as those of others.* This is true even in the case of the 1867 Treaty with Austria, when the Austro-Hungarian kingdom was formed, or in the case of the Warsaw Pact and the CMEA (COMECON) after the Second World War. The lack of a sense of compromise could have been the reason Hungary was never a founding member in very important international organizations like the League of Nations or the United Nations, witnessing the period during which multilateralism began on a substantial scale. The Warsaw Pact and CMEA can be easily set aside because of special circumstances where the voluntary nature of participation can at least be questioned.

Hungary's connections with multilateralism really began only in the 1950s, when she was accepted as a member of the United Nations following a long and controversial admissions procedure.

About sources and authors

The literature on international organizations and multilateralism is not a very rich one in Hungary. The reasons for this are complex. Matters concerning international organizations, like those connected with foreign affairs generally, have often been handled as top secret, or at least as matters that concern a narrow circle of experts only. Materials pertaining to international organizations were circulated among these experts and were kept in the archives, sometimes very rich and well organized 'libraries', of ministries in charge of the given topic. The publication of books and articles about the United Nations and other international organizations was started only in the mid 1970s, and emerged during the 1980s on a greater scale, when relevant questions and problems came to be regarded as public. Because of these circumstances, the authors of books and articles, almost without exception, were initially the experts of ministries and other state organizations which dealt with multilateralism and who served as representatives in different international organizations, mainly in UN bodies.

General views on multilateralism

Notwithstanding the fact that multilateral thinking came late to Hungary, there were and are scholars well aware of the specific features of multilateralism, its pros and contras. One of the most well-known scholars was the late János Nyerges.[1] In his book *The Battlefield of the Gaming Table*, he observed that

> [m]ultilateral negotiations have become a general part of the recent life of interstate relations. The method of multilateral negotiations created a new institutional network, a new framework, too: that of international organizations. These provide nowadays the frame, the stage, on which international relations play a role in politics, military affairs, economy and culture. This state of affairs feeds back onto bilateral negotiations.[2]

Later this author summarizes the most important features of multilateralism (multilateral negotiations) as a) the precedent; b) 'the division of the booty'; c) the simultaneous game; d) conflict-solving and group interests; e) forms and procedures; f) institutional forms. Nyerges provides a full picture of multilateral negotiations, highlighting the main features and the advantages. This book could be (and really was for a while) the textbook of multilateralism.

Views about the United Nations system

a. General opinions of Hungarian experts

Among the not very numerous Hungarian publications about the United Nations, an important place is filled by two books edited by Professor Mihály Simai.[3] He introduces the earlier book with a question: 'Is it important and worthwhile that the UN, its central and specialized institutions, deal with crucial global problems, even though this organizational system is such that resolutions are not compulsory and the possibilities are very limited for fulfilling these resolutions?' His positive response bears extended quotation:

> Firstly, . . . it is a very difficult task to seek and find common interests in the conflicting system of values of the different countries. The UNO has already served mankind greatly by helping to determine such common interests. Secondly, the participating states, . . . member countries of the UNO, feel and value the great questions of our era above all on the bases of their own respective situations, their internal economic troubles and social problems, and how these surface to cause collisions. In the fora of the United Nations this given helps member countries to measure the real possibilities of their own endeavors and to change their aims and plans accordingly. This process is often accompanied by 'painful' experiences, experiences difficult to accept. . . . Thirdly, the World Organization helps the governments of all member countries by discovering the essence, the causes and consequences of the great international problems, because its functioning makes possible not only the deeper, better and more complex realization of these problems, but also the forecasting of expectable troubles, as well. Fourthly, the United Nations Organization can help to organize world programs that can further ease the great problems and worries of mankind. . . . The government and public of the Hungarian People's Republic appreciate the activity of the United Nations Organization in helping peaceful coexistence and international cooperation.

In the later book edited by Professor Simai, Mátyás Domokos evaluates the UN's role from the Hungarian point of view in 'The significance of our membership in the United Nations Organization'.[4] Hungary became a full member of the UN only in 1955, ten years after its founding. The reasons were connected mainly with the cold war: the US and their allies regarded Hungary as a non-sovereign country because of its close relationship to the Soviet Union. Because of the long acceptance procedure

– Hungary applied for membership back in 1947 – this goal became a very dear one for the Hungarian state and public. With respect to these hopes, Domokos observes that

> International organizations offer opportunities in several forms for the fulfillment of national goals, be these political, economic or otherwise in character. In connection with Hungary's membership in the UNO, and with the rights, opportunities and obligations stemming from this, it is necessary to deny the misbelief that international organizations can solve, ipso facto, the problems of the world quickly and durably.... For these 'expectations' do not take into consideration that *the international organizations cannot do more than what is decided by their member countries, the fulfilment of which depends upon their sovereign wills. The preference for national decisions over collective actions is a reality of our era, with which we will have to calculate for a long time.* Notwithstanding all of this, the UN system offers advantages which stimulate countries to join it.

b. Hungarian views about the future of the United Nations

Mihály Simai considers the future of the United Nations.[5] In 'Changes forming the future of the United Nations', he puts this question at the outset: 'Is the UN obsolete?' and continues:

> [T]here are many who [conclude] that the UN could not fulfill its aims, or could do so only to a very limited extent. Among critics are politicians who say that its framework and instruments are obsolete without any question. Others, criticizing the UNO, say that international conflicts, because of their character and intensity, fall outside the framework. Thus this organization became unable to fulfill its tasks.... Nevertheless, it would be a great mistake to 'write off' the UN. It reached an age double that of its predecessor, the League of Nations, upon its 40th anniversary. And though the longer life is not necessarily a proof of efficiency, the balance of activity of the organization is not a negative one.... Despite all the problems, the United Nations Organization survives.

Why has the UN survived?

- The cold war made necessary the permanent activity of the Security Council and generally the 'high political' role of the UN.

- The democratic principles and practice of the UN were and are the only viable methods to handle world problems.
- '*Global problems*' appeared and proved susceptible to treatment only on a global plane.
- The United Nations remained the only global organization able to offer machinery for use by the countries of the entire world, and this machinery can be used relatively quickly and efficiently if the need arises. No other bilateral or multilateral organization was formed that could replace the UN.

Simai offers some propositions as to how to improve the work of the UN:

- Coordination within the UN system must be significantly improved. Superfluous and unnecessary overlapping and parallelism must be eliminated.
- When certain resolutions are approved by the General Assembly, it is necessary to decide clearly which specialized agency of the UN will be responsible for the implementation of the given projects or tasks. An organization should be created in the UN system which is able to control and evaluate the activity of every given UN organ, and the whole system as such.
- The operation of the Secretariat of the United Nations should be improved, including the quality of the secretarial work. To enable the UN to play a more important role in the world, it is necessary to eliminate bureaucratism in the organization.
- The substance of the work of the United Nations must be altered in several fields. While keeping the properly developed priorities like disarmament, limitation of the arms race, the creation of a new, more regulated and more democratic world economic order, and the solving of crucial global problems, it should also be a central and important task to make forecasts about development problems and crises of world politics and the world economy.

This evaluation about the endurance and the future of the United Nations was quite apt at the time of its writing. Nevertheless, by 1992 the world had changed significantly, and these changes, first of all the change of power relations between the two superpowers, the US and the USSR, made an important impact on the UN, too. Consider the future role of the United Nations within the new world situation.

In 1990 the 'socialist world system' ceased to exist, and in 1991 even the Soviet Union disappeared as such. This began to trigger important and previously inconceivable consequences in the life and operation of the United Nations:

- Already by 1990, as a result of the weakening of the USSR, it became possible to accept a resolution in the Security Council which expressed 'universal interest' but really meant the interests of the US and the 'Free World'. This was the resolution against Iraq after her aggression against Kuwait, on the basis of which the US and allied western nations successfully fulfilled their military 'Operation Desert Storm' in 1991. The approval of the western sanctions against Iraq by the Soviet Union in the Security Council proved that the USSR had finished with its communist, 'anti-imperialist' ideology, and saw the beginning of a historically new era in the UN. The Yugoslavian crisis further defined the emerging era by demonstrating Russian collaboration as well as its limits.

One might think that the 'happy days of the UN are here again', because the founding members of the UN, notably the US and Russia, could agree upon all the important problems of the world because of the disappearance of ideological and political differences between the two superpowers, or more accurately, because of the disappearance of the USSR.

But life will not be so beautiful. Conflicts of new character and origin will arise, not only between past enemies, but among past and recent allied nations as well. It will be so because *for half a century the threat of communism was the main element of cohesion among non-communist countries, and the chief instrument of leadership in the hands of the US, the main 'locomotive' of political and economic integration in the West.* Yet herein lies paradox. *Precisely because of the momentous change, the role of the UNO as a multilateral forum for the arrangement of international disputes and conflicts, for the meeting of global problems, will not decrease, but increase in the future.*

c. Regional organizations: the Economic Commission for Europe

For Hungary, being a European country, the most important regional organization of the UN system has been the Economic Commission for Europe. This is especially so because Hungary became a member of the ECE in 1947, long before becoming a full member of the UN. As János Szita explains in his *Horizons of the All-European Economic Cooperation*:[6]

The Economic Commission for Europe…deserves special attention among the European economic cooperation institutions. This is the only European international organization where there is continuous and many-sided cooperation among the countries of the Continent on the governmental level.

Professor Szita advances critical comments on the activity of the ECE in terms of organization, performance and politics. He also makes several suggestions to improve the work of ECE.[7] In essence these proposals are as follows: more independence for the ECE; concentration on the problems of East–West economic relations; special emphasis on common regional problems (environmental protection, for instance); the *solution* of concrete economic problems, and not merely the formulating of recommendations; integration of the ECE to global UN projects; clarification of the position and the ways of cooperation between ECE and the emerging union of European institutions.

This book was chosen from several possible ones in order to express Hungarian opinion about the ECE. The brief review shows how old some issues are relative to the reform of the UN system, even if some of them have an entirely different meaning today after the systemic changes in eastern Europe.

d. Specialized agencies of the UN system – Hungarian participation and valuation

As mentioned above, Hungary, having been a medium-developed small country, was objectively very much interested in being a member of multilateral international organizations, particularly the specialized agencies. Hungary has joined all the important specialized agencies of the United Nations, or takes part in their work. Hungary was a full member in some of these organizations long before becoming a member of the UN. It is impossible to deal with all these organizations here, so we mention only the most important examples.

UNESCO

Hungary became a cooperating partner of UNESCO in 1947 and since then has been an active participant in its work, surely the reason why Hungarian literature on UNESCO is relatively rich.

The Forty Year Old UNESCO and Hungary[8] provides a fairly good evaluation of UNESCO. Professor Béla Köpeczi[9] lauds the agency as a universal organization of scientific, educational and cultural cooperation that fulfills a great task in the development of international relations in the fields of science and education, has done a lot in the interest of the cultural progress of developing countries, and has helped the intellectuals of the world to meet each other.[10]

WHO

Professor Imre Hutás writes approvingly of the World Health Organization:[11]

The most spectacular achievement of the four-decade activity of WHO was the world-wide abolition of smallpox. There were other, less spectacular results, in consequence of which the population of the world became more healthy. This achievement was due to the purposeful international controlling and coordinating activity of WHO. WHO announced such principles in its health strategy, which basically changed the ideas about health care compared with previous ones. WHO consistently proclaimed that in our era public health care cannot be carried out by isolated small units which are independent from each other and different in principles and practice, but only by health systems on the national and regional levels, in which systems the preventive, prophylactic activity is at least as important as the medicative one. Health systems must be operated on the basis of well determined, realistic plans.... WHO initiated the 'basic needs oriented' principles in public health and physician education and training. By these principles, WHO created the new foundations of the planning and training of health personnel.... The activity of the World Health Organization cannot be easily measured only by figures and data, but we surely can say that it fulfilled and fulfills such a role...which significantly contributes to the creation of a more just world order.

FAO

FAO was founded in 1945, but Hungary became a member only in the early 1960s. Hungary's participation in the work of FAO is not related to FAO's main task – the easing or solution of the world's food problems – but with other activities, namely standards of the agriculture and food industry, water-economy, and recommendations for more efficient use of agricultural resources. Since agriculture always has been and remains a very important sector of the Hungarian economy, the recommendations of FAO looking toward more efficient agricultural and food industries were welcomed. One of the most important forms of Hungary's cooperation with FAO is the creation and operation of so-called 'model plants' in farming and animal husbandry in order to help developing countries use similar methods. All Hungarian works about FAO emphasize the practical benefits of participating in its work.[12]

Evaluations of multilateralism and the UNO after the systemic change in Hungary

As has been stressed throughout this chapter, official Hungary greatly appreciated the United Nations and its specialized organizations after the Second World War, especially during the Kádár era. This esteem arose partly because Hungary's participation meant international acknowledgment of the regime, and partly because the country badly needed the international cooperation that was denied her bilaterally for a long time. How have things evolved since 1990, since the former political, social and economic system has been changed?

a. In the programmes of the parties within the Hungarian Parliament

A snapshot of domestic politics serves as background to change. In the free elections in May 1990, six parties gained enough votes to get into Parliament. Ranked by number of seats, these were the Forum of Hungarian Democrats (FHD), Union of Free Democrats (UFD), Union of Young Democrats (UYD), Hungarian Socialist Party (HSP – one of the successors of the split former ruling party), Independent Small-Owner, Farmer and Civic Party (ISOFCP), and Christian Democratic Peoples Party (CDPP).

Thorough study of these parties' programmes yields the following picture. The program of FHD (the strongest party of the governing coalition) makes many references to international organizations, to the will for integration, and to the EC, though UNO is not mentioned. The programme of the UFD (the second strongest party in the Parliament, but recently in opposition) stresses the importance of international law, of the EC and international organizations, but makes no direct reference to UNO. Nothing about multilateralism appears in the programme of UYD except a sentence about international human rights. The programme of HSP contains a lot about international organizations and the UN, since this party is the successor of the former state-ruling party, and the 'international relations' chapter was ever a compulsory part of official party documents. In ISOFCP's 'Program of the National Revival' there are many references to international institutions, but mainly very short ones, the mention of different international organizations without detailed policy options. CDPP has no comprehensive programme, but offers booklets on different topics (education, health, agriculture and so on). There is not a word about multilateralism or international organizations in any of them.

We might observe that these parties, with the exception of HSP, were not in power at the time of the declaration of their programmes, which might be the reason for their relative ignorance of the importance of international organizations, above all the United Nations. It is worth adding, however, that all the parties in the Parliament regard the relationship and cooperation with the evolving community of Europe as being very important. Is this just pragmatism, or a sign of devaluation of the UN system?

b　In the statements of politicians, academics and experts

As mentioned earlier, the Gulf War was a very important event in the history of the United Nations. In March 1991, a Round Table on Security Policy and Defence Research was held in Budapest for Hungarian researchers. The question of the role of the UN was raised. One part of opinion reflected satisfaction and hope: the time has come when the UN can operate really efficiently in the solution of world conflicts as the result of consensus of the world powers.

Surprisingly, experts (mainly in international law) near the new political parties in the government and in the opposition expressed different views, as follows.

The United Nations, and first of all the Security Council, was always an instrument in the hands of the superpowers to enforce their wills upon the small nations. In the time when there was systemic contradiction among the representatives of the two systems, especially from the mid 1970s, some space for manoeuvring was available for the smaller countries of the world. The preparation and operation of the Gulf War raises the fear that through the United Nations the great powers can arrange any crisis in the different regions of the world against the national interests of small or medium-sized countries.

The phrase 'national interests' bears emphasis. During the past few years in Hungary this is the expression most commonly used by politicians of all parties and by the media. The reasons are complex: it might be the aftermath of the four decades of Soviet occupation, the long-lasting traditions of Hungarian nationalism, or the fact that masses of the people were prompted to back the changing of the system by nationalist slogans and the promise of a rich 'European' Hungary.

Negative opinions such as these above are quite widespread in different publications and statements. Many think that Hungary's problems must be solved by European institutions, first of all by the help of Germany and of the European Union. Those who regard the UN's role and importance as a decreasing one seemingly got ammunition from the argument that early on the EC played a greater role in the Yugoslav crisis than did the UN.

According to some analysts, this tendency against multilateralism can be related to the influence of those politicians and historians who think that the isolationist policy of Admiral Horthy between 1924 and 1940 would be a good example for a conservative Hungary. But notwithstanding opinions to the contrary, official government statements and actions prove that Hungary still regards the UN as a very important organization in terms of its practical role in the world.

Summary

This review of the Hungarian literature and viewpoints about multilateralism and the United Nations system seeks to present and analyze as much information about the topic as is possible in the given framework. The exercise provides a basis for drawing some conclusions. Synthesis of Hungarian opinion presents a picture in which the United Nations system, and generally the role of international organizations, is a positive one. This affirmative evaluation was stronger in the mid 1970s and 1980s, becoming more controversial at the beginning of the 1990s. The situation after the end of the 'Communist World System' is really quite a new one, simpler and more complicated at the same time. In any event, Hungarian opinion continues to reflect that the UN will play an important role in our rapidly changing world.

Notes

1　Dr. Nyerges was a public official and scholar. As a younger official of the Ministry of Trade, he accompanied Count Mihály Károlyi to Geneva when the talks on the accession of Hungary to the UN Economic Commission for Europe were going on in 1947. Later, he headed the department responsible for international organization in the Ministry for Foreign Trade and served as Special Envoy of Hungary to the International Economic Organizations until his retirement in 1986.

2　*Zöldposztós csatatér-A nemzetközi tárgyalások anatómiája* [*The Battlefield of the Gaming Table: The Anatomy of International Negotiations*], Budapest: Gondolat Kiadó, 1985.

3 Mihály Simai is an economist, member of the Hungarian Academy of Sciences, and university professor. He was general director of the Institute of World Economy of the Hungarian Academy of Sciences. Earlier he served in the Secretariat of the United Nations in New York. More recently he has been Chairman of the Council of the United Nations University. His earlier edited work is *Az ENSZ és a világproblémák* [*The UNO and the Global Problems*], Budapest: Kossuth Köbtvjuadó, 1977.

4 'ENSZ tagságunk jelentósége', in Simai, ed., *Az ENSZ napjainkban* [*The UNO in Our Days*], Budapest: Kossuth Könyvkiadó, 1985, pp. 81–100. Domokos is an economist, a career official in the Ministry for Foreign Trade and the Ministry for Foreign Affairs, and former Ambassador of Hungary to the UN in Geneva and in the United Kingdom.

5 Simai, 'Az ENSZ jövöjét formáló változások', in Simai, ed., *Az ENSZ napjainkban*, pp. 17–44.

6 *Az összeurópai gazdasági együttmúködés távlatai*, Budapest: Kossuth Könyvkiadó, 1975. Szita is a career diplomat of the Ministry for Foreign Affairs, former Ambassador of Hungary to the UNO in Geneva, in the United Kingdom, and in Italy. He has also served as honorary scientific counsellor in the Institute of World Economy of the H.A.S.

7 *Ibid.*, pp. 331–2.

8 Salgó Lászlóné, *A 40 éves UNESCO és Magyarország*, Budapest: Hungarian UNESCO Commission, 1986.

9 Academician, then Minister of Education of Hungary, former Secretary-General of the Hungarian Academy of Sciences and world-renowned historian.

10 *A 40 éves UNESCO és Magyarország*, Introduction, pp. 5–7.

11 Member of the Hungarian Academy of Sciences, ex-Secretary of State in the Ministry of Health. 'Az egészségügyi együttmúködés globális rendszere [The Global System of Public Health Cooperation]', in Simai, 1985, pp. 211–29.

12 See Lipovecz Iván, 'Az ENSZ és a világélelmezési gondok [The UNO and the World Food Problems]', in Simai, 1977, pp. 169–90.

8
Latin American Views of International Law Principles and the United Nations System

Alberto Cisneros-Lavaller*

Introduction

The main object of this chapter is to review the contemporary Latin American literature – in its most representative trends and lines of thought – that has addressed the United Nations as a system or analyzed international principles of certain importance during the last two decades. It examines the work of many authors who have studied such a field, conceived in the broadest sense. However, since Latin American literature pertaining to the subject has been so rich from the very beginning of the existence of these countries, not to mention the beginnings of modern international organization, it would be almost inexcusable not to consider initially the general principles and foundations of the core literature that engendered what could be recognized as a 'Latin American International Law' before surveying the most modern schools of thought. To understand Latin American approaches to multilateralism, one must understand Latin American approaches to international law.

Origins

An International Law for the Americas has been evolving since the beginning of the nineteenth century. Its rules and principles were established at the birth of the states of the Americas as independent nations, therefore it is linked to their freedom. These countries faced the need to adapt themselves to some norms that were universal (to a general international law), but also they proclaimed as a vital principle their right to

* I wish to thank Lic. Nora Fischbach for her assistance in bibliographic compilation as well as preparation of several parts of this chapter.

be free – acquired through liberation movements – and sought to offset the unequal status in which they were placed by the prevailing international law as a consequence of the wars for independence. Thus, they contended that their fights against colonial powers were truly international wars instead of rebellions. They also declared the illegitimacy of European intervention in the area, and the unlawfulness of territorial acquisition in the Americas by mere occupation. In order to deter future intentions or avoid future conquest, they also reaffirmed the inexistence of *res nullius* territories through the application of the *uti possidetis iuris* rule, formulated as early as 1810, with which they established the boundaries of the new states, coinciding with those of the administrative divisions of the colonial era.

Without doubt, the International Law of the Americas had its origins in Spain during the sixteenth century. It probably had its foundations in the thought of Francisco de Vitoria, who rejected the justification for the Spanish conquest of the Americas. The existence of a truly American International Law is based on the thesis that in this continent there has arisen a set of problems, and in turn a set of rules, which are both proper and different from those of Europe. Together these rules constituted a law structured in and for the area.

When the states of the Americas became independent, the first rules proclaimed were: (a) the right to affirm their independence; (b) non-intervention; and (c) non-acquisition of territories by mere occupation. Thus American International Law was born by adopting principles that contradicted those of general international law.

Though independence was a major theme, other developments foreshadowed the coalescing of independent states in organized efforts. Several states entered bilateral treaties of friendship and alliance during the 1820s. Pan-Americanism is an ideal with which the peoples of the new states greeted their independence. Bolivar, for instance, spoke as early as 1815 of the need to constitute an Inter-American Congress. He insisted on this innovation upon several occasions thereafter.

One of the most important events in the development of American International Law was the Congress of 1826. Several American states' representatives met to pass resolutions and prepare the Treaty of Union and League of Perpetual Confederation with which the Congress concluded. This pact had as its main goal the sovereignty and independence of American states. From this Congress in particular emerged the most important principles of American Law: a) good offices, negotiation and mediation as means to achieve the peaceful resolution of conflicts; b) abhorrence of war; c) condemnation of conquest; d) solidarity in

defence against a foreign aggressor, or collective self-defence; e) collective security; and f) territorial integrity. At the same time, other principles, such as the egalitarian status of nation-states and the *uti possidetis
iuris* rule, were also foregone conclusions of that Congress.

Other Inter-American congresses took place. They contributed to the
establishment of a continental international conscience as well as a
body of law to meet particular American needs. After 1889, these congresses' contributions became more efficient and concrete. For instance,
in line with the inclination against belligerency, Drago inspired the
doctrine that carries his name, a doctrine establishing the illegitimacy
of the use of force in trying to compel the payment of debts. Hence
public debts could not legitimately serve as the impetus for foreign
armed intervention. The Drago doctrine was first invoked by Argentina
upon the occasion of acts of force perpetrated by European powers in
1902. Later the doctrine became a cornerstone of international law
when accepted by participants at the Second Peace Conference in The
Hague during 1907.

The assertion that such principles comprised an American International Law was advanced by some authors. Strong debates occurred with
the publication of one of the works of Carlos Calvo called *El Derecho
Internacional: Teorico y Practico* (International Law: Theory and Practice).[1]
But Amancio Alcorte in particular criticized Calvo on the issue of
whether American International Law is peculiar or universal.

At the first Pan-American Scientific Congress, held in Santiago, Chile,
in 1908, the debate re-emerged due to a study introduced by Alejandro
Alvarez. He expounded and justified the roots of American International
Law by advancing two basic arguments: a) the existence of peculiar
problems in America (not applicable to Europe) on which these countries have ruled, *or* the existence of problems of a general nature and
character, with no international agreement upon them; b) the existence
in Europe of general problems and situations that do not apply to the
American domain. The Brazilian delegate, Sa Vianna (Professor at the
University of Rio de Janeiro), aired his disagreement, contending that
one cannot speak about the existence of an American International Law,
only of principles that were born in America and that could contribute
to building up the general body of international law.

Recent writings in review

One may infer from the preceding exposition that in Latin America,
international law underpins the study of multilateralism. Moreover,

'Latin American International Law' has given rise to a number of principles and practices found in the UN Charter and elsewhere in organized international life. Now I focus explicitly upon representative trends and their exemplars from the 1970s onward. With the intention of shedding light upon this very broad area, writings are classified in categories. I identify and comment upon the following: theory and methodgy; cooperation and global dimensions; Latin America as a continent; Central America as a Peace Zone; community development; and teaching and research.

a. Theory and methodology

A number of studies exhibit a Latin American viewpoint in considering issues of a theoretical nature. For instance, in his *Malvinas y Regimen Internacional* (*Malvinas and the International System*), Juan Carlos Puig uses that conflict to analyze the structure and functioning of the international system.[2] With regard to the functioning of the global system, the author discerns two different and contending approaches: the *atomism* and the *international community law* theories. According to atomism, states are the key actors of international politics, and they become more significant as their power increases. This approach favours the predominance of the great powers in the international system.

The international community law theory suggests a different interpretation. It implies that international interactions should be determined by certain general principles which in turn pave the road to rules of law governing all international relations.

Puig concludes that neither of the two is completely adequate. Atomism fails because it merely reflects the reality of international structures that belonged to the nineteenth century and does not correspond with current reality. The other theory also falls short because it represents only a legal perspective, essentially a normative one, leaving aside the examining of social reality.

The book's main contention is based upon a study of the international system that properly assesses the real structure and functioning of the whole system through a comprehensive analysis of international community law within three dimensions: norm, social reality and justice. This thesis provides grounds for a framework that coherently amalgamates in the analysis not only the legal approach but also that of international politics. Such a comprehensive framework is utilized to stress the main criteria that govern the international community. Puig offers the view that these desiderata could help in the formulation of policies and strategies that will be functional to current international structures.

In a less recent work, *Doctrinas Internacionales y Autonomia Latinoamericana (International Doctrines and Latin American Autonomy)*, Puig offers a thorough analysis of international law and international relations for the last third of this century.[3] His work shows the deep transformation undergone by the international system and its growing and definite aspiration to consolidate justice on a global scale.

His work is divided into two sections. In the first, he synthesizes the most fashionable doctrines of international law, pinpointing accomplishments as well as failures, and confronting the latter with the virtues of triangulation: norm, social reality and justice. This section deals more with what international law 'should be' than with what it 'is'. The second part of his work focuses on the theories that relate to international relations, with its main characteristics, downfalls and the like. This concludes with a theoretical framework that frames the current international arena in accordance with the 'atomist' requirements of Latin American countries.

The study also exhibits different approaches taken by diverse specialists such as lawyers, political scientists, practitioners, decisionmakers and Latin American politicians. They are constantly, in international fora as well as in the formulation of their own countries' foreign policies, looking for gradual and progressive increments of political space, that is for authentic independence from the big powers.

b. Cooperation and global dimensions

Other Latin American authors concentrate on large problems or global aspects of international institutions. This is the case with L. Valencia Rodriguez, who in a retrospective of international cooperation reviews its different historical stages with the idea of comparing diverse processes that took place in international conferences leading to the shaping of international organizations with more permanent goals and more general competence in nature and scope.[4] These developments and processes, according to Valencia Rodriguez, forced the review of the essence of some traditional concepts and ideas, such as that of state sovereignty. The discourse and debate that the author portrays is linked to the analysis and recommendations suggested by the Special Committee on Principles of International Law. With these principles in mind, he analyzes friendly relations and cooperation among states.

In another comprehensive perspective, Simon Alberto Consalvi analyzes the confrontation between the US and the USSR. His 1988 work is entitled *La Paz nuclear: Ensayos de Historia Contemporanea (Nuclear Peace: Essays in Contemporary History)*.[5] The author singles out a Latin American viewpoint on global problems.

c. Latin America as a continent

Other works hold Latin America as their main focus for analysis. Cisneros-Lavaller examines Latin American conflict and cooperation.[6] He contends, among other hypotheses, that the states of Latin America need to consolidate their independence from the big powers at the economic as well as the politico-diplomatic level.

In his *Un Momento Historico de America Latina* (A Historical Time for Latin America), Colsalvi summarizes the origins and birth of the Permanent Mechanism for Consultation and Political Convergence advanced by Latin American nations.[7] The author finds that the Mechanism has been working positively for integration, cultural and scientific exchange, education, and regional 'dialogue', all of these important elements toward the unity of Latin America and the Caribbean. Moreover, this instrument is seen as an adequate response awaiting diverse challenges that Latin America may be facing during the next decade.

Jimenez de Arechaga analyzes the phenomenon of collective security for Latin America and how this is linked to the UN system.[8] Tackling a similar problem, A. Linares concentrates on the study of the project sponsored by the USSR at the 31st UN General Assembly session regarding no use of force in international relations and the peaceful solution of disputes.[9] Hector Gross Espiell links collective security in Latin America with the signature of the Tlatololco Treaty for non-nuclear proliferation in the area.[10] And finally, Zelaya Coronado, former Deputy Secretary-General of OAS, emphasizes the coordination between the regional and global security systems as exhibited by the OAS and the UN in order to enhance the peaceful solution of conflicts.[11]

d. Central America as a peace zone

Other writings follow a subregional focus. Assessing the strategic value for international cooperation and peace that Central America and the Caribbean have as regional enclaves, Fabio Castillo and Ariel Soto investigate these areas using an interdisciplinary approach.[12] Theirs is an attempt to relate harmonious regional development to international legal instruments by analyzing the characteristics and political implications for peace of the subregion. The working proposition they expound from the outset is that Central America and the Caribbean should be considered transit areas, a characterization that will positively influence economic, political and military relations that the subregion is fostering with other nations outside the area. The principal actors that would use this transit zone would try to establish, according to their interests, symmetrical relations with the subregional countries in order to guarantee the peaceful existence of these commercial routes. Castillo and Soto conclude that all states located in the area should declare the region a Peace Zone in order to bring about greater cooperation for the whole area.

e. Community development

With respect to substantive scope, community development deserves inclusion because it is closely linked to efforts of international institutions to solve problems specific to Latin America. Ezequiel Ander-Egg, for instance, concentrates on the analysis of social reality in Latin America, using for this purpose the method of observation.[13] His efforts focus on domination structures imposed upon less developed countries. His book seeks to provide a response to these challenges since the structures of domination can have a negative impact, offsetting the progress of development in Latin American countries.

This author singles out the need to build new models and techniques to study community development in order to achieve the effective participation of marginal social strata of the population in developmental processes. The traditional approach of integration-marginality-development has failed, according to his assessment. Therefore, new ideas such as the ones spelled out by UN documents could shed new light on how to confront the problem of community development. His work is an effort to collect, systematize and arrange the main works of the UN related to the subject of community development, works that approach this problem for analysis on local or regional as well as global levels.

f. Teaching and research

Some interesting Latin America writings analyze questions on international organization by emphasizing current problems of teaching and research. Among them, Gross Espiell might be cited.[14] He grapples with the problem of teaching public international law in Latin America. As a personal witness, he evaluates as poor the quality of teaching of this subject.

His main argument contends that there is a need to enrich the traditional approach with international reality. So, beyond the analysis of international uses, traditional bibliographical sources, unilateral deeds with international impact, jurisprudence, and general principles of the

Gentry Law, public international law badly needs studies on the historical framework, the geopolitical as well as the political context, and the global reality within which law is applied.

According to his perspective, the teaching of international law should take into account the new realities that comprise a 'New International Law' while comparing it with the traditional approach. In its 'modern approach', international law should include the principles upon which this law is based, such as peace, security, solidarity, and also dimensions with political, economic, social, cultural and human content. The non-centralized character of the current international community, the absence of coalitions to sanction violations of law, the elements that operate as regulators of the rights and duties of actors of different character – among which the state prevails – are among the most important factors that should be taken into account when teaching international law.

Finally, Gross Espiell stresses that international normativity ought to be studied in relation to the criteria of efficiency and effectiveness. Thus it is also necessary to engage in an active, realistic, critical and polemical type of teaching that will confront ideas with a sense of progress, normativity and reality.

Another work worthy of inclusion is the proceedings of The Third Seminar on the Teaching of International Law that was held in Mexico City in April 1986,[15] which emphasize the obstacles in teaching international law. Guidance on epistemological issues and methodology are offered.

Other authors concentrate on regional or country analysis of international law teaching and research. Puig focuses on the cases of Venezuela and Mexico, in so doing compiling a number of efforts to teach and research this subject.[16] His work is a contemporary bibliographical endeavor of Latin American *pensa* about the study of international public law. It offers a critical analysis and suggestions for eventual reform and the betterment of programs.

Alberto Szekely, to the contrary, concentrates on how international law is taught in Mexico within its national context.[17] His work offers a critical appraisal of the teaching of the subject in that country. He intends to arouse a debate among Mexican and Latin American international lawyers with respect to the challenges they should confront and solve in order to enhance the quality of teaching international law.

Other works deal specifically with research. This describes *El Sistema Interamericano y su Futuro Plan de Investigacion (The Interamerican System and its Research Plan).*[18] It develops a detailed plan for research by members of the OAS staff, particularly those who work in the legal department of this international organization. The research plan looks to bridge the gap between everyday routine work and academic theory. It provides guidance for researching several subjects in the short and long term, and also suggests the necessary steps for research development. With its threefold aim, the work reviews the literature, explains research planning, and organizes and provides a sense of direction for investigating the main subjects concerning the Inter-American System and the OAS.

In the first section, the bibliographical review concentrates on the subjects that have been considered priorities by the academy. It also focuses on those subjects that have been neglected by the scholarly community and reviews the main trends of research.

The second part relates to the designing of research topics in conjunction with the flaws identified by the bibliographical review of the first section. An effort is made to systematize problems and questions hierarchically. Thus some sense of priority among research projects is conveyed. The preferred context for research is also indicated, for instance whether in a regional or a global perspective.

Finally, this work points out that research effectiveness in the Washington area largely depends on being linked to the local academic community. Thus improvement in relations between international bureaucrats and scholars is badly needed.

Concluding remarks

How do Latin American scholars view international principles and the UN system? The following observations are necessarily but not exclusively the most important with which to begin.

Firstly, the approaches that dominate in this area are those which relate to legal matters more than societal matters. This means that Latin Americans seem to be more concerned with the 'should be' of international relations than with 'what is'.

Secondly, few current works analyze the UN system from a political science or international relations viewpoint.

Thirdly, the problems that afflict Latin America are those upon which they act (this is natural, of course) without considering global or world order problems very much. However, it seems that contemporary efforts are not as important as were the endeavours of earlier times following independence when Latin Americans were able to forge important doctrines that helped build up the general body of international law.

Fourthly, Latin Americans are preoccupied with bridging the gap between teaching and research. They want to improve both from a Latin American point of view, yet they depend on the US for research and development to a large extent.

Finally, there is a keen interest in enriching their analysis with socio-political reality. It seems they know what they lack, are debating the incorporation of these contents in the mainstream of the subject, but still lack a contemporary assessment of their own to make a contribution that could on a worldwide basis be regarded commensurate with what they had contributed by the turn of the last century.

Notes

1   Buenos Aires, 1943.
2   Buenos Aires: Depalma Editores, 1983.
3   Caracas: Univ. Simon Bolivar, 1980.
4   *Fundamentos y Propositos de las Naciones Unidas*, Quito: Editorial Universitaria, 1970.
5   Caracas: Monteavila, 1988.
6   *America Latina Conflicto o Cooperacion*, Caracas: Editorial Proimagen, 1986.
7   Caracas: Ed. Pomaire, 1988.
8   In *Primeras Jornadas Latinoamericanas de Derecho Internacional*, Caracas: UCAB, 1979.
9   *Ibid.*
10 *Ibid.*
11 *Ibid.*
12 *Declaracion de Zona de Paz y Cooperacion en Centroamerica y el Caribe.*
13 *Problematica del Desarrollo de Comunidad a traves de los documentos de Naciones Unidas*, Fondo Editorial Comun, 1970.
14 *La Ensenanza del Derecho Internacional Publico en la actual situacion de America Latina*, 1986.
15 *Tercer Seminario sobre la Ensenanza del Derecho Internacional*, Mexico, 1986.
16 *America Latina: Ensenanza del Derecho Internacional Publico*, Caracas: Unesco, 1987.
17 *La Ensenanza del Derecho Internacional en México*, 1987.
18 Washington, 1980.

9
A Study of Multilateralism in Iran: the United Nations and the Iran–Iraq Conflict

Djamchid Momtaz

The attitude of the United Nations during the eight-year conflict between Iran and Iraq stimulated, a few years after the beginning of the war, a strong interest within scientific and academic circles in Iran. Most of the work done at this time, though limited, addresses the issue of the Security Council's responsibility in the event of an infraction of the peace or of an act of aggression, as well as its role regarding the respect of human rights on the part of aggressors.[1]

The United Nations and respect of the *jus contra bellum*

On 22 September 1980, 22 divisions of Iraqi motorized troops made a surprise advance into Iran in order to occupy an area of approximately 30,000 square kilometres. Given the definition of aggression formulated in the UN General Assembly's Resolution 3314 of 14 December 1974, this Iraqi advance must lie at the base of any debate as to whether Iraq should be deemed an aggressor or not.[2]

Faced by this armed aggression, Iran took action, exercising its legitimate right of self-defence, as provided for in Article 51 of the UN Charter.[3] The deficiency of the UN Security Council, as well as its refusal to take the 'measures necessary to maintain international peace and security', provided a legal basis for the pursuit of military operations on the part of Iran.

a. Refusal to acknowledge Iraq's act of aggression

The day after Iraq's penetration of Iran's borders, the UN Secretary-General brought this act of aggression to the attention of the Security Council. In spite of the severity of the situation, the Council went only so far as to express, on 23 September 1980, its profound distress in witnessing the conflict expand.[4] It was not until 28 September that the Security Council decided to adopt Resolution 479. Clearly ignoring the fierce combat taking place on Iranian territory, the Council refused to recognize Iraq's armed advance as an act of aggression.[5] Instead the conflict was qualified as a 'situation between Iraq and Iran'.[6] Contrary to the practices it had used with regard to previous instances, the Security Council had now shunned its responsibility by requiring neither a ceasefire nor a withdrawal of forces from international borders.[7]

The iniquity and partiality[8] of this first resolution regarding Iran became undeniable when the Security Council, having remained quiet for a period of more than twenty-one months (a period during which Iraq was able to consolidate its positions in Iran), decided finally to come out of its lethargy.[9] In view of Iran's military pressure, which succeeded in liberating the majority of its territories and which threatened the principal Iraqi cities, the Security Council unanimously adopted Resolution 514 on 12 July 1982.[10] It is believed that the Security Council in this way intended to aid Iraq by rearticulating the principles of sovereignty, independence and territorial integrity. Not only did the Security Council call for a ceasefire, but it also required that all forces retreat to the internationally recognized boundaries.[11] When, on 19 February 1986, Iranian forces succeeded in crossing the Chatt-El-Arab and seizing the peninsula of Fao, the Security Council reacted by adopting Resolution 582. In this resolution the Security Council referred to the illegality of any acquisition of territories obtained through force, whereas it had remained silent when Iraq had occupied vast stretches of Iranian territory.[12] One can hardly fail to notice a pattern symptomatic of the Security Council's attitude. The period from 1982 to 1987, during which Iran posed the greatest threat to Iraq, corresponds with the phase of the conflict in which the Security Council adopted the greatest number of resolutions.[13]

b.   Refusal to recognize the exercise of legitimate defense by Iran

As a victim of armed aggression, Iran immediately took those measures provided for in its legitimate right to self-defence, as defined in Charter Article 51. While refusing to take the 'measures necessary' to re-establish peace, the demand which the Security Council was addressing to those involved in Resolution 479 amounted to denying the victim of this act of aggression the right to continue its struggle in legitimate defence.[14] Taking into account the absence of a simultaneous demand for the retreat of forces from the internationally recognized borders, this resolution put Iraq at an undeniable advantage, for Iraq could now remain in its positions inside Iran. This explains the dispatch with which Iraq accepted the resolution.

Starting in July 1982, Iran's approach to the natural right to legitimate defence changed slightly. Now Iranian forces had succeeded in liberating the greater part of the territories which had been occupied, and were initiating operations inside Iraq. For the first time the Security Council, in Resolution 514, declared itself profoundly concerned about the prolongation of a conflict which could endanger peace and security, and asked for a ceasefire. This organ and, shortly thereafter, the UN General Assembly, through its adoption of Resolution 37/3 of 22 October 1982, put the brunt of responsibility on Iran for prolongation of the conflict by referring to its unwillingness to accept the ceasefire.

The question arises as to the juridical nature of the resolutions adopted by the Security Council without any reference to Chapter VII of the UN Charter. Almost without exception,[15] these resolutions did not carry obligatory force.[16] Iran was therefore never expected to conform to the conditions of and accept the ceasefire. The view has been upheld, in accordance with this thesis, that Iran, the only judge of the efficacy of measures adopted by the Security Council, had the right to pursue the exercise of legitimate defence so long as it had not received sufficient guarantee from the Council. In citing this doctrine, a number of jurists have stressed the punitive end of legitimate defence. Qualified as international crime, a war of aggression brings to bear not only the penal responsibility of the authorities which undertook it, but also, on the level of civil responsibility, the obligation to pay war reparations. In these circumstances Iran had the right to pursue the exercise of its legitimate defence until the Security Council should adopt the necessary measures.[17]

For a long time, Iran has felt that the first measure the Security Council had to take was to recognize the existence of an act of aggression perpetrated by Iraq against Iran. By asking the Secretary-General to explore, in consultation with Iran and Iraq, the possibility of having an impartial body look into the question of responsibility for this conflict, the Security Council, on 20 July 1987, and within the framework of Resolution 598, finally approached the matter in this manner. Nonetheless such an initiative was seen as feeble and not very promising.[18] It was again noted that only the Security Council has the authority to recognize the act of aggression, and that under no circumstances could it delegate this power elsewhere.[19]

It is for this reason that Iran refused once more to follow the injunctions of the Security Council. In effect, the Security Council required that all parties involved adhere to a ceasefire as a prerequisite to its taking any action. Iran's military superiority on the front explained its intransigence. It must be kept in mind too that Iran made it a point to reject the ceasefire in order to have the Security Council focus on the question of responsibility for the conflict, thereby leaving the door open for future negotiations.[20] The defeats that Iran suffered following its rejection of the resolution led this state, in a spectacular about-face, to accept, on 18 July 1988, the Council Resolution, with the hope that an impartial third party would make known Iraq's responsibility for creating the conflict in the first place.

While awaiting the formation of this impartial investigative party, the report of the UN Secretary-General, dated 9 December 1991, on the application of Resolution 598[21] was to acknowledge that Iran was right. The Secretary-General recognized in effect that the Iraqi attack could not be justified by the UN Charter, with the rules and principles of international law, or with some principles of international morality, and therefore Iraq carried the responsibility for the conflict. In the opinion of the Secretary-General, the fact that Iran had made some movement on Iraqi territory before the conflagration did not justify Iraq's aggression toward Iran, following which Iraq occupied Iranian territory for the duration of the conflict, in violation of the prohibition against the use of force, considered to be one of the rules of *jus cogens*. It was this tardy recognition that, in his message of 22 March 1992, with the advent of the Iranian new year, the Ayatollah Ali Khamenei, Iran's 'spiritual guide', extolled as 'the grand victory of the nation'. It is all the same regrettable that the Secretary-General should have found it useful to suggest, in the interest of peace, that the impartial party be put in place, as foreseen by Resolution 598, thereby depriving Iran of the possibility of bringing to bear the penal responsibility of the Iraqi authorities, as well as of assuring that war reparations be paid as a measure of Iraq's civil responsibility – a proposition which the Security Council does not seem to have entertained very seriously, since no mention of it has been made.

The United Nations and respect for the *jus in bello*

In spite of its failure to apply the rules of *jus contra bellum*, starting in 1983 the Security Council found itself beginning to respect the *jus in bello*. Even in this area, its declarations and resolutions have been qualified as being shy and partial regarding the interests of Iran, an opinion supported by the Council's reactions following the use of chemical arms and the attacks made on neutral ships in the Persian Gulf.

a.   The use of chemical weapons

The Security Council's refusal to carry out its responsibilities in the matter of peace and international security is what led Iran to boycott this body. Iran's political stance was counterbalanced by consistent contact with the Secretary-General and with a full-fledged expression of confidence in the person of Javier Perez de Cuellar. It was believed that this political confidence in the Secretary-General would pay off; as proof one has but to look at the report prepared on 20 June 1983 in response to demands made by Iran on the evaluation of damages to civil properties. The inventory of violations of those obligations with which Iraq found itself confronted[22] was to encourage Iran to put more before the Secretary-General in the area of respect for human rights and, more particularly, with regard to Iraq's use of chemical weapons.

Consistent with the earlier pattern, and following Iran's complaints concerning the use of chemical arms, the Secretary-General sent a number of investigative missions. In every case the reports submitted to the Secretary-General and immediately communicated to the Security Council concluded, to the great satisfaction of Iran, that chemical weapons were being used. Nonetheless, the lax reactions of the Security Council gave rise to new criticisms regarding this body.

From 1984 to 1988, the Security Council went only so far as to adopt more declarations, while the importance of the question would have merited the adoption of resolutions in their full effective form.[23] As it turned out, the Council was to have recourse to the more formal procedure only at the end of the war, at which time it adopted Resolution 612 of 9 May and Resolution 620 of 26 August 1988. Aside from these resolutions addressing exclusively the use of chemical weapons, the declarations touched on the matter only in the general context of the war. It should have been necessary to condemn Iraq's use of chemical arms independently of the respective positions of the belligerent parties regarding the Security Council's resolutions.[24] Yet only after the cease-fire did Resolution 620 express the profound consternation of the Security Council regarding the intensive and frequent use of these bombs against the Iranian people,[25] and to express these sentiments without naming or condemning Iraq. The absence of firmness by the Council and its failure to adopt effective measures encouraged Iraq to violate, throughout the duration of the war, and with complete impunity, the Protocol established in Geneva during 1925.

b. The attacks on neutral merchant vessels

Even though Iraq took the initiative to attack neutral tankers by instituting, on 7 October 1980, a zone of exclusion around the Iranian
terminal on the Island of Kharg, the Security Council refused to condemn this. By Resolution 540 of 13 October 1983, the Council
demanded that both warring nations immediately halt all hostilities in
the merchant shipping routes. It was claimed that the co-authors of the
plan for this resolution had been encouraged by France, thereby justifying the location in Iraq of super tankers used in attacking tankers.[26]

Resolution 552 of 1 June 1984 was voted under the initiative of the
member states of the Gulf Cooperation Council, alarmed by the attacks
Iraq was making on tankers going to or coming from the ports of Kuwait
and Saudi Arabia. This resolution condemns only the attacks made by
Iran and does not mention the more numerous attacks made by Iraq,
which prompted those attacks undertaken by Iran against neutral vessels.[27] It is interesting to note that the Security Council considered the
attacks to be a threat to the security and stability of the region and that
they had serious repercussions for international peace and security. This
claim was used as justification for the alacrity with which the Council
reacted to the demands of the member states of the Gulf Cooperation
Council. The firmness with which the Security Council acted with
respect to attacks on neutral merchant vessels constituted a reference
point for those who believe that its reaction to the violations of the
Protocol established in Geneva during 1925 were too timid.[28]

Conclusion

All the studies cited undeniably hold against the Security Council its
neglect to play the role that the Charter imposed regarding the maintenance of international peace and security, and for not having taken
the measures that would have been necessary to discourage Iraq's
repeated violations of human rights. This default by the Security Council contrasts with the speed and effectiveness with which it reacted
during Iraq's aggression against Kuwait. On 2 August 1990, the same
day Iraqi forces entered Kuwaiti territory, the Security Council was
adopting Resolution 660 within the framework of Chapter VII of the
Charter. In this resolution the invasion was condemned and it was
demanded that Iraq retreat immediately and unconditionally to those
positions it had occupied prior to the attack. Following this, the Security
Council adopted, still within the framework of Chapter VII, a whole

series of resolutions condemning Iraq's violations of human rights during this conflict.

It should be noted, though not going so far as to justify, that the default of the Security Council was at least in part due to current opinion on Iran which, for the duration of the first conflict in the Persian Gulf, was the overriding view of the international community. The taking as hostages of the diplomatic personnel of the American Embassy in Teheran, and the holding of these hostages despite many efforts to have them released, including a ruling by the International Court of Justice, made this country something of an international outcast.

In these most difficult moments the support of the permanent members of the Security Council and the sympathy of the international community were lacking. Moreover, being unfamiliar with the mechanisms of the United Nations, and overwhelmed by domestic problems, the Iranian authorities were unable to see the importance of diplomatic action.[29] On the other hand, Iraq knew how to reorient the action of the Security Council in such a way that it would serve Iraqi ends in this particular situation.

Be this as it may, and in spite of the criticism directed at the Security Council, it does not seem that the amount of confidence placed in this body was very seriously damaged. Resolution 598, adopted in the framework of Chapter VII of the Charter, by which the Council directed itself to engage, with success, in a peace process, is considered the point of departure of a new era in the affairs of this body, at which time the end of the cold war permits glimpses of a promising future.[30]

Stress is put on the necessity to get around the shortcomings of the United Nations system by assuring a return to the spirit in which the Charter was written[31] without ignoring the positive experiences acquired. It is in this manner that the return to the operations in maintaining the peace, whose positive results are unanimously recognized,[32] should be pursued.

Translated from the French by Gunnar R. Sewell

Notes

1 These studies are all rendered from the Persian language: M.J. Mahalati, 'L'évolution de l'attitude du Conseil de Sécurité à l'égard de la guerre imposée', *Rapport de Séminaire No. 4*, Publication de l'Institut d'Etudes politiques et internationales, March 1986, pp. 53–66; A. Alem, N. Mossafa, B. Mostaghimi, M. Taramsari, under the direction of D. Momtaz, *L'agression de l'Irak contre l'Iran et la position des Nations Unies*, Publication du Centre des Hautes Etudes Internationales de l'Université de Téhéran, 1987; M. Zandieh, 'L'analyse de

l'attitude du Conseil de Sécurité', *Journal de Politique étrangère*, 2, April–June 1988, pp. 137–53; A. Malecki, 'La guerre imposée et le Conseil de Sécurité de l'Organisation des Nations Unies', *ibid.*, pp. 155–87; M.J. Larijani, 'Actions internationales de la République islamique d'Iran au sujet de la guerre imposée', *Rapport de Séminaire No. 8*, Publication de l'Institut d'Etudes politiques et internationales, January 1988, pp. 13–20; N. Sagafi Ameri, *L'Organisation des Nations Unies et la responsabilité du maintien de la paix et de la sécurité internationales*, Publication de l'Institut d'Etudes politiques et internationales, Téhéran, 1989; D. Momtaz, 'Le droit naturel de légitime défense dans la guerre irano-irakienne', *Etude des aspects de l'agression et de la défense*, 2, 1989, Téhéran, pp. 185–92; M.R. Ziaei-Bigdeli, 'La Légimité de la guerre et du recours à la force en droit international', *Journal de politique étrangère*, 5, Summer 1991, pp. 387–416; H. Falsafi, 'Le Conseil de Sécurité et la paix mondiale', *Revue de recherche juridique*, No. 8, Autumn–Winter 1990–91; A. Hedayati-Khomeini, *Le Conseil de Sécurité et la guerre imposée par l'Iraq à la République islamique d'Iran*, Publication de l'Institut d'Etudes politiques et internationales, Téhéran, 1991; N. Mossafa, 'L'évolution du concept du maintien de la paix', *Journal de politique étrangère*, 5, Summer 1991, pp. 363–86.

2　A. Alem, p. 59.
3　D. Momtaz, p. 186.
4　A. Hedayati, p. 70.
5　A. Maleki, p. 178.
6　A. Alem, pp. 110–11.
7　A. Maleki, p. 158; A. Alem, p. 115.
8　A. Hedayati, p. 92.
9　*Ibid.*, pp. 78, 82.
10　A. Maleki, p. 161.
11　A. Alem, pp. 110–11.
12　A. Hedayati, p. 112.
13　This coincidence is one of the principal theses of A. Hedayati.
14　A. Alem, p. 102.
15　H. Falsafi, p. 55.
16　A. Hedayati, p. 84.
17　D. Momtaz, pp. 187–8.
18　M.J. Larijani, p. 17.
19　A. Hedayati, p. 147.
20　*Ibid.*, p. 162.
21　UN Document S/23273.
22　A. Alem, p. 136.
23　*Ibid.*, p. 107.
24　M.D. Mahalati, p. 327.
25　A. Hedayati, p. 208.
26　*Ibid.*, p. 98.
27　A. Maleki, p. 165; A. Alem, p. 108.
28　A. Alem, p. 107.
29　A. Hedayati, pp. 78–9.
30　N. Sagafi, pp. 95, 97.
31　M. Zandieh, p. 152; N. Sagafi, p. 107.
32　N. Mossafa, p. 382; M.R. Ziaei-Bigdelli, p. 414.

10
African Perspectives on Multilateralism: the View from Anglo-Africa

A.I. Samatar

Introduction

The closing stages of the 1950s and the first decade of the 1960s were times of great dreams and expectations in most of the Third World. These dreams were engendered by decolonization and the possible inception of a new international order informed by the noble principles of equity, liberty and prosperity. Expectations focused on the promise of a fruitful four-way marriage between the munificent precepts of the United Nations system and other multilateral organizations, the prosperous liberalism of the times, the technological skills and surplus capital of the developed segments of the world, and the vast untapped human and natural wealth of Africa, Asia and Latin America.

Against this background, a number of well publicized initiatives, perhaps best symbolized by the United Nations Development decades of the 1960s and 1970s, were launched. By the early 1970s, however, the assumptions of human solidarity and a euphoric tone of empathy were severely undercut by grave global economic crises (including energy), geopolitical competition, and the relentless and powerful undertow of an underlying logic of unequal partnership. The inaugural moment of this new phase of antagonism, across the great divide of core-periphery hierarchy, was officially underscored by the now familiar proposal by the Third World (originally the Group of 77) for a New International Economic Order (NIEO). Several sets of UN General Assembly resolutions, adopted in the early 1970s, pointed to an acute asymmetry of global economic relations between the industrialized societies of most of Africa, Asia and Latin America. A few years later, more demands for equity were expressed by the Third World, including a call for a New World Information Order (NWIO).

Initially, a few developed countries paid attention to these Third World concerns. However, even this meagre interest was overtaken by the spiralling deterioration of the international economy, culminating in the deep recession of the late 1970s and early 1980s. Consequently, the views of the core states and most multilateralists were dominated by a single mission: the resuscitation of the world capitalist order. As a result, social democratic ideals in the advanced industrial societies, Third World needs, and the basic ethos of the United Nations were all either blatantly jettisoned or drastically redefined. A belligerent, neo-imperialistic ideology radiated from the metropolises of global power, which became set on bending international institutions and the *geist* surrounding them to the unilateral interests and will of these dominant social forces. For the countries and peoples outside the core, the 1980s have passed into history as years of crushing debt burden, onerous structural adjustment policies, retrogressing quality of life (including acute levels of malnutrition and starvation), a degrading environment, and grave abuses of human rights. The 1990s wrought conditions no better.

Perhaps more than any region, it is in Africa where the early senti-ments of enthusiasm for a constructive multilateralism were most audible, and the echo of subsequent frustrations and disillusionment are loudest. This mutation of African outlook should come as no sur-prise; after all, with the unenviable distinction of having the most beleaguered of all continents, Africans see themselves as the group having most to gain or lose depending on the nature and fate of multilateralism.

The following bibliographical and evaluative essay follows the histor-ical trajectory outlined above and offers a representative sample of the literature from English-speaking Africa. Needless to say, the para-mount (but not exclusive) theme is *development*. Given the dire condi-tions of the majority of Africa's peoples, the cutting edge of the contemporary African voice is critical and condemnatory. However, this should not be construed as a complete loss of faith either in the original tenets of the United Nations system or in the future possibility of constructing a more efficacious multilateralism. The chapter will highlight examples of upbeat literature, then offer representations of the more grim and bitter, and conclude with a few thoughts on how these discrepant views might be integrated into the making of a more salutary multilateralism.

The affirmative

Two strong but somewhat Janus-faced voices come from an individual and an organization. The first is Amadou-Mahtar M'Bow, former Director-General of UNESCO (1974–86); the latter is the United Nations Economic Commission for Africa (UNECA or ECA). M'Bow has the distinction of rising to one of the highest appointments of an African in the United Nations system, while the ECA is generally acknowledged as the critical vehicle for the expression of Africa's economic condition. Both (particularly) articulate the menace that threatens African lives but, at the same time, speak positively of the work and promise of the United Nations system and multilateralism. I will offer a synopsis of each to be followed by a number of other writings more sanguine about the United Nations' contribution to African development.

M'Bow takes stock of the decade of the 1970s and looks into the 1980s and beyond.[1] He suggests that these are times of great difficulties. The tough challenges that face the world community include widening disparities in terms of access to resources, rampant disease and debility, and illiteracy. Combined, these are the bedrock of inequality and injustice. Despite the fact that the United Nations system was imagined and designed to address divisive issues that often compound tension – tension which, in turn, undermines peace – it continues to be dogged by 'narrow, short-sighted views'. The weight of these attitudes, so antithetical to the original vision, is heavier when they are espoused by the powerful. If the United Nations system is to stay on course and, consequently, to pursue the 'collective long-term interest of the human community', the choice, according to M'Bow, is stark: consensus and attention to the fundamental incongruities of contemporary global affairs or further descent into ruinous antagonism and mutual hatred.

M'Bow is a believer in the United Nations system. He is convinced that the United Nations is one of the few global structures that is capable of connecting intimately two pivotal factors: moral strictures of peace, equity and reciprocity, and the impressive scientific and technological prowess already achieved by human beings. Having a fair chance of accomplishing this historic feat and, in the process, subduing ignorance and war – one of the greatest issues facing all countries – hinges on a renewed confidence in, and support of, the United Nations system.

The United Nations Economic Commission for Africa's programme statement is critical of some of the major agents of the present multilateralism (for instance the International Monetary Fund and the World Bank) while equally positive toward the United Nations and a reformed multilateral relations as the basis for a new age conducive to African development and participation.[2] This document postulates that the most notable attributes of Africa since the late 1970s are disintegration of productive and infrastructure capabilities and frighteningly low economic performance. Average annual growth rates of only 0.4 per cent, and a per capita income decline of 2.6 per cent, have created a condition of generalized pauperism, in which women, youth, the disabled and the elderly are suffering most. The fundamental structural weakness of the African political economy, so vulnerable, is attributed to the combined effect of the predominance of subsistence and mercantile activities, a fragile and 'disarticulate' productive foundation (that is, decreasing rate of investment and worsening balance of payment deficits) accompanied by inappropriate technology, neglected rural life and informal sectors, a depleted ecological base, brittle institutions, and an accentuated dependency on external linkages (for instance, exports and factor inputs). In short, life for most Africans is caught in a cruel grind of poverty and diminishing productive capacities.

Given the above, the end of the 1970s brought Africa to a crossroad: a descent into a further harrowing decline of living standards or an immediate effort to arrest degeneration and, therefore, revitalize production. Concomitant with the unanimity over the state of the continent, two strategies for rehabilitation were proffered. The first was an African initiative, *The Lagos Plan of Action* (1980), which stressed the inception of self-sustaining development and collective self-reliance as principal targets; the second was the now equally famous 'Berg Plan', *Accelerated Development in Sub-Saharan Africa* (1981), commissioned by the World Bank. The ECA document argues that *The Lagos Plan* did not make any progress since the African economies were devastated by the collapse in price of their primary commodities, rising indebtedness, the drying up of net flows of capital, high inflation, and an encircling ecological doom typified by long droughts and mounting denudation. With the African ambition thus enervated, coupled with the monetarist policies enacted by the core states, multilateral agencies such as the IMF and the World Bank (essentially relay stations for the core's economic agenda) became dominant forces in the search for workable strategies.

The IMF's and the World Bank's diagnoses of the African condition are, essentially, predicated on the assumption that ill-conceived economic policies as well as irresponsible fiscal management by African states are the source of the current calamities. Consequently, revival depends on how successfully the public sector is curtailed, in addition to attaining external and internal financial balance (that is, getting the accounts right). These propositions, known as Structural Adjustment Policies or SAP, have given specificity by focusing on: control of the money supply, a credit squeeze, exchange rate and interest rate adjustments, trade liberalization and price reforms, and rendering competitive market forces the fulcrum of economic life.

The ECA argues that enough evidence is in on the effectiveness of IMF/World Bank prescriptions. Not only have these policies cavalierly disregarded African initiatives as enunciated by *The Lagos Plan of Action*; they have, additionally, deepened the 'disarticulation' of African economies that have adopted the policies of the IMF and the World Bank. Some of the more obvious fallouts of the implementation of SAP, according to the ECA, are dearth of sustained growth, continuing decline of the rate of investment, deteriorating budget profile and balance of payments deficits, more burdensome debt service requirements, and total neglect of the critical human sectors of education, health and employment. The conclusion to be reached, therefore, is that the resurrection of African economies (that is, restoring growth) by undertaking fiscal and external balances and the unmitigated application of market forces is unrealistic as well as untenable. Such a goal can only be achieved by giving full attention to the structural basis of the general deficiencies and 'bottlenecks' of the economies of Africa. It is in the light of the above that the ECA, with the blessings of the United Nations Development Programme (UNDP) and the United Nations Programme of Action for African Economic Recovery and Development (UNPAAERD), unveiled a new African initiative, *The African Alternative Framework to Structural Adjustment Programmes*, which has the following eight features.

One, it is 'holistic' in the sense that directions and criteria together with ways of implementation are closely tied to the central elements of both adjustment and transformation. In other words, holism implies a cohabitation of the admittedly needed immediate structural reorganization and the requirements for long-term development. Two, rather than pushing African economies to an inordinate reliance on external contributions, optimum effort should be exerted to mobilize and wisely invest local resources. Third, proper development needs an appropriate environment that successfully celebrates the unavoidable relations between the public and private sectors. Four, *The African Alternative* emphasizes the axiom that human beings are at the heart of any viable strategy. As a result, issues of motivation and equity are keys to reinvigoration. Five, economic recuperation and long-term development of the continent require genuine democratic order in which popular participation is an organic part of reconstruction. Six, while there is a common physiognomy of African economies, *The African Alternative* stresses flexibility in the face of each country's peculiar condition and complexity. Seven, challenges from the prevailing international order and continental circumstances dictate that African countries quicken the pace and deepen cooperation among themselves as they undertake adjustment and transformation. A pivotal item of this solidarity is the integration of three basic areas: physical and social infrastructure, production, and markets. Finally, *The African Alternative* conceives of outside contributions not as an exercise in manipulation of the beggarly by the powerful; rather, the document's spirit and recommendations are in line with a new communion between donors and Africans resulting in a mutual understanding to confront one of the greatest challenges of the present epoch. For Africa, any new or reconstructed multilateralism must pay close attention to the plight of the continent, and listen to the authentic voices of its people.

A more effusive celebration of the United Nations system is the common thread of the rest of the affirmative perspectives. Wellington Nyangoni begins his analysis by suggesting that membership in the United Nations system has given African countries an opportunity to make or shape global affairs.[3] Two notable factors are responsible for this: the remarkable role played by the United Nations in decolonization and the enormous count of African membership. Individually and collectively (as the largest bloc), African states are, according to Nyangoni, making an impact on international legal and diplomatic practices and the creation of an international public opinion and morality (for instance, on the Law of the Sea, international piracy, and the protection of the environment). Successes in these areas have emboldened African states, together with other members of the non-aligned movement, to work for a reorganization of the international economic system by conceiving NIEO. African activities continue to benefit the United Nations by bringing up new ideas and issues that energize the workings of the whole system.

But African countries and the United Nations system are not always in sync with each other. For instance, African states, through the Organization of African Unity (OAU), have campaigned for the recruitment and placement of more sympathetic cadres in the international civil service, particularly in the senior posts. While some success has been attained in a number of divisions of the United Nations bureaucracy, including the Secretariat, the Economic and Social Council, and the United Nations Conference on Trade and Development (UNCTAD),

African members and their allies feel that there is some distance to travel before the management of the United Nations system becomes an agreeable mixture of competence and compassion with regard to issues important to the South. This, Nyangoni tells us, is a salient item in bringing Africa and the United Nations system closer together.

In the end, Nyangoni thinks that African aspirations and the Charter as well as the functions of the United Nations blend well. Africans need a platform to express their thoughts on the great questions of peace, justice, economic well-being, and human rights. The foundations of the United Nations system and its guiding principles are the embodiment of these same African concerns. This confluence of philosophy and interest is so sound that 'the more powerful the UNO becomes, the more African states . . . will use it for resolving disputes and conflicts within the international community'.

John Afolabi's dissertation underlines the fact that colonial domination of Africa, until about 1960, froze African active involvement in any endeavour to construct universal or regional orders.[4] But with the birth of the United Nations and the subsequent dawn of independence, Africa's place in global interaction has assumed a more worthy profile. Perhaps the issue that most attests to this coming of age is the role the countries of the continent have played in the long and meandering negotiations that culminated in the Third United Nations Conference on the Law of the Sea. Unlike the 1958 and 1960 conferences, in which African pressure was hardly feasible and which did not accomplish much, African participation this time contributed to the progress achieved in international rule making. According to Afolabi, part of the reason for the endorsement of this Law is attributable to African tactics in 'coalition making . . . leadership, [and] lobbying', and a commodious spirit offered by the United Nations system. The latter is particularly significant in two ways: strong propagation of the idea of the common interest of humankind (especially in the wake of studies on the effect of growth on global resources) and the consecration of the principle of equal participation. Together these traits of the United Nations system act as an antidote to international relations based on the calculus of state-centred power while simultaneously keeping alive the hope of a future multilateralism reinforced by equality and solidarity among the citizens of the planet.

The OAU is the conduit for K. Mathews' engagement of Africa's place in multilateral affairs.[5] Mathews sees the OAU as the prime continental organization for the channelling of Africa's input into the central mission of the United Nations, the advancement of global cooperation.

Equally part of the mission of the OAU is the shepherding of a continental outlook that is non-aligned. Taken together, these two elements express the coherence of African hopes toward the United Nations system. Since the signing of the Agreement on Cooperation with the United Nations in 1965, the OAU has emphasized both the common principles and the opportunities for African states to capitalize on the resources of the United Nations system. For the past two and a half decades, this kinship between the two organizations has helped virtually eliminate colonialism, declared Africa a de-nuclearized zone, endorsed a demilitarized Indian Ocean, established a United Nations Commission on Transnational Cooperation and a Centre on Transnational Corporations, and laid effective siege to apartheid in South Africa. For Mathews, the OAU and the United Nations system are ideal partners for the construction of a more inclusive and just world order.

The vesicatory

For over a quarter century now, Samir Amin has been at the forefront of the study of African political economy and its relations with the outside world. His work of 1990 is a testament to how the international order is singularly guilty of the humiliation and near annihilation of the continent.[6] His advice to Africans and to the people of the periphery in general is to disconnect and work toward a political economy of self-reliance.

Amin contends that the elemental factor in Africa's intensifying underdevelopment and powerlessness is the yet unrealized revolution in agriculture. This failure is so central that all 'other aspects of backwardness flow from it . . . ' – including industrialization. Consequently, population increases (over 2.5 per cent) and rapid urbanization (between 5 and 9 per cent) that are not sustained by industrial development have compounded the deformities of economy and governance. Amin does not, of course, argue that this African condition is determined by some immutable tradition or original sin; rather, he postulates that an explanation should be sought in the relationship between the productive labour of African peasants and the larger system of which it is a part. This relationship, best described as highly exploitative integration, serves the interest of the 'system of dominant capitalism' as well as allied indigenous classes. If it was one of the main achievements of conquest to alienate and capture African peasant labour, independence has not altered this arrangement. In fact, argues Amin, we are living through the institutionalization of neo-colonialism, essentially business as usual.

A second locus of the crisis of development in Africa is the state. The weight of transnationalism (that is, the globalization of core capitalist power), writes Amin, vitiates or 'sets limits' on local capacity to build public power and therefore facilitates the easy triumph of despotism across the continent. Originally concocted, usually forcefully, by colonial powers, and negotiated with the blessings of these very powers or, in a few cases, won over with tremendous cost and in the teeth of continuing hostility, the post-colonial state can neither act as 'a progressive agent' for successful national accumulation nor create the ambience for democratic political life. Deprived of a strong yet accountable state, African governance is bedeviled by cacophonic claims and disintegrating cleavages (for instance ethnic, class and strata) that exacerbate its already inferior status vis-à-vis transnational power. It is, Amin suggests, in the emanations of culture where ultimate imprints of transnational dominance (for instance generalized anomie, loss of identity and nerve) of African peoples are most manifest. With an eye for comparative history, Amin writes:

> As in the West, the individual climbs out of the disaggregation of traditional collectives, but here climbs into an atmosphere of confusion. The decomposition of social values has more the effect of changing them than of purely and simply destroying them, for the reason that mentalities are slow to change, but also that the evolution of social and economic structures fails to give rise to a coherent entity.[7]

Amin's final diagnosis is a sharp one: the combination of these crises adds up to the 'recompradorization' of the continent. How to address this serious retreat is the burden of the rest of the book. Amin thinks there are two regular alternatives usually paraded: statism or liberalization. The first offers very minimal yields in both economic and political goods. To a certain extent, this is the lesson from the collapse of East Europe and a number of fading experiments in the Third World. Liberalization, on the other hand, as an adjustment to the injunctions of the world-system, has already shown itself to be a licence for the pillaging and acute marginalization of Africa. From high interest rates which induce capital flight, substitution of local price controls to world market prices (with their hidden subsidies), devaluations that show precious little positive impact on balance of payments, to de-industrialization and the deterioration of social infrastructure, liberalization thus construed and imposed has led to a 'regressive and stagnant equilibrium'. To transcend this stasis, according to Amin, requires three mutually reinforcing processes. First, the imagination and concretization of a 'national and popular' development project is necessary. Antithetical to continued integration into the current world order, this implies an 'autocentric' strategy of accumulation in which the rewards for productive work are directly connected to an increase in productivity. In other words, the production of producer goods is to be devised so that it tightly relates to the production of mass consumer goods. The political corollary of such a strategy is the 'delinking' of the local economy from the global capitalist division of labour and the remaking of the state into an agent advancing such an agenda.

Second, Amin admonishes Africans to strengthen inter-African cooperation and relations with the rest of the South. Such a cooperation will be radically different from the usual monetary and customs unions and African common markets, for these conventional attempts at unity not only continue linkages with the colonial metropoles, but also deepen regional inequities. The new cooperative effort could arrest the current descent into underdevelopment and neo-colonialism by undertaking planned agricultural, industrial, financial and military resources, along with the optimal application of talents. Coupled with a new rationality antithetical to external dependence and unequal internal structures, 'planned complementarities' strengthen local development as it simultaneously stimulates larger collective empowerment.

Third, a successful transformation of this malfunctioning global economy, and the subsequent transcendence of concentrated impoverishment (verging on extinction in some areas), requires a new world order: polycentrism. This is quite different from polarizing transnationalism (pyramided on the submission of economic and social life to the 'worldwide law of value') which triggers further compradorization of Third World societies, punishment and domestication of labour at the core, and the rehabilitation of Eurocentrism under the aegis of the United States. Polycentrism is a new multilateralism based on a plurality of regionalized productive systems. Such an order, according to Amin, could give space to 'national popular' reconstruction of the North, the South, and the East.

Dovetailing with Amin's paradigmatic frame, Azzam Mahjoub and his contributors take for granted the culpability of the prevailing international order in the underdevelopment of Africa.[8] From Algeria to Mozambique, many African countries have declared their conviction to deal frontally with the major contradiction that results from the clash between nation-building and subordination to transnationalization. Mahjoub and his colleagues argue that a critical choice for African peoples is between merciless battering of adjustments to the uncontrollable vagaries of the present world-system, or 'delinking' – the latter defined as a strategy for autonomy and the building of internal strength. This choice represents the axis on which the great issues of African development are being fought. The authors examine seven countries (Egypt, Algeria, Tanzania, Ethiopia, Zimbabwe, Uganda, Burkino Faso and Ghana) to find out how much headway they have made. The broad common denominator is that their respective present histories have, at one time or another, thrown up social forces which articulated a commitment to face up to bequeathed heteronomous development and subsequently built a more autonomous society.

The general consensus, important particularities of each case notwithstanding, holds that 1) most regimes did not undertake an authentic or better empowerment of the popular forces in their respective societies, making development dependent on the whims and idiosyncrasies of the new ruling bloc; 2) ruling groups made few if any even half-hearted forays into the extension of their African affiliations; and 3) these countries have not succeeded in neutralizing the logic of worldwide market-driven prices (different from those underpinned by proportionality of social labour). As a result, the economies continue to manifest some of the dire effects of global unequal development such as vulnerability and sectoral disparities; and 4) African states continue to be encapsulated by an international order whose velocity adversely affects any meaningful attempts at nation-building – the latter necessary for genuine participation in the making of a true multilateralism.

Another strictly political economy work which links the horror of African circumstances to the buffeting of world order is Fantu Cheru's.[9] His basic thesis is that despite the end of colonialism new forms of subjugation are taking root. One deadly kind of this late twentieth century conquest is conveyed by way of the prescriptions of the IMF and World Bank. Broadly based on neo-classical economic themes and specifically identified as 'structural adjustment' strategies, these are deep infiltrations into African life that are so regressive and exploitative that, in Cheru's eyes, they are tantamount to a 'recolonization' of the continent.

Cheru fleshes out the immediate and devastated state of Africa: nearly a quarter of African peoples are either complete paupers or on 'the verge of poverty', with income per capita of less than $115; Africans make up over half the world's refugees and the displaced; the continent has over $175 billion in debt, with less than twenty cents of every borrowed dollar staying in investment; and most African countries display an acutely alienated state power.

In the case study section, Cheru examines five Central and East African countries (Zambia, Tanzania, Kenya, Ethiopia and Sudan). He finds that regardless of ideological orientation and economic strategy, all have suffered immensely from the implementation of IMF and World Bank 'advice'. Using the criteria of democracy, self-reliance, accountability, ecological sustainability, and sovereignty, he concludes that an intimate involvement with current multilateralism is antithetical to African development. Subaltern Africa, therefore, should disentangle itself from the tentacles of the current global order (distinct from autarchy) and be extremely sceptical of any 'new' multilateralism lest it proves to be old wine in a new bottle.

S.K.B. Asante's contribution is based on the assumption that regional cooperation and ultimate integration is the surest way to overcome 'Balkanization' and vulnerability in an international milieu that is dominated by giants.[10] Tracing the intellectual lineage of South–South cooperation to NIEO, Asante examines the case of the Economic Community of West African States (ECOWAS), established by the Treaty of Lagos in 1975, as a test case for collective empowerment. The measurements of the study include intensity of economic exchange, collaboration in research and development, common investment in education and communications, and collective use of regional natural resources.

The last two pieces of this excoriatory genre touch upon the issue of security. D.K. Orwa brings together the politics of the cold war, the United Nations, and the complexity of the struggle for independence in the African country of Congo during the 1960s.[11] Besides its historical contribution, the work's significance lies in its message with regard to the United Nations system, global powers, and Africa.

Orwa propounds a number of theses. First, despite the continual declarations of commitment to 'self determination' and liberty, the United States ignored these very principles when it came to the rights of Africans. Second, contrary to the celebrated perception that the involvement of the United Nations in the Congo crisis had forestalled a destructive superpower tug-of-war, United Nations actions (particularly those of Secretary-General Dag Hammarskjöld) derailed Congo's nationalist political direction. Third, African nationalist and progressive leaders of the future should not be taken in by the rhetoric of dominant powers (notably the US) and colonial powers, and should not put much credence in United Nations declarations.

Orwa analyzes the issues, times and personalities surrounding the assassination of one of Africa's rising nationalist leaders, Patrice Lumumba. After careful review of the evidence (including recently declassified materials), he concludes that while the United States was initially predisposed to support Africa independence, American fixation on Soviet strategic behaviour and, less conspicuously, a desire to turn Third World nationalism into a benign force, set the framework for US attitudes toward Africa. Lumumba was the quintessential African nationalist. He was well aware of the pillage and cruelties of Belgian colonialism. He was equally mindful of the indispensability of combining the struggle for political independence with the reduction of foreign (particularly Belgian) control of the economy, and especially the vast mineral wealth of his huge country. Lumumba and his supporters were immediately confronted with other Congolese sympathetic to the West, including the colonial metropole. It is Orwa's contention that Lumumba had confidence not only in the correctness of his position, but also in the role of the United Nations as a truly international and humane organization that was committed to justice and the well-being of the African people. Lumumba paid dearly for this naïveté.

The conclusions of this work are instructive. First, marshalling a great deal of evidence, Orwa establishes the fact that 'the CIA assassinated' Patrice Lumumba. Second, the United Nations and Secretary-General Hammarskjöld were not, to say the least, 'the impartial arbiter' that they were made out to be. Third, the United Nations, already handicapped by ignorance of the complexities of the situation, undermined its credibility by giving in to the imperial designs of the West. Fourth, African leaders and peoples should not invest too much hope in a new global order or multilateralism initiated and led by the United Nations. The killing of Lumumba and the subsequent imposition of the US-supported corrupt dictatorship of Mobutu, a regime that ran to the ground one of Africa's wealthiest countries, are testimony to why Africans 'must never have any illusions that the United Nations can serve [Africa's] interest'.

Bassey E. Ate suggests that African security is an index of a new and agreeable multilateralism.[12] Thus far foreign powers, who dominate the current world order, have been the main architects of regional security in the continent. The continuing presence of military bases, facilities, security treaties, arms sales and personnel training attest to the pervasiveness of foreign (notably superpower and ex-colonial) strategic interests. Driven by their competition as well as the maintenance of the general order of capitalism, dominant states are bent on preserving their lordly reach into African affairs.

Continental organizations like the OAU are seen by the West, writes Ate, 'as multilateral instruments for teleguiding [their] security interest'. This is affirmed by the US refusal to accept, and subsequent torpedoing of, Gaddafi's leadership of the OAU in 1982. Ate sees all this as a measure of African weakness and the 'power vacuum' in the continent. In the end, the author offers two scenarios which could converge with a new global security order. First, a deteriorating material life coupled with worsening human rights could create the context for a conception of African security different from the current attitudes of the dominant states and their African allies. This will be equivalent to a challenge to the 'state-centred, neo-colonial' status quo. Second, the rise of indigenous modes of military power (for example Nigeria and South Africa) could establish local capacity sufficient to 'delegitimate' external intrusion. With either one in place, the continent could help create a new global security order.

Concluding remarks

Despite marked differences in tone, focus and immediate conclusions, the two categories of writers presented here share at least four premises: the utterly exposed conditions of Africa, the culpability of previous and contemporary world orders, development as *the* defining issue of the continent, and an almost disconsolate call for the reconstruction of the 'world-system'. Where they diverge is in their interpretation of the United Nations system. One group sees it as the agent of a beckoning universalism; the other construes this system as at best tangentially relevant or at worst an instrument of the dominant states.

Generally, African views converge on what is seen as a peculiar contradiction that seems to underpin the current moment in history. On one side lie the glories and further promises of human intelligence – the Promethean face. Here we are witness to the proven genius to create wealth, build massive systems of knowledge, canonize human dignity, appreciate peace, and feel for the environment. On the other side of this divide lie shame and failure. The manifestations include harrowing magnitudes of deprivation (tantamount to global apartheid), privatization of knowledge and its misuse for short-term gains, flagrant violations of human rights, proliferation of the means of mass destruction, and desiccation of the natural habitat. If the transformation of world order and the strengthening of the United Nations system are *sine qua non* for effective treatment of the above disjunction, runs the weight of African thinking, some novel steps should be undertaken immediately. Foremost among these is an urgent need for a compelling global vision and the ethic carried by multiple voices, for a new multilateralism – one based on pluralistic mutuality. Pluralist, so that our unique civilizational heritages and particular identities are respected and nurtured; mutual, so that basic affinities of humanhood are bolstered minimally as a theriaca in the event of slippage into degenerate nativism. With this mindset, Africans would then forward the conception of a more just global political economy, one that is antithetical to underdevelopment, conducive to all societies' meeting the basic needs of their citizens, sensitive to a fragile world environment, and one that enshrines democratic political life.

Notes

1 Amadou-Mahtar M'Bow, *Building the Future: UNESCO and the Solidarity of Nations*, Paris: UNESCO, 1981.
2 UNECA, *African Alternative Framework to Structural Adjustment Programmes for Social, Economic Recovery and Transformation*, Addis Ababa: UNECA, 1989.
3 Wellington W. Nyangoni, *Africa in the United Nations System*, Madison, NJ: Fairleigh Dickinson University Press, 1985.
4 John O. Afolabi, 'The Impact of the African States on the Third Law of the Sea Conference: Its Ramifications for the Emerging World Order', PhD dissertation, University of Miami, 1980.
5 'The Organization of African Unity in World Politics', *Nigerian Journal of International Affairs*, 13, No. 1, 1987.
6 *Maldevelopment: Anatomy of a Global Failure*, translated by Michael Wolfers, London: Zed; also Dakar: Third World Forum, and Tokyo: United Nations University, 1990.
7 *Ibid.*, p. 99.
8 Azzam Mahjoub, ed., *Adjustment or Delinking? The African Experience*, translated by A.M. Bennett, London: Zed; also Dakar: Third World Forum, and Tokyo: United Nations University, 1990.
9 *The Silent Revolution in Africa: Debt, Development, and Democracy*, Harare: Anvil, 1989.
10 *The Political Economy of Regionalism in Africa: A Decade of the Economic Community of West Africa States*, New York: Praeger, 1986.
11 *The Congo Betrayed: The UN–US and Lumumba*, Nairobi: Kenya Literature Bureau, 1985.
12 'A Note on the Superpowers and African Security', *Nigerian Journal of International Affairs*, 11, No. 2, 1985.

11
Pragmatism, Displacement and the Study of Multilateralism
James P. Sewell

This concluding chapter offers an interpretative overview of world literature on multilateralism and the UN system. The combined effort preceding and underlying it sought to honour a criterion of extensiveness. Our work cannot be deemed exhaustive since we do not examine scholarly bodies of literature from all geopolitical and cultural quarters of the planet. Nor does this final chapter comprehend every question that might be asked about the literatures included. Furthermore, questions asked do not invariably become questions answered. Yet even silences acutely observed can bear fruits of improved understanding. Active reading of previous chapters will already have precipitated insights into the study of multilateralism. One task of this final chapter is to flag certain analytical gaps that might otherwise remain unobserved. May our project's lacunae, recognized and unrecognized, serve as others' stimuli. Although this study's domain and scope encourage no claim to conclusiveness, its contributors' findings do point toward general conclusions. These conclusions sustain an interpretation of multilateralism.

The interpretation proceeds as follows. Common questions posed to orient contributors at the beginning of the project afford useful points of discourse. Thus at the outset we focus findings by comparing various responses to these questions. Both their reactions and their reticences yield inferences as to where observers stand – and occasionally as to where they are going. Often reports on a literature depart revealingly from the original suggested terms of reference, in particular with respect to theoretical tendencies discerned by contributors. These adventitious offerings in turn create a need for raw new concepts to integrate unforeseen implications with anticipated sorts of findings. By characterizing patterns that appear across contributors' essays, the concepts of *pragmatism* and *displacement* enrich the interpretation of literatures

190

on multilateralism. Finally, I offer a concluding comment on the study of multilateralism.

Findings and interpretation

Recall the series of questions suggested for consideration by contributing essayists and previewed in the Introduction. Here is their fuller version.[1] What is the balance of interest in scholarly endeavours between emphasis on the UN system and on other forms of multilateralism? What is the balance among different disciplines (international law, international economics, international relations, political science, history, for instance)? How are the boundaries between various disciplines understood with reference to multilateralism? Are different functional scopes of multilateralism dealt with by different groups of scholars; for example, do UN system specialists focus on peace, security and disarmament issues; economists on economic issues; others on environmental or ecological issues? What are the principal theoretical mindsets or -isms, for instance (though not exclusively) realism, neorealism, functionalism, neofunctionalism, Marxism? Have there been trends favouring one or another perspective? Is there consideration of the future of multilateralism and of the UN system, for instance on the issue of 'reform' of the UN, or does there occur a more radical critique of the UN system or some of its components? These questions we now relate to contributors' findings.

As suggested in this book's introduction, its research design prospectus from the United Nations University's Multilateralism and the United Nations System (MUNS) prioritized universal-participant conjunctures over particular-participant ones. Nevertheless, as suggested by the MUNS prospectus, most essayists do manage to address literature on 'regional' organizations, at least in passing. Indeed, Károly Nyíri submits that circumscribed-membership institutions have offered more tempting research prospects than has the UN system as Hungarians rehearsed their membership in the European Union's predecessor organizations as well as in the North Atlantic Treaty Organization (NATO). Participation in the UN Economic Commission for Europe (ECE) provided regionally-oriented lessons for Hungarians, as did participation in the Council for Mutual Economic Assistance (CMEA or COMECON) and in the Warsaw Treaty Organization. Full access to the UN system came later. The earlier experiences all contribute to a Hungarian legacy of familiarity – if not invariably to comfort – with multilateral arrangements limited to certain sets of members.

In Holland, however, United Nations units receive so much attention by observers that the Dutch team of literary surveyors, headed by Monique Castermans-Holleman, necessarily could allocate relatively little space to such other important and academically popular institutions as the EU, NATO, the Western European Union (WEU), the Conference for Security and Cooperation in Europe (CSCE, now OSCE), and the Council of Europe. The Netherlands seems willing and able to participate actively in multilateral institutions that function relative to domains of widely varying dimensions. One might remember that Dutch legacies of universalism and particularism began early and apparently mingled happily. The Hague conferences at the turn of the century preceded the League of Nations, and BeNeLux preceded the larger institutions of Community Europe. Dutch scholarship bespeaks a long and affirmative tradition of multilateral practice within smaller and larger institutions.

As reported by Hassan Nafaa, the League of Arab States draws critical attention by some scholars in Egypt. Pan-Arabism similarly attracts writers, not only from Egypt but also from elsewhere in the Arab world.[2] Jean-Philippe Thérien touches upon francophone writings dealing with particular-member institutions. The study of international organization, as part of the study of international relations, remains 'associated extremely closely with regional studies' within francophone milieux. In neither the Arab world nor *la francophonie* does this literature appear to overwhelm the literature treating the UN system.

US-based studies of integration thinned, curiously, as Europeans advanced palpably, albeit haltingly, on their long journey toward unity. But studies of NATO, most often taking the form of policy prescriptions, abounded steadily in the United States throughout the cold war despite shifting circumstances that drove alternating alliance tendencies of fusion and fission.

Both Latin America and Africa offer instructive examples of the interplay between studies directed to organized regionalism and those directed to universalism. As Alberto Cisneros-Lavaller reminds us, the ideals of inter-Americanism long precede the United Nations: they date from the nineteenth century. In Latin America, much of the debate between scholars of particularist and universalist proclivities has been expressed over the decades – as is true of other issues – through the medium and language of international law. Today's particular-participant arrangements within Latin America and the Caribbean invite prospecting, and a literature on these multilateral arrangements awaits assessment beyond the scope of Cisneros-Lavaller's essay.

Writings that treat both universal- and particular-member organizations are reviewed by A.I. Samatar. Samatar finds an 'effusive celebration' of the United Nations system in a number of writings. Those by Wellington Nyangoni and K. Mathews emphasize productive working relations between the Organization of African Unity (OAU) and the United Nations system. On the other hand, the important statements published by the United Nations Economic Commission for Africa (ECA) sometimes criticize other parts of the United Nations system.[3] The writings in Samatar's 'excoriatory genre' stress sub-regional, regional or South-oriented multilateralism. For instance, S.K.B. Asante eyes the Economic Community of West African States (ECOWAS) as an organized attempt at empowerment. Others implicitly prescribe African treatment for Africa's ills by counselling distrust of the United Nations, self-reliance on a continental scale, or both. Samir Amin's scathing critique of the status quo leads to his call for Africans to disconnect from existing engagements while strengthening relations, among themselves and with other parts of the South. In sum, Samatar's overview provides a rich mix of writings, some stressing complementarity, others stressing contradiction between the United Nations system (or elements thereof such as the International Monetary Fund and World Bank) and 'regional' undertakings.

Yevgenia Issraelyan's explication of Soviet/Russian scholarship and Zhang Xinhua's overview of Chinese scholarship converge on a telling issue.[4] Regional arrangements 'can render great service', as Issraelyan summarizes the views of several authors, if the activities of these organizations proceed 'in a manner consistent with the UN Charter, and if their relationship with the UN is governed by the Charter's guiding principles'. In the same essay Georgii Morozov buttresses this viewpoint with his contention that 'multiformity of inter-state relations implies' vigorous multilateral diplomacy along with 'universal international cooperation' that can be secured only by the United Nations system.

Chinese scholars too offer conditioned praise, going so far as to regard 'regional organizations as the most substantial manifestation of multilateralism', in the words of Zhang Xinhua. From Chinese vantage points, the organizing of the Third World in quest of development goals contributes mightily to the growth of regionalism. Similarly to some African writers, Chinese commentators extol the virtues of South–South cooperation. Yet like their Russian counterparts, Chinese scholars enter a caveat, holding the effectiveness of respective regions' organized activities to depend upon their congruence with the UN Charter and its principles. An attribute of regionalism so conceived seems to be its openness and non-exclusivity, contrasting especially with regional arrangements for collective self-defence during the cold war incarnations of organized treaty alliances. Concern that regional organizations serve principally to legitimate hegemonist designs and spheres of influence seemingly has abated.

Notwithstanding MUNS signals to emphasize all-inclusive forms of multilateralism within the severe constraints of space allocated to contributors, 'regional' or particular-membership multilateral complexes also receive substantial attention in the critical surveys by contributors. Scholarly writings on these complexes have increased in most parts of the world, reflecting and often lauding actual developments. No doubt the casting of a wider net would yield an additional array of instances. Southeast Asia, to note only one other part of the world, offers important regional multilateral developments unaddressed in the present collaborative study.

Today's emphasis upon a symbiosis of multilateral forms marks a contrast with an older generation of writings in which regional organizations, especially selective-defence treaty establishments, were sometimes deemed a 'problem' for the United Nations system.[5] With certain exceptions, writings examined herein suggest benign, even mutually beneficial relationships between institutions comprising larger and smaller overlapping congregations of participants.

The logic of impersonal collective security safeguards poised to counter a hypothetical fellow signatory run amok, and that of pre-targeted collective self-defence against a particular outsider, abide uncomfortably together. Similarly, the global commercial markets sought by members of the General Agreement on Tariffs and Trade (GATT) and now the World Trade Organization (WTO) contrast in principle with the intensified trade among themselves sought by particular subsets of WTO members through limited-area free trade arrangements, let alone concerted efforts behind common trade barriers cultivating more ambitious projects of economic union. Yet these abstractions pitting inclusivity against exclusivity overstate facts on the ground and differ from contemporary perceptions as expressed in written form. For recent literature reflects a working assumption that particular-membership organizations cooperate fruitfully with the United Nations system in seeking solutions to many obdurate problems of the present human condition.[6] Similar to the relations among states, relations among multilateral organizations apparently have grown happier as well as closer. Writings on UN, OSCE, EU and NGO relations with NATO may take a different direction following the latter's 'robust' action against Serbia.

The practice and study of international law long antedate that of international organization. International law arises from inherently multilateral processes, especially as reflected by its sources in general international conventions and international custom. From international law more than any other disciplinary field emerged the study of multilateralism, our surveys suggest.

The process by which international law yields organization, then cradles the study of organization, proceeds as follows. States found intergovernmental organizations upon multilateral treaties. These conventions give rise to institutions serving as contractual devices that register the express accord of ratifying governmental members. They also serve as constitutions outlining the purposes, organs and primary procedures ostensibly agreed by their state members. Fundamentally, then, multilateral international law indicates how consenting participant governments have agreed to act, hence are supposed to act, within the figurative premises of each organizational creature of their wills. And since this international law asserts how governments have explicitly agreed they *will* act, surely it must guide the scholar in tracing how governments *do* act. Moreover, the evolution of international law and especially its growth serves as proxy to a broadening scope of substantive problems comprising the programme of humankind and inscribed upon the collective agenda of international organization.[7] To study international law thus is to comprehend international organization. So goes a major justification for the study of international law as a means to understand patterns of multilateralism.

International law originated within a system of states more decentralized than the organizing international relations of the twentieth century. To a modest extent international law has accommodated international organizations among its subjects.[8] Yet the continuing emphasis upon states as its principal subjects fits international law to serve as salutary corrective of a common mental tendency to assign personalities to intergovernmental organizations and thereby to obscure the states that give and sustain their life. This corrective is salutary because the focus of prescriptions by governments when they create an international organization soon shifts from proper behaviour by themselves to proper behaviour by their organizational 'it'.

The tendency for governments to exonerate themselves while scapegoating their artifice can be termed the problem of *displacement*. Displacement signifies the attempt to shift accountability from the displacer (notably a government and its publicists) to the displacee, here a multilateral institution. When governments displace their failings on to an intergovernmental organization, they also tend to project proposed reforms on to this organization rather than addressing reforms to themselves. In this respect journalists follow their home government's lead. And scholars too generally follow these tendencies. Displacement by a preponderance of participants leads to an institution held responsible without holding authority.

International law, then, can counterbalance inordinate emphasis upon an institution's autonomy from the member states that constitute and maintain this institution.[9] Of course international law can mislead the observer by implying too little institutional personality, especially if the school of legal study guiding this observer ('realism') denigrates multilateral organizations as subjects. Furthermore, international law as an approach to understand and explain multilateralism also presents other major liabilities along with its assets.

Two such liabilities warrant summary recognition. Notwithstanding its dynamic growth and its several sources, the body of international law offers prescriptions, thus sustains justified anticipations, only for a limited range of behaviour. International law does not even purport to address much of what is done by states, let alone by other types of actors.

Even within this limited range, international law proves only a problematic guide to what states and other actors, especially the governments of large states, actually do. The purposes written into the charter of an intergovernmental organization by its founding member governments represent no more than a fleeting verbal convergence of intentions, and quite possibly less. Practice supplants conventional procedure without necessarily bequeathing customary law. Not surprisingly, 'Is international law really law?' stirs debate upon many planes of discourse, not merely within introductory academic courses on this subject. Discrepancies between normative expectations and actions thus stem both from the limited scope of what international law prescriptions cover and from the unruliness of state subjects within this limited scope.

In any event, the significance of international law in establishing intergovernmental organizations led understandably to international law as the initial approach in studying these organizations. As well as elsewhere, a formative role for international law as guide to understanding occurred in the United States, where the interwar period witnessed a number of books pertaining to the legal design and sometimes to the lawmaking or 'legislative' output of international organizations.[10] After the war, however, political science became the chief academic base for scholarly studies in multilateralism and for the most part political scientists left aside questions asked by international lawyers.[11]

In Chapter 1 we observed an extended period of declining American interest in the study of international organizations. To some extent the study of international politics and the study of international relations more generally have separated from political science in the United States. Insofar as international organization has staged a comeback, this comeback has accompanied the burgeoning study of international relations. Yet the recent interest in 'governance' bespeaks an effort to situate multilateralism anew within a context of politics, a context that heretofore emphasized (if it was not limited to) the politics of state polities, in our epoch nation-state polities.[12] Thus the American study of multilateralism bids to fashion new terms for convergence with the American science of politics, whether accommodated within the field of political science or established separately from it.

More recently, observers tilling other scholarly fields within the US have shown an interest in multilateralism. Environmentalists, for example, transcend political boundaries as the problems they examine carry them increasingly beyond the state. A common trait of multilateral studies in the US is the relatively low level of attention paid to walled institutions in favour of attention to less formalized patterns. This deemphasis of intergovernmental organizations characterizes all academic fields, and accompanies the American abhorrence of becoming fenced in by multilateral confines and a strong, almost visceral preference for unilateral, revocable US initiatives.

Jurists along with political scientists and researchers on international relations constitute the scholarly contingent writing upon multilateralism in the Soviet Union and subsequently in Russia. Most recent studies are done by specialists in international relations, security and disarmament issues, and international law. Yevgenia Issraelyan indicates that the history of the United Nations, economic matters, and ecology receive treatment by experts in several fields. She speaks for almost all contributing authors in concluding that even though 'various matters are covered and different sciences involved, the studies are not interrelated, remaining separated within the framework of their respective disciplines'.

By others' accounts, too, international law leads the way in the study of multilateralism. International law specialists were foremost among the distinguished scholars who published on the United Nations system before the government in Beijing assumed the UN seat of China. Zhang Xinhua observes that in recent years research and writing 'are highly dispersed, as reflected in the multitude of disciplines involved in the study of' multilateralism. As is true elsewhere, in China no 'independent, clear-cut special area of research has yet emerged' to integrate the study of multilateralism and the United Nations system. Chinese scholars appear to seek consensus as to their findings. Contrast this Chinese tendency to mute individual interpretation in favour of common scholarly ground with the highly individualized American generation of concepts thereafter most often made rapidly obsolescent in academic discourse. Given the premium upon 'science' in the US, the latter practice contributes, paradoxically, to rendering the cumulative fruits of inquiry more of a mirage than these might otherwise prove. Yet the liability of countenancing ephemeral findings linked to disposable concepts does not mean that a contrary disposition toward collective closure in reaching scholarly judgments proceeds without its own costs.

In the developed francophone world of France, Belgium, Canada and Switzerland, the study of international relations stems from international law and the history of diplomacy. International relations in turn gives birth to the study of multilateralism. But because 'the study of international organizations is in all respects a subset of the study of international relations', as Jean-Philippe Thérien writes, 'the underdeveloped status of francophone literature on international organizations appears in no small way to be a consequence of the underdeveloped status of francophone literature on international relations'. Nor has international relations (let alone its offspring, international organization) 'yet succeeded in distinguishing itself from its originators', in particular international law. And this 'identity crisis' bears consequences: 'the underdevelopment of francophone literature stems in large part from the hold exercised by the juridical tradition', according to Thérien. Just as states and intergovernmental organizations are the subjects recognized by public international law, so these are the units acknowledged in the study of international organizations. Transnational corporations and non-governmental organizations receive increasing attention in francophone works, but they are not much incorporated into the study of multilateralism, tied as is this study to international law. The investigation of international organizations today straddles several disciplines without really bridging them. Nevertheless, the rudimentary autonomy of multilateralism, certainly not a stage of premature individuation limited to *la francophonie*, has in French-language literature yielded distinctive and valuable pathways to understanding. The sociological approach, a strong cultural anthropological bent and development law are among them.

In Egypt, similarly, teaching and research on multilateralism originated in departments of international law. But establishment of the Faculty of Economics and Political Science at Cairo University, along with departments of political science in other universities, 'contributed to the emergence of a new generation of scholars armed with additional tools and methodological approaches' yielding 'different perspectives', as observed by Hassan Nafaa. The evolution of Egyptian foreign policy bequeathed additional breadth to the research agenda on multilateralism. High-politics crises of the 1950s and 1960s impacted studies, as did Egypt's 'increasingly intensive interaction with Arab, Afro-Asian, non-aligned and Islamic countries'. In particular, fresh waves of scholars undertook the investigation of regionalism and regional organizations, problems of development, and disarmament. In Egypt and elsewhere in the Arab world, political research centres facilitated interaction among specialists who then produced multidisciplinary studies. From the accounts of contributing authors, it would seem that modes of investigative integration have progressed further in this part of the world than in other domains offering reports about research on multilateralism. Yet notwithstanding such coordinated multidisciplinary approaches, international law retains strong independent influence in the Arab world through what is known as the 'French school' of studies addressing international organization.[13]

To examine multilateralism within the context of international law is both traditional and fashionable in the Netherlands. Monique Castermans-Holleman and her co-authors cogently explain why: 'the Dutch have shown a great interest in developing international law and establishing the rule of law because of strong commercial interests . . . and a weak military position'. Article 90 of the Netherlands Constitution admonishes the government to 'promote the development of the international legal order'. Just as Holland pioneered in the conception of multilateral organizations large and small, so too did Dutch writers and practitioners long beforehand contribute mightily to the development of international law.

Academic or disciplinary boundaries operate relatively insignificantly when the Dutch study multilateralism. Practice and theory seem virtually to form a seamless web of pragmatic endeavor. The apparent absence of debate on how best to understand and explain multilateral phenomena strikes an observer.[14] One senses that throughout the Netherlands reigns a consensus so firmly established as to the unmitigated value of multilateralism that observers focus their attention not on why multilateral phenomena proceed as they do so much as on how, practically speaking, multilateral processes can be rendered even more productive. Given this consensus, reachable norms of international law continue to play a significant role. Political controversy persists in American and Hungarian studies[15] on basic questions about how avidly, even whether the home state should engage at all in UN multilateral institutions. Studies in the Netherlands proceed as though such issues have long since been settled and only matters about more effective and efficient implementation now comprise everyone's agenda.

'To understand Latin American approaches to multilateralism, one must understand Latin American approaches to international law', insists Alberto Cisneros-Lavaller near the beginning of Chapter 8. In Latin America as elsewhere practical considerations preceded theorizing. To touch upon circumstance thus aids understanding of how international law came to occupy a dominant position in Latin American studies of multilateralism.

Starting early in the nineteenth century, the newly-independent states of the Americas fashioned of international law a means to buttress their formal freedom. Several innovative norms of an 'International Law of the Americas' served a continuing struggle to open political space by ensuring autonomy, in the first instance from European colonial powers. The International Law of the Americas initially tended to legitimate a decentralized system of legally equal sovereign states. Yet early communitarian proclivities likewise manifested themselves, according to Cisneros-Lavaller. Peoples of the new states voiced Pan-Americanist sentiments, supported bilateral treaties of friendship, and convened an Inter-American Congress. Some normative elements outlined *in 1826* at one such Congress offer awesome prefigurations of twentieth century multilateral precepts. For Congress delegates then adopted, within a Treaty of Union and League of Perpetual Confederation, principles exalting territorial integrity, disapproving of war, and proscribing the fruits of conquest, along with procedures sanctioning pacific settlement when possible and either collective self-defence or collective security when necessary.[16]

Given the fecund legacy of such contributions to the framework of international norms, perhaps it is small wonder that Latin Americans have continued to study multilateralism primarily by way of international law. Only in recent years, as Cisneros-Lavaller says, have scholars from other disciplines such as political science sought to account for the discrepancy between what is and what ought to be.

In Iran, similarly, international law offers the main set of reference points to understand multilateralism, including its liabilities. Drawing on learned writings, Djamchid Momtaz employs international law concepts and evidence in building a case that the United Nations Security Council acted continually on behalf of Iraqi interests and against Iranian interests during the years of war between these states. Measured by international law standards and the evidence evoked, the Security Council falls far short of its role agreed by state members of the United Nations in ratifying the Charter. More recently, a return to these Charter norms 'permits glimpses of a promising future', according to Momtaz. International law, then, initially provided the means for states to construct a multilateral mechanism that would enhance their peoples' security. Thereafter it enables observers to judge how well this mechanism – and the Council's constituent states – perform with regard to the maintenance of international peace. Yet Momtaz's study itself suggests implicitly the exercise of political insight along with its deployment of international law criteria to adjudge multilateral failure.

Hungary demonstrates a quite different pathway to the study of multilateralism. As Károly Nyíri states, throughout 'her 1100-year history, Hungary never happened to be in an alliance *where she would have realized that common rules serve her interests in the same way as those of others'*. Such a perception regarding the inefficacy of 'common rules' would not have boded well for attitudes about international law, including the basic law giving rise to intergovernmental organizations. Nor did Hungary's exclusion from UN institutions during years of the cold war spur an impulse to reassess the moving frontier of international norms and organizing relations. For Hungary the practice of multilateralism began only during the 1950s, public consideration of this experience even later, in the 1970s and especially the 1980s. Even then the locus of concern with multilateralism remained circumscribed. Traditionally, issues of Hungary's participation in intergovernmental organizations, 'like those connected with foreign affairs generally' over the centuries, were treated 'as top secret, or at least as matters that concern mainly a narrow circle of experts only'. After the war, this Kissingerian elite closely held materials pertaining to multilateral diplomacy in ministerial archives and restricted circulation of these materials to themselves. When at last published studies on multilateralism began to appear, unsurprisingly they owed their authorship not to scholars in international law or other academic disciplines, but to reflective men schooled in the practice of diplomacy – that is, to practitioner-scholars. Notable among these are János Nyerges and Mihály Simai.[17] The title of Nyerges' work of 1985 indicates clearly how Hungarians were seeing multilateralism: *The Battlefield of the Gaming Table: The Anatomy of*

International Negotiations. Nyíri remarks that this study remained for some time 'the textbook of multilateralism'. But international law now serves the practice and study of multilateral diplomacy in Hungary. Experts in this field close to the emergent political parties have for instance voiced cautionary notes about the impact of multilateralism, in particular the post-cold war Security Council, upon Hungary's 'national interests'.[18] Thus continues the long tradition of circumspection toward engaging in common international endeavors.

Without exception, the writings on multilateralism examined by A.I. Samatar bespeak scholarly dedication to reversing the impoverishment and indignities of Africa. African commentators bear witness to 'harrowing magnitudes of deprivation (tantamount to global apartheid), privatization of knowledge and its misuse for short term gains, flagrant violations of human rights, proliferation of the means of mass destruction, and desiccation of the natural habitat'. Africa's human predicament sets a stern test for the Persian adage that everything is difficult but everything is possible.

The application of received international law does not promise alleviation of these ills, to infer from scholarship originating in anglophone Africa.[19] For instance, the multilateral performance that is measured and found wanting against Charter legal norms by studies within Latin America and within Iran is instead measured and found wanting against an 'original vision' – and, one might add, against subsequent multilateral resolutions on behalf of many kinds of development – by studies within Africa. The third United Nations Conference on the Law of the Sea (UNCLOS) does depart from these African attitudes about the practical and explanatory deficiencies of international law. Yet even in assessing the process by which the Law of the Sea came about, African commentary stresses the multilateral creation of new norms by African 'coalition making...leadership... lobbying' rather than the adaptation of established norms to current circumstance. Pride in political achievement and worldly coming of age seem stronger here than satisfaction with legal improvisation.

Political science (including international politics) and especially international political economy best describe the disciplinary orientation of most studies in Samatar's review. Writers who see UN multilateralism as propitious on the whole[20] tend to focus upon political phenomena. These more sanguine scholars emphasize the fulcrums by which African states may exert leverage in modifying a system that all regard as functioning to their disadvantage and detriment. Group voting in the plenaries of multilateral institutions and in thematic global conferences such as those called to protect the environment presents a tempting stratagem. Concerted effort to place Africans at strategic posts within multinational staffs African writers hold to yield position power. Scholarly inquiries by the hopeful devote extensive consideration to political approaches promising salutary change.

Others see in United Nations institutions and (in the case of at least one scholar[21]) even in African multilateral organizations the instruments of their perpetuated subjugation. Studies by these observers, particularly Samir Amin's major book entitled *Maldevelopment* in its English translation, describe a coffling or chain-gang effect of sorts within the world-system. Such influences as the International Monetary Fund's Structural Adjustment Policies (SAP) and the globalization of production and finance -- liberalism as ideology and dominant-state capitalism as practice -- are seen as contributing to weakened, perverted states, corrupted and oppressive local despots, and debased, demoralized and often disintegrating nations forced to proceed, if at all, economically in lock step under direction of their extra-continental overseers, while reduced to communicating with each other by rattling the metaphorical chains that bind them in common enslavement. These findings give rise to radical prescriptions: Africans must disentangle, disconnect or delink from all offending forms of multilateralism, indeed from all offending relationships. They must likewise envision and create or re-create 'autocentric' (though not autarchic or statist) and 'polycentric' systems by critical acts of self-reliance supplemented by collective self-reliance.

Africa needs development, various schools of commentators agree. Ahmed Samatar's two categories of writers converge among other respects in 'an almost disconsolate call' to recast the global system, not merely to transform their own continent and its constituent parts. An evaluation of multilateralism turns affirmative or 'vesicatory' (as Samatar labels the grimly and bitterly negative writings) depending on whether the writer believes that multilateralism yields change benefiting Africans. African works affirming multilateralism usually issue as political science; those condemning multilateralism manifest themselves as political economy. More specifically, the latter form prognoses based on dire findings of structural/material deformity and capped by political potions the dependence on which would seem to require doubt-defying leaps of faith.

Having reviewed the academic orientations (disciplines, fields, functional specializations) of those who write about multilateralism, let us acknowledge explicitly that not only academics prepare scholarly studies. Hungary offers the most striking illustration of extra-academic scholarship among our chapter contributions by introducing practitioners who, for historic reasons, led the way in publishing before academics began to do so. But other cases reveal a mix of practitioner authors with academics. All contributors' essays provide at least some evidence of practitioner scholarship. Many individual instances efface the distinction between academics and practitioners; some authors act in both capacities, simultaneously or sequentially. Maurice Bertrand of France, Boutros Boutros-Ghali of Egypt, John W. Holmes and Robert W. Cox of Canada, James Jonah of Sierra Leone, Johan Kaufmann of the Netherlands, János Nyerges and Mihály Simai of Hungary, and Sadako Ogata of Japan, among others, have served their home states or intergovernmental organizations (or both), contributing scholarly writings along the way. Moreover, a growing corpus of literature evincing both practical comprehension and critical distance often comes forth as the work of NGOs.[22]

Moreover, international law as an academic orientation, and a prevalent one on a global scale, tends to blur the boundary between theory and practice. By definition law is normative, whether measured as a distance transcending practice, expounded in multilateral forums deliberating action or in the classroom. Its ineluctable normativity lowers the threshold between these two loci of legal activity. And Article 38(1) of the International Court of Justice Statute enshrines 'the teachings of the most highly qualified publicists of the various nations' as a source (albeit a lesser source) of international law. Those who write about international law thus potentially create it by their acts of scholarship.

Perhaps the essay contributions on studies from the United States and from *la francophonie* least showcase practitioners' writings. No doubt space limitations in relation to the number of academic items deemed to warrant inclusion in these two chapters largely explain the relatively modest listings of publication credits accorded to practitioners.[23] Yet differences between the substance of the academic studies and that of the practitioner studies, especially in the United States, invite further attention, as Jean-Philippe Thérien implies. To this matter I return briefly below when considering the principal theoretical mindsets or -isms reflected in essays from various provenances.

Whether their authors are practitioners, academics or both, most writings reviewed address significant 'real'-world problems. These are problems whose significance stems either from the seriousness and immediacy of a challenge posed for human life, from ineffectiveness of the multilateral means expected to cope with such a challenge, or from both. Problems of inadequate or misguided means lend themselves to examination below in pondering how scholars see the future of multilateralism and the demands for its 'reform' or more radical treatment. Here scholarship concerned primarily with problems as challenges to humankind invites attention. What theoretical mindsets or -isms inform this body of substantive writings from many parts of the world?

I have already indicated that much of the literature reviewed reflects an orientation to international law. This orientation may be described as the examination or the setting up of standards – rules – as to what a limited range of behaviour, primarily by states, should but especially should not be. Let us call this mindset 'legalism'. Legalist studies appear in the literature of every contributor's domain, and are especially prominent in the chapters on Latin America and Iran.

Legalism aside, the bulk of studies canvassed fits most comfortably into a category designated as *pragmatism*. Pragmatism refers to a belief that the purpose of thought is to guide action, that the meaning of ideas is to be sought and their value gauged in terms of their practical bearings within a particular historical complex. As action, pragmatism relates to the affairs of a state or community; insists upon an integral relationship between means and ends (if it accepts this distinction at all); adapts to changing circumstances as these make themselves felt; deals with events arising in such a manner as to take account of and utilize their interconnections; and concentrates on achieving immediate results. Pragmatism unabashedly evinces an orientation of problem-solving.

Pragmatism derives less from conceptions about the world than from sensory perceptions of worldly challenges. Pragmatism's putative closeness to 'reality' may embolden its practitioners to regard more abstract notions as *derivatives*, derivatives of conjectures that bear little earthly relation to existential conditions. Taking these derivatives as harmless irrelevancies, pragmatism thereby disqualifies itself as a critical theory.

Yet like other perspectives, pragmatism embeds theoretical or ideological suppositions. For instance, during an extended historic era when states continue to offer the salient cockpits of action within the global system, pragmatism will be state-centric without necessarily recognizing this.[24] 'Obviously, we have a problem here', the pragmatic writer characteristically implies in a matter-of-fact manner unembellished by much verbal fanfare. It takes no sophistication in comprehending theories or detecting ideologies for a detached observer to realize that the particular definition of this problem bears a self-evident relationship to the scholar's vantage point and probably to interests shared by others within the scholar's home space. Similarly, the proposed practical treatment will bear an apparent relationship to the scholar and like-minded beings.[25] Most pragmatic writings tacitly exhort fellow citizens on behalf of action with reference to their state.

The pragmatist plays it as it lays.[26] How 'it' (the problem) lays will receive analysis, probably including how 'it' got there. But pragmatism stresses the making of the immediate play more than contemplating contours of the past or comparing outcomes from previous plays, more too than reckoning where the next play may lead.

Unlike some other perspectives, pragmatism eschews grand designs and favours incremental steps that as a consequence, though without evident forethought, contribute to an endless process of construction and reconstruction. Were the building of theory its aspiration, pragmatism would seek to do so in this same modest, gradualist manner. But theory building does not constitute pragmatism's chief aim. In both the endeavours of thought and action, and to the extent that it accepts their difference, pragmatism presents not a carefully articulated framework so much as a temperament. Pragmatism reacts to opportunities and problems alike; indeed, it seizes upon problems as opportunities. Thus the pragmatic temperament expresses itself in the coupled proclivities to ameliorate and to capitalize upon difficulty. Once moved to act, the pragmatist muddles along until the current problem no longer pinches and ceases to afford leverage for achieving self-oriented objectives.

Pragmatists thrive on their sensitivity to exigency. Pragmatism advances encumbered by no trigger of abhorrence for any mode of action, including that of multilateralism, if multilateralism best works. The pragmatist rises above 'principle' when the producing of results requires doing so.

Pragmatism thus understood characterizes writings from most parts of the world surveyed in this collaboration. In particular it marks the literature from the Netherlands, where questions of whether, why and how much to engage in multilateralism seem long since to have reached working consensus and thus have passed from the cutting edge of scholarship. Surely the Dutch are masters of multilateral-ship. Yet pragmatism also informs the otherwise quite different literature from Hungary and the politically-oriented or 'affirmative' portion of the literature from Africa. Moreover, pragmatism finds some representation in the essays on Russian and Chinese literatures. The former advances several important psychological ponderables for the successful practitioner of multilateral-ship. And Hassan Nafaa refers explicitly to a 'pragmatic' era in Egypt. Given this geopolitical breadth in production of pragmatic writings, one gains the impression that over time pragmatism more than any other perspective describes the literature on multilateralism.

If the defined problem and its proposed alleviation relate primarily to a state and the interests imputed to it, and especially if the analysis or prescription features power and power's use either as means to maximize these state interests or its quest as end in itself, then the writing may be termed *realism*. Realism tends to regard multilateral institutions as arenas where governments maintain instructed delegates to get a few – by no means most – of the things they want, and to prevent some of the things they do not want from happening. Intergovernmental organizations thus output the sum of or some other function of inputs from member states. (Realists and especially neorealists do not regard the potency of all states' institutional inputs to be equal. US presidential candidate Pat Buchanan describes the UN as 'a creature of the United States'; MIT economist Paul Krugman says that everyone knew it was 'just Bob [US Secretary of the Treasury Robert] Rubin behind that mask' called the IMF.)[27]

But realism so described proves less productive than might have been expected as a category to which studies of multilateralism may be assigned.[28] For one thing, the forms of power elucidated by scholars from Thucydides through E.H. Carr, if not beyond,[29] do not key the studies of multilateralism reported upon above. And writings that focus upon power tend not to inquire into multilateralism.[30]

The nature of what multilateral participants seek suggests a further reason that pragmatism better than realism characterizes many studies cited in the contributions above. Adapting an idea advanced by Arnold Wolfers, let us suggest that the governments of states seek 'possession' goods and 'milieu' goods. Possession goods, if realized, belong exclusively to the possessor. Their possession by one actor means the dispossession or want of possession by any other. Possession goods tend to be sought in the world at large rather than in multilateral arenas. They are apt to figure in the literature of realism.

Milieu goods, however, are shared goods. They benefit more than one state. One state's milieu consists of other states as well as its natural environment. Milieu goods require some measure of joint consent and further collaboration to achieve. No single state can stem global warming; no one state can assure the preservation of most species; no state, acting alone, can govern the actions of the states constituting its environment. Not even the greatest of states commands the system capacity to control its milieu. Multilateralism provides a relatively effective and efficient means to resolve intentions, then concert efforts leading to the realization and maintenance of milieu goods. Pragmatists accept this and act accordingly. And scholarship follows practice.

Essays on the literature contain differing assessments of the functional approach to international organization – that prescription credited principally to David Mitrany and characterized by the building of international community and its institutions through initial efforts to cooperate in solving common presenting problems. Some writings implicitly adopt a functional approach to multilateral organizing; these overlap the sizeable category of pragmatism considered above. Yet functionalism assumes a meta-pragmatic stance since functionalists purport to take a longer view of consequences than abatement (and exploitation) of the problem immediately at hand. For instance, Zhang Xinhua describes Chinese scholars as welcoming collaboration upon 'projects of common interest, moving from the easy to the difficult so that suspicion among member states can be reduced and effective co-operation achieved'. Other writings evoke functionalism explicitly in order to evaluate the Mitranian argument, often by a comparative approach. Zhang Xinhua cites Yang Yuguang as finding the functionalist promise of non-political, universal-membership endeavours to have 'its echo in regional situations'. Hassan Nafaa reports that functionalism and related theories have neither proved helpful in creating Arab unity nor useful in accounting for the course such ineffectual efforts at unity have taken.

Some Soviet scholars attacked functionalism. Yevgenia Issraelyan cites Vladimir Fedorov's *The United Nations and the Problems of War and Peace* as one exemplary critical survey of western scholarship that takes special exception to functionalism. Fedorov views functionalism as an effort to depoliticize the United Nations and reduce it to dealing with minor matters instead of confronting disarmament and security issues. Functionalism here is seen to serve ideological purposes. Credence for this view is provided by Monique Castermans-Holleman and her collaborators. The authors of the Dutch contribution summarize an article by M. Couwenbergh and H. Siepel that traces the early politicization of the United Nations Environment Programme (UNEP) by the Third World on behalf of development claims to accompany consideration of measures for protecting the environment. UNEP's subsequent *de*politicization and relegation to technical matters devoid of development implications then is accomplished, in the authors' view, to safeguard 'the interests of the dominating western countries'.

The term 'neofunctionalism' has been used in reference to writings that acknowledge and pay homage to Mitrany's contribution, yet fault its defects. A notable line of criticism emphasizes Mitrany's admonition to eliminate politics. Critics instead see politics as a dynamic in creating (and accounting for) community while imparting the salience deemed necessary to cause governments effectively to grapple with problems. Newer versions of functionalism also seek, beyond or in denial of Mitrany's prescriptive aims, to conceptualize and empirically to apply functionalist insights for purposes of analyzing and explaining pertinent international phenomena.[31] Jean-Philippe Thérien reports that author Panayotis Soldatos carries forward the functionalist tradition a step further to post-neofunctionalism.[32]

Marxism or historical materialism best characterizes the Soviet literature, the 'vesicatory' portion of the African literature, particular writings from *la francophonie*,[33] and especially many of those from China. The latter case calls for special attention, since by contrast with most other bodies of literature characterized by what Robert W. Cox calls problem-solving theory, much of the Chinese literature as conveyed by Zhang Xinhua approximates critical theory.[34] Here pertinent attributes of critical theory include its capacity somehow to attain a vantage point beyond 'the prevailing order of the world', and from this position to inquire 'how that order came about'; to regard existing 'institutions and social power relations' as conditioned and conditional, thus raising questions about 'how and whether they might be in the process of changing' already; to focus choice upon 'alternative orders which are feasible transformations of the existing world', and thereby 'to clarify this range of possible alternatives', in part by discerning 'how . . . change may be influenced or channeled'. Circumstances of uncertainty amid palpable if ill-defined upheaval and a sense of growing contradiction arouse reflections leading to critical theory 'as people seek to understand the opportunities and risks' of the crisis that binds them.[35]

Consider Zhang Xinhua's interpretation by these lights. His synthesis of Chinese scholarly findings proceeds essentially as follows. Two profound changes have dramatically transformed the global system. Third World states have risen and strengthened their role within international arenas. At the same time, the superpowers have declined (even disintegrated in one instance) relative at least to their former co-dominance. Today the United States presents a telling contradiction with its limitless objectives and limited power.

Chinese scholars see the emerging heterogeneous world system as one of growing 'multipolarity' marked by increasing participation of

multiform entities: states large and small, interstate and non-state organizations and groups both global and regional, international political
movements, global and regional political party organizations, transnational corporations and other entities. Looking back, bipolarity can now
be seen as 'a transient phenomenon wherein the old pattern of Euro-
powers governing international relations' gave way to the 'historical
inevitability' of multipolarity. But the realignment of world forces as
multipolarization progresses does not receive a uniform blessing by
Chinese scholars. Some see multipolarization as peace-bearing, others
as dangerous.

After a long historical period, the multiple poles will converge, according to Feng Tejun. In the meantime, multipolarity serves as prerequisite
for multilateralism. Multilateralism in its fruitful period can have
emerged only as the rise and coalescence of some international actors,
the decline of others, and the amplitude of significant new actors – that
is, the configuration of multipolarity – has proceeded. To this temporal
projection I return briefly with some concluding questions when closing.

The American discourse on multilateralism and international organization includes representation of all the mindsets originally listed. Yet
certain tendencies stand out, for instance to the keen eye of a non-
American observer inclined to demonstrate findings by drawing distinctions. Jean-Philippe Thérien sees in much of the literature from the US a
pattern of positivism.[36] Positivism here implies an approach that hon-
ours its particular image of the natural sciences by postulating the
separability of data from investigator (or controlled from controller) so
as to operationalize empirical testing – or manipulate conditions – that
will render objective findings, or produce measurable results. Some
critical theorists link positivism with the effort to control society after
traditional bonds and constraints have been undone by industrialization – let alone by global trade, transstate hot money, and electronic
transactions. According to Brian Fay, 'the process of rationalisation
pushes outward from its original economic base – where the development of natural science seemed most important – so that it finally
comes to include politics as well – in which the development of a
technically exploitable social science is thought to be an urgent necessity'. Rationalizing the exchange of goods and services suggests the
pertinence of rationalizing the rule of social forces driven to turbulent
unpredictability by economic change: '*because* of its conceptual connections with the idea of control...a positivist social science has...
relevance and institutional backing...in modern life'. For positivism so

conceived, the surest way to predict outcomes would be to command them.[37]

Thérien reports francophone distrust of 'the excessive theorizing and quantification' prevalent in American writings and holds that these show 'little concern for the dangers of conceptual reification'.[38] The notion of regime in US literature has in francophone commentary been treated 'mostly as a passing fashion, or even as a retrograde step fostering the rise of neorealism'.[39] Thérien doubts that the 'succession of concepts' of which regime is but one example 'has made the theory of international organizations a cumulative process'; in this respect the American science of politics fails to advance as adjudged by its own standards. More importantly, in Thérien's view, 'francophone writing on international organizations displays far greater ideological pluralism' and acceptance of diverse ways toward comprehension than American positivism, with the latter's drive to banish other modes of understanding to the hinterlands of scholarship. Furthermore, the francophone literature presents 'a less ethnocentric, more universalist vision of the world' and a readier willingness to criticize 'the established political order' than scholarship in the US.

American positivism sustains a belief that the existing system manifests a given set of conditions at once explicable and impervious to deliberate alteration. Scholarly-fostered acceptance of the status quo lies also at the heart of Fay's indictment of policy science. His observation recalls the crusade to depoliticize multilateral institutions that we noted in Chapter 1: 'Reification, the impoverishment of political discussion, and political domination are latent features...which interlock and reinforce one another.' Together these breed a public spirit like the 'wise resignation' to the laws of social life that Auguste Comte had extolled as part of his positivistic religion. 'Far from being politically neutral, as its proponents claim, the idea of a policy science is one of the deep, important, and enduring ideologies of our own time, one which is all the stronger in that it claims to be "objective" and "scientific"', maintains Fay. 'Unmasking the ideological content of this doctrine' opens 'the possibility for a social order along quite different lines from our own'.[40] What *is*, then, is not *necessarily* so; beyond questions of 'why?' arise liberating, affirmative questions of 'why not?'

By insisting upon a radical disjuncture between subject and object, positivism influences practice in a manner especially germane to our study. The supposed disassociation of observer from observed commends itself to applications that treat multilateralism as distinct from multilateral participants, the United Nations system as distinct from UN member states. In so doing, positivism abets displacement.

Finally, consider examples of what contributing scholars see, or wish to see, in the future for multilateralism. The surveys of various literatures above contain many criticisms and exhortations to 'reform' the United Nations system or certain parts of this system.[41] To illuminate reformist thinking, it seems useful to distinguish writings according to what, in their respective authors' views, should be reformed.

Most reform proposals call for alteration of a particular UN organizational unit's mandate, its structures, procedures, personnel, policies, or financing. In assessments above, the IMF and the World Bank (IBRD) draw the greatest revisionist attention. Even the UN Economic Commission for Africa criticizes policies of these Bretton Woods fraternal twins. Beyond Africa, critics of the Fund and Bank noted in this study include observers in *la francophonie*, in Latin America, and in China. A common complaint is that the financial institutions (IFIs), especially the IMF, exact conditions upon assistance – structural adjustment or SAP – straitjacketing governments and harming the poor. For understandable reasons the phrase 'IMF riots' has gained currency over the years. Chinese critics urge restructuring to make the economic institutions more multilateral and thus more equitable. Maurice Bertrand draws from the deficit in effectiveness of UN economic institutions a different lesson: the need for an 'economic security council'.

The UN Security Council receives criticism in the essays on literature from the French-speaking world, Hungary, the Netherlands, and especially Iran. A common remedy suggests that this UN board for the management of violence expand its membership so that able-to-pay powers such as Japan and Germany become permanent members, with or without veto capacity. Some remedial versions prescribe a further expansion of Council membership to include additional representation from the South. The remedy proposed on behalf of an aggrieved Iran seems in principle far more elegant: let the Council simply follow the letter and spirit of the United Nations Charter. Reformist writings assayed here report no concern about the opaqueness of deliberations by the present permanent five members or about the inadequate accountability of all Council members.[42] Nor do these writings devote much attention to the advancement of judicial independence within the UN system, for instance in the form of an international criminal court enjoying meaningful autonomy from the Security Council. Quite possibly the Council's imprimateur upon NATO peace compellence in Serbia will stimulate further investigation in various quarters.

Democratization by the establishment of a parliamentary assembly proportionally representing world population does receive endorsement by Russian jurists Galina Dmitrieva and Igor Lukashuk. Others beyond Russia suggest such a plenary representing non-governmental organizations. The proposal for a 'binding triad'[43] features a procedure whereby General Assembly decisions would bind all UN members if approved by qualified majorities weighing in to fulfill three criteria: two-thirds of the Assembly claiming two-thirds of the world's population and two-thirds of the UN's financial contributions. This proposal has reached *la francophonie* and elsewhere from its birthplace in the US. Andrei Sakharov thought the UN, UNESCO and other multilateral organizations 'should compose a rudimentary world government based exclusively on human values', according to Yevgenia Issraelyan. Sakharov's ideas live on. Another small group of Russian scholars believes the United Nations system should be replaced by a different form of governance attuned to requirements of the changing global order, since the UN system 'embodies the past and present world, in other words, the world based on force'. Elgiz Pozdniakov and Irina Shadrina criticize the UN system and counsel abandoning it in favour of a world confederation of states.

Different though they may be from each other, these reformist writings share an attribute. All focus attention either upon organs and organizations of the United Nations system or upon the United Nations viewed as a complex of institutions. Whether modest alteration, addition, transformation or demolition is the prescription, UN structures serve as the objects considered pertinent for reform. And yet, an important part of the United Nations system remains beyond or outside this focus: the state members necessary to make the United Nations a system.

Reform of the participation by member states receives scant but notable attention in the essays above. True, the scathing, despairing literature from Africa reviewed by A.I. Samatar implies drastic state action toward the financial agencies and other parts of the UN: total disengagement and self-reliance or collective self-reliance. Scholars based elsewhere report proposals to reform the system by upgraded participant engagement. Yevgenia Issraelyan writes that 'an oncoming generation of scholars concludes that, to a greater or lesser extent, all the states members of the UN, including the Soviet Union, are responsible for its low effectiveness'. She adds that 'the redirection of Russian foreign policy...gives hope for new opportunities in cooperation at the UN'. And Zhang Xinhua prioritizes member state reform over Charter or organizational reform in citing Jiang Shikui's plea that state members commit themselves 'to the moral obligations and responsibilities

UN Charter so that the functions of the United Nations
:ned and its system be perfected'.

comment

Clearly the UN's member states matter fundamentally in determining
how well the UN system performs. Some writers explicitly acknowledge
as much. Yet this portion of the reform literature is small and no doubt
will remain small, given the useful function that multilateral institutions perform as lightning rods, whipping boys or other forms of political cover. The extent to which reformist literature focused on UN units
exceeds that focused on participation by UN member states offers a
measure of the incidence of displacement. And today's widespread displacement is deleterious to understanding, to effective multilateral
action, and to accountability. This is my first summary conclusion.

Secondly, 'successful' earlier response to worldly challenge tends to
yield an enduring pattern of behaviour, embellished often by refined
theoretical, even mythical attire, and sustained by local punditry. Displacement favours stylistic continuity: Why change established ways
when erudite scholarly writings and media opinion-mongers instead
counsel 'reform' of external contrivances in order to meet new or
newly-appreciated exigencies? Hungary's historic legacy bequeaths continuing suspicion toward multilateral involvement, suspicion diminished though not superseded by a slender popular affirmation toward
membership in NATO. The Netherlands, contrariwise, learned early to
create, not merely to benefit from legal and other institutional multilateral opportunities. British leaders carried the historic insular role of
continental balancer to twentieth century multilateral institutions,
bringing an habitual posture of aloofness punctuated by occasional
intervention, a posture modified in due course with the recognition
that Britain now looms greater within selective multilateral councils
than without them. Canada was 'born allied', in James Eayrs' phrase;
came of age with Lester B. Pearson's Nobel Prize for Suez peacekeeping;
and continues to exercise a multilateral inclination virtually as perdur-
able as the US impulse to take unilateral action.[44]

Thirdly, the multiplicity of literature here termed pragmatism
deserves to be assessed by standards pertinent to its authors' aims as
well as by criteria advanced on behalf of other epistemological sensibilities. How convincingly do authors commenting in a pragmatic vein
justify the importance of dealing with the problems that they define for
resolution, and with what cogency do they set forth feasible steps to do

so? Academics might usefully become more conversant with the pragmatic literature on its own terms, even while accepting that pragmatism does not attempt the same feats as do scholarly –isms. To compare pragmatic contributions across cultures and nations may lessen the scholarly tendency to ideologize, in the name of theory, on behalf of parochial interests. Moreover, active acquaintance with others' pragmatic formulations guards high-flying theorizers against losing touch with what is happening on the ground. Such connectedness by their professors also serves students who from their acculturation may lack the most elementary knowledge about concrete institutions. A multilateralizing world increases the shortfall of current educational offerings from the requisites for preparing informed, comprehending citizens.

Pragmatic writing offers the critical analyst an opportunity to situate the pragmatist within a structure thereby rendered more richly susceptible to elucidation, since such writings relate to the political space and other circumstances bearing upon their author. Those who theorize reflect exigency indirectly, whereas those who write pragmatically reflect it directly. Regard briefly one application germane to the present collaboration. The distance between pragmatic writings and theoretical writings may help to illuminate the orientation of a state that serves tacitly as their common frame of reference. This distance remains wide in American literature, for instance; it is negligible in Dutch literature. The predominance of pragmatic multilateralist writings by commentators may characterize states adapted to a world wherein only negotiation of the tumultuous currents of multilateral action can mitigate many of the difficulties facing humankind. No doubt the pragmatic works that accompany such an adaptation sustain a cost in critical thinking; moreover, they lack conceptual adornment and analytical distinction by academic standards. Yet no assurance of superior comprehension attends abstract sophistication. Of course reading abstraction as ideology can likewise be turned to advantage in apprehending the global system. Here I simply wish to add that comprehension of this system, and of any 'meta-mindset' that may integrate various –isms,[45] implies familiarity with pragmatic writings no less than a grasp of scholarly publications.

Lastly, on the assumption that we want to journey self-consciously toward a more effective and accountable multilateral UN system, we also need studies that provide a trail guide, compass and travellers' advisory notes. Historical materialism charts limitations more than it inspires alternative possibilities. Thus it shares the strengths and weaknesses of classical realism, a realism mindful that the forces of history contend by no means only through the state. Visionary writings, including much of the 'reform' literature, exhibit a different liability to the extent they propose castles in the air but only fanciful means to reach their construction sites. Nor do other approaches satisfactorily orient today's explorer, however well some may still actuate today's practitioner. An era that front-ends politics with virtually every issue in every arena on every plane renders largely irrelevant both functionalism and neofunctionalism – though the approach of assuaging enmity through structuring adversaries' focus upon the amelioration of common practical problems will forever bring promise to rancorous, seemingly intractable conflicts.

In the present study we seek to make more transparent as well as more accessible world literature on multilateralism and the UN system. Conceived intentionally, designed or redesigned to accommodate many-sided deliberation, supportive of consent and the purposeful action vitalized by consent, walled institutions make a difference.[46] The significance no less than the burgeoning of multinational walled institutions our essays attest. These essays offer differing lights by which to view the manifold phenomena of multilateralism. But neither the essays nor the studies that they examine integrate a more effective, accountable multilateral system with plausible ways of approaching it.

The Chinese literature, in its presentation by Zhang Xinhua, projects a global system to which I return in closing. Multilateralism is said to be conditioned by 'multipolarity',[47] an historically inevitable stage characterized by the proliferation of multiform state and non-state entities, along with a decline of superpower ability (or willingness) to commit abroad scarce resources on the scale that marked the Euro-centric period of bipolarity. Multipolarity, another manifestation of '–polarity', hence antinomian like taut bipolarity, promises neither peace nor the fruits of peace. Indeed some Chinese scholars, also scholars elsewhere, stress the dangers that multipolarity intensifies or introduces beyond the cold war. But after a long historical period, according to Feng Tejun, the poles of multipolarity will converge.

How, more precisely, does multipolarity condition multilateralism?[48] Does a reverse effect also exist; that is, does multilateralism moderate the polar tension of relations among actors within a multipolar system, thereby altering multipolarity? Can multipolarity influence even the most recalcitrant unilateralist into modified multilateral behaviour? In short, what research agenda is implied by a dynamic of multipolarity with multilateralism? And more fundamentally, how can one recognize multipolarity or verify that it obtains rather than some other system, for instance unipolarity? Would the kaleidoscopic alliances of polyglot minutemen mustered by successive leaders of some modern-day Paul Revere state qualify as multipolarity? Would shifting leadership by varying multilateral participants in ameliorating different issues, like the rotating leadership that Canada geese migrating in V formation are said to assume, signify multipolarity? Or would multipolarity instead be indicated by multilateral stalemate in the face of grave and mounting dangers?

Notes

1 Robert W. Cox, Coordinator of the United Nations University Programme on Multilateralism and the United Nations System, formulated these questions.
2 Emerging Islamic 'regional' organizations touched upon by Hassan Nafaa invite attention beyond this survey.
3 Notably the International Monetary Fund and the World Bank.
4 For another perspective on Russia and China in the post-cold war era, see Robert Boardman, *Post-Socialist World Orders: Russia, China and the UN System*, New York: St. Martin's, 1994.
5 Inis L. Claude, Jr.'s *Swords Into Plowshares*, for instance, classes regionalism as one of six 'constitutional problems' distinct from seven 'approaches to peace' that make up a substantial part of this seminal work.
6 A work reflecting the new symbiosis of different organizational forms is Thomas G. Weiss, ed., *Beyond UN Subcontracting: Task-Sharing with Regional Security Arrangements and Service-Providing NGOs*, London: Macmillan, 1998.
7 Of course the glass edifices of multilateralism have in turn come to hothouse the norms of international law.
8 The Advisory Opinion of the International Court of Justice on *Reparations for Injuries Suffered in the Service of the United Nations* is a key case in assigning international personality to the United Nations. See *I.C.J. Reports, 1949*. Phrases that signify restricted standing of intergovernmental organizations in international law include 'limited international personality' (as for previous components of Community Europe including the European Coal and Steel Community, the European Economic Community and EURATOM), and 'international public corporations' or 'supranational corporations' (as in the case of IBRD and IMF).
9 Judge Richard Goldstone offered an example of keeping states in perspective when he left his position as chief prosecutor for the International Criminal Tribunals for the former Yugoslavia and Rwanda: 'No international court, in my view, is ever... going to have its own police force, its own army, to go and arrest people. Any international court is going to have to rely on the cooperation of governments, of state members of the United Nations. Our warrants of arrest have to be executed by national police forces. National governments have to give the orders. If our investigators want to go and consult even with willing witnesses...it's...inappropriate for an international prosecutor's office to send investigators into any country without the knowledge and consent of the government concerned.... Sovereignty is ...very jealously guarded...by all governments. It's the main reason...we

don't have an international [criminal] court already. It was promised in the genocide convention in 1948; it's never happened. Governments don't like to be subject and subject their citizens for trial by courts other than their own. It's the reason extradition applications are so cumbersome and so seldom succeed.' US National Public Radio, 'All Things Considered', 2 October 1996.

10 See for instance P.B. Potter, *An Introduction to the Study of International Organization*, New York, 1928; D.H. Miller, *The Drafting of the Covenant*, New York, 1928; Quincy Wright, *Mandates and the League of Nations*, Chicago: University of Chicago Press, 1930; Manley O. Hudson, *International Legislation*, 7 vols. covering 1919–1937, Washington: Carnegie Endowment, 1931–1941; Clyde Eagleton, *International Government*, New York: Ronald Press, 1932, 1948; C.G. Fenwick, *International Law*, 2nd ed.; New York, 1934; Leland M. Goodrich and E. Hambro, *Charter of the United Nations: Commentary and Documents*, Boston: World Peace Foundation, 1946.

11 In the United Kingdom, diplomatic history carried forward the study of international organization, asking questions rather different than those posed by political science.

12 *Global Governance: A Review of Multilateralism and International Organizations* began publication in 1995.

13 It is interesting to note that from the perspective of Jean-Philippe Thérien, neither a distinctive French approach nor a French school exists.

14 The public controversy over whether Dutch delegations to the General Assembly should include or exclude non-professionals merely highlights the marginality of disagreements on how best to proceed in practical affairs.

15 Also perhaps in Iranian studies.

16 The Drago doctrine regarding the illegitimacy of force to compel payment of debts, advanced in the context of congresses late in the nineteenth century, found wider acceptance during the Second Peace Conference at The Hague in 1907.

17 Simai continues to publish studies on multilateralism. Beyond the sources cited by Nyiri, see for instance 'The Five Decades of the United Nations: Accomplishments and Limitations', in Klaus Hüfner, ed., *Agenda for Change: New Tasks for the United Nations*, Opladen: Leske + Budrich, 1995, pp. 17–38.

18 The Hungarian Centre for Security Policy and Defence Research organized a Round Table in March 1991 that enabled both critical and supportive comments about the Security Council in the context of the Gulf War.

19 Jean-Philippe Thérien, on the other hand, maintains that development law stands as one of the chief contributions of *la francophonie*.

20 Some otherwise favourably disposed criticize the World Bank (IBRD) and especially the International Monetary Fund (IMF), regarding these as 'relay stations for the core's economic agenda'.

21 Bassey E. Ate holds that the West sees continental organizations such as the Organization of African Unity (OAU) 'as multilateral instruments for teleguiding [their] security interest', according to Samatar. Somewhat to the contrary, S.K.B. Asante, another writer of Samatar's 'excoriatory genre' regarding multilateralism, scrutinizes the sub-regional Economic Community of West African States (ECOWAS) 'as a test case for collective empowerment'.

22   NGO literature on multilateralism is for the most part not addressed in the present study.

23   Jean-Philippe Thérien insists that the study of international relations remains open to practitioners in *la francophonie*, quite possibly more open than in the United States.

24   David Armstrong remarks wryly that 'there is something paradoxical about works which, on the one hand, dismiss notions of the state as a purposive being, but, on the other, sketch out recommendations for United States foreign policy'. 'International Organisation', in Smith, ed., *International Relations: British and American Perspectives*, p. 181.

25   For a classic study of the sociology of knowledge and its application to sharpened political acuity, see Karl Mannheim, *Ideology and Utopia*, New York: Harcourt, Brace, 1936.

26   After Joan Didion's *Play It as it Lays*, New York: Simon and Schuster, 1979.

27   Cable News Network, 'The McLaughlin Group', 13 March 1998; Public Radio International, 'Marketplace', 18 February 1998.

28   This is not to say there are none. Claude's classic *Swords Into Plowshares* elucidates power, especially US power, while analyzing multilateral dynamics. Cox and Jacobson, *et al.*, in *The Anatomy of Influence: Decision Making in International Organization*, investigate how decisions are taken in intergovernmental organizations and who most influences these decisions, exploring, as part of this investigation, power and its stratification 'in reference to states'. Franck's *Nation Against Nation* contends vigorously that the United States can win if it stays in the multilateral contest, plays hardball, and (in a metaphoric reference to the different game of basketball) mounts a full-court press.

29   'Neorealism' has been treated as an American successor to classical realism and exemplified by Hans J. Morgenthau's *Politics Among Nations*, New York: Knopf, 1948, with subsequent editions and Kenneth N. Waltz's *Theory of International Politics*, Reading, MA: Addison-Wesley, 1979. But neorealism has also been regarded as a deviant version of classical realism; see for instance Robert W. Cox, with Timothy J. Sinclair, *Approaches to World Order*, Cambridge: Cambridge University Press, pp. 49–59, 91–3, 153–4, 505, 514. See also Cox, ed., *The New Realism: Perspectives on Multilateralism and World Order*, New York: St. Martin's, 1997.

30   Nye's *Bound to Lead* illuminates some emergent forms of power within the present historical context. Their application supports the author's argument that one-on-one, the United States can, with the proper leadership, continue to lead when pitted against any single state challenger for such a role.

31   For two examples of the literature sometimes labeled thus, see Haas, *Beyond the Nation-State*, and Sewell, *Functionalism and World Politics*. Concepts congruent with or owing something to Mitrany's functional approach include integration, spill-over, task expansion, engaging, transnationalism, learning, confidence-building measures (CBMs), autonomy (compare Mitrany's 'technical self-determination'), impact, and world society.

32   Soldatos, *Le système institutionnel et politique des Communautés européennes dans un monde en mutation: théorie et pratique*, cited in Chapter 4.

33   Jean-Philippe Thérien reports that two textbooks and Daniel Holly's studies focused upon UNESCO exemplify 'neo-Marxist inspired analyses' in *la*

francophonie. But the reach of francophone literature, including Thérien's own contribution, extends to meet criteria of critical theory even when writings do not rely upon historical materialism.

34 On 'problem-solving theory' and 'critical theory', see Cox, *Approaches to World Order*, pp. 87–91, 525–6.

35 *Ibid.*, pp. 88, 89, 90, 525.

36 For a brief consideration of why and how positivist and post-positivist issues matter to some international relations scholars, see Smith, 'Positivism and Beyond', in *International Theory*, especially pp. 11–13.

37 'A positivist social science, technical control, and industrialism: these are mutually reinforcing features of modern social life.' Fay, *Social Theory and Political Practice*, London: George Allen & Unwin, 1975, pp. 46–7. Fay deploys Auguste Comte's epigram to assert the relation of positivist theory to practice: ' "From Science comes Prevision, from Prevision comes Control." ' *Ibid.*, p. 37. Mark A. Neufeld, *The Restructuring of International Relations Theory*, Cambridge: Cambridge University Press, 1995, quotes Kenneth N. Waltz as maintaining that one's ' "urge to explain is not born of idle curiosity alone. It is produced also by the desire to control, or at least to know if control is possible." ' Neufeld, p. 157. On the futility of control, or at least of beneficent results from exercises in social engineering, see James C. Scott, *Seeing Like a State: How Certain Schemes to Improve the Human Condition Have Failed*, New Haven: Yale University Press, 1998.

38 Fay defines reification as 'making into a thing'. To reify means to treat 'what are essentially conventional activities... as if they were natural entities which have a separate existence of their own, and which operate according to a given set of laws independently of the wishes of the social actors who engage in them'. *Ibid.*, pp. 58–9. Compare Neufeld, pp. 41–2.

39 Neorealism Cox describes as 'a science at the service of big-power management of the international system'. In positivist terms, neorealism perceives state actors to be bound by an international 'systemic', though some states are more bound than others. 'Powerful actors are "causes" of change in the behaviour of less powerful ones, and the structure of the system "causes" certain forms of behaviour on the part of the actors.' Cox, *Approaches to World Order*, pp. 57, 51.

40 See Fay, pp. 20, 24, 59, 60, 64. I am grateful to Rod Church for introducing me to Fay's work.

41 Chapter 1 on literature by American writers contains a discussion on variations of 'reform' and the precariousness of reliance upon this word for clarity of meaning.

42 These and related issues are considered in Sewell and Mark B. Salter, 'Panarchy and Other Norms for Global Governance: Boutros-Ghali, Rosenau, and Beyond', *Global Governance*, 1, September–December 1995, pp. 373–82, and in Sewell, 'The Questionable Authority of the United Nations Security Council', Working Paper No. 7, Multilateral Institutions and Global Security series, Centre for International and Security Series, York University, 1997. See also 'Frontline: Spying on Saddam', *http://www.pbs.org/wgbh/pages/frontline/shows/unscom/* on the Internet. More generally on democratizing international institutions, see Stephen Gill and James H. Mittelman, eds., *Innovation and Transformation in International Studies*, Cambridge: Cambridge University

Press, 1997; Michael G. Schechter, Martin Hewson and W. Andy Knight, *Global Governance for the Twenty-First Century: The Realistic Potential*, London: Macmillan, forthcoming.

43 In the US, this proposal is most closely associated with Richard Hudson, his writings and his advocacy.

44 See, for instance, 'Multilateralism Still the First Option for Canada', *Review '85/Outlook'86*, annual publication of the North–South Institute, 1995–96, Ottawa, pp. 1–16; David Black and Claire Turenne Sjolander, 'Multilateralism Re-constituted and the Discourse of Canadian Foreign Policy', *Studies in Political Economy*, 49, Spring 1996, pp. 7–36.

45 I am obliged to an anonymous UNU reader for suggesting this possibility.

46 'We shape our buildings', said Winston Churchill in reference to the British House of Commons; 'thereafter, they shape us'.

47 In her summation of themes within Russian literature, Yevgenia Issraelyan also uses this term in a matter-of-fact way. The word *multipolarity* does not appear frequently in American literature.

48 For a more thorough assessment of global forces bearing upon multilateralism, see Schechter, ed., *Innovation in Multilateralism*, London: Macmillan for the United Nations University, 1998, also Schechter, ed., *Future Multilateralism: The Political and Social Framework*, London: Macmillan for the United Nations University, 1998.

Books and Articles Published (or to be Published) through MUNS

Robert W. Cox, 'Multilateralism and World Order', *Review of International Studies* 1992, 1, 161–180. Based on a 'concept paper' written at the launching of the MUNS programme.

Yoshikazu Sakamoto (ed.), *Global Transformation: Challenges to the State System*, Tokyo: United Nations University Press, 1994. Based on the symposium held in Yokohama in 1992.

Keith Krause and W. Andy Knight (eds.), *State, Society and the UN System: Changing Perspectives on Multilateralism*, Tokyo: United Nations University Press, 1995. Based on the symposium held in Toronto in 1992.

Robert W. Cox (ed.), *The New Realism: Perspectives on Multilateralism and World Order*, London: Macmillan for the United Nations University Press, 1997. Based on the symposium held in Fiesole, Italy, in 1993.

Stephen Gill (ed.), *Globalization, Democratization and Multilateralism*, London: Macmillan for the United Nations University Press, 1997. Based on the symposium held in Oslo in 1993.

Michael G. Schechter (ed.), *Innovation in Multilateralism*, London: Macmillan for the United Nations University Press, 1999. Based on the symposium held in Lausanne in 1994.

Michael G. Schechter (ed.), *Future Multilateralism: The Political and Social Framework*, London: Macmillan for the United Nations University Press, 1999. Based on the symposium held in San José, Costa Rica, in December 1995.

James P. Sewell (ed.), *Multilateralism in Multinational Perspective: Viewpoints from Different Languages and Literatures*, London: Macmillan for the United Nations University Press, 1999.

Robert W. Cox, *Multilateralism and the United Nations System: Final Report*, United Nations University Press, March 1996.

Sequel to the MUNS programme

Michael G. Schechter, Martin Hewson and W. Andy Knight, *Global Governance for the Twenty-First Century: The Realistic Potential*, London: Macmillan, forthcoming.

Tables of Contents of Titles in MUNS Subseries

Robert W. Cox (ed.), ***The New Realism: Perspectives on Multilateralism and World Order***, **London: Macmillan for the United Nations University Press, 1997.**

Stephen Gill (ed.), *Globalization, Democratization and Multilateralism*, London: Macmillan for the United Nations University Press, 1997.

Michael G. Schechter (ed.), *Innovation in Multilateralism*, London: Macmillan for the United Nations University Press, 1999.

7 Expanding the Limits of Imagination: human rights from a participatory approach to new multilateralism
Abdullahi A. An-Na'im
8 Indigenous Peoples and Developments in International Law: toward change through multilateralism and the modern human rights frame
S. James Anaya
9 AIDS and Multilateral Governance
Peter Söderholm
10 Gender, Social Movements, and Multilateralism: a case study of women's organizing in Russia
Elena Ershova, Linda Racioppi and Katherine O'Sullivan See

Michael G. Schechter (ed.), *Future Multilateralism: The Political and Social Framework*, London: Macmillan for the United Nations University Press, 1999.

1 Editor's Introduction
Michael G. Schechter
2 From Civil War to Civil Peace: multi-track solutions to armed conflict
Kumar Rupesinghe
3 Multilateral Security: common, cooperative or collective?
Raimo Väyrynen
4 Back to Heterodox Questions: progress with regress through competition
Javier Iguiñiz-Echeverria
5 A Signal Failure: ecology and economy after the Earth Summit
Peter Harries-Jones, Abraham Rotstein and Peter Timmerman
6 Environmental Rights: multilateralism, morality and the ecology
Tariq Osman Hyder
7 The Quest for Human Rights in an Era of Globalization
Richard Falk
8 Globalization, Multilateralism and the Shrinking Democratic Space
Claude Ake
9 High-Speed Growth, Crisis and Opportunity in East Asia
Walden Bello
10 Engineering Space in Global Governance: the emergence of civil society in evolving 'new' multilateralism
W. Andy Knight
11 Multilateralism from Below: a prerequisite for global governance
Marie-Claude Smouts

James P. Sewell (ed.), *Multilateralism in Multinational Perspective: Viewpoints from Different Languages and Literatures*, London: Macmillan for the United Nations University Press, 1999.

1 Congenital Unilateralism in a Multilateralizing World: American Scholarship on International Organization
James P. Sewell

Michael Schechter, Martin Hewson and W. Andy Knight,
***Global Governance for the Twenty-First Century: the Realistic
Potential*, London: Macmillan, forthcoming.**

Index of Persons' Names

Index of Subjects

Academic Council on the United
  Nations System, *see* ACUNS
accountability, 23, 24–5, 41, 186, 212,
  214, 216
actors (*acteurs*), international
  organizations as, 84
  see also autonomy, of
    intergovernmental organizations
ACUNS (Academic Council on the
  United Nations System), 24, 115,
  118, 120
Afghanistan, 119
Africa, 129, 175–89, 192, 193, 202,
  206, 209, 212, 213
  see also individual states
African Alternative Framework to
  Structural Adjustment Programmes,
  179–80
Al-Ahram Center for Political and
  Strategic Studies (Egypt), 104
Algeria, 184–5
alliances, *see* contact groups; regional
  phenomena
Al-Siassa Al-Dawlya (Egypt), 104, 109,
  111
American International Law, *see*
  International Law for the
  Americas
Americans for the Universality of
  UNESCO (AUU), 19
Anglo-Saxon school, of Egypt, 109–10
anthropological approach, 89
Arab–Israeli conflict, 104, 106, 112
Arab League, *see* League of Arab
  States
Arab world, *see* Egypt; *individual states*
Argentina, 159
arms control, *see* disarmament
ASEAN (Association of Southeast Asian
  Nations), 64
assertive multilateralism, 19
Association of Southeast Asian
  Nations, *see* ASEAN

atomism, as theory of international
  law, 160–1
autocentric strategy, 184, 203
  compare statism
autonomy, of intergovernmental
  organizations, 83, 84, 125, 151,
  212, 219
auxiliary role, US, 28

balance of power, Great Britain as
  balancer, 214
Battlefield of the Gaming Table, 146,
  201–2
behaviouralism, 9, 30
Belgium, 78, 82, 93, 187, 198
BeNeLux, 192
Berg Plan, for Africa, 178
Berlin, 22
Bertelsmann, xvi
binding triad, 92, 213
biosphere, 22, 23, 25, 43, 47, 49, 54,
  62, 74, 75, 89, 100, 118, 124–6,
  135, 136, 151, 176, 178, 180, 186,
  188, 197, 203
  see also UNEP; Ecological Security
    Council, proposed
Bonn, 22
Bosnia, 20, 21, 27–8
  see also Yugoslavia, former
Brazil, 159
burden sharing, *see* assertive
  multilateralism
Burkina Faso, 185
Bush administration, 18

Cambodia, 115, 119
Canada, 12, 20, 22, 31, 32–3, 78, 99,
  198, 204, 214, 217
  see also functional principle; Ottawa
    Process
Caribbean, 162, 192
  as peace zone, 162–3